Patterns
in Shakespearian Tragedy

Patterns
in Shakespearian Tragedy

IRVING RIBNER

NEW YORK

BARNES & NOBLE INC.

First published 1960
Reprinted 1962
© *1960 Irving Ribner*
Printed in Great Britain by
Robert Cunningham and Sons Ltd, Alva

FOR R.G.R.

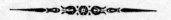

Contents

Preface

━━━━━◆━◆◆◆◆━◆━━━━━

I cannot hope fully to acknowledge the many books and articles on which I have drawn in the following pages. Although I have written in opposition to A. C. Bradley's principal tenets in his influential *Shakespearean Tragedy*, my great indebtedness to him will be everywhere apparent. I have drawn also upon the writings of E. E. Stoll, and among more recent critics I have learned much from G. Wilson Knight, J. F. Danby and the late Samuel L. Bethell. My debt to Hardin Craig, my former teacher, goes back a long way. I have made some attempt to record more specific indebtedness in the notes, but for the many writers I have omitted this blanket statement must of necessity suffice.

The numbering of the Globe text has been used for all Shakespeare references. To the editors of *The Journal of English and Germanic Philology, Shakespeare Quarterly, English Studies, Tulane Studies in English* and *Tulane Drama Review*, and to the directors of the New York University Press, publishers of *Studies in the English Renaissance Drama; In Memory of Karl J. Holzknecht*, I am grateful for permission to re-use some materials already published. Some parts of this book were delivered as lectures in 1959 at the Sorbonne, the University College of North Wales in Bangor, and King's College, London. I am glad of this opportunity to thank Professors Michel Poirier, J. F. Danby, Geoffrey Bullough and their colleagues for the kindness shown me on those occasions.

I have gained much from the criticism and suggestions of R. W. Corrigan and R. C. Whittemore of Tulane University, and particularly from those of H. C. Morris, with whom I have had to argue every point along the way. I have profited also from discussions with Miss Enid Welsford of Newnham College, Cambridge. The kindness of T. R. Henn of St. Catherine's has gone beyond the mere reading of the manuscript.

The John Simon Guggenheim Memorial Foundation and the Research Council of Tulane University have given me periods of relief from teaching which have helped make the book possible. It could not have been written at all without the interest, sympathy and sufferance of one to whom it is fondly dedicated.

CHAPTER ONE

Introduction

The following chapters will attempt to trace Shakespeare's development as a writer of tragedy from *Titus Andronicus* through *Coriolanus*. Many such attempts have been made, and it is part of Shakespeare's greatness that others will continue to be made, for Shakespeare's art is infinite in its variety and in the many dimensions it offers for critical examination. Any analysis of Shakespeare's achievement must be a partial one, a reflection of what the particular critic finds most significant and of what his own intellectual milieu has conditioned him to seek. Here Shakespeare's growth will be considered primarily in terms of the cognitive function of tragedy, its value as a way of knowing which, in its distinctive manner, postulates a moral order. This is but one of many possible approaches.

Tragedy is an exploration of man's relation to the forces of evil in the world. It seeks for answers to cosmic problems, much as religion seeks them, for it is a product of man's desire to believe in a purposive ordered universe.[1] I propose to treat Shakespeare's development as a growth in moral vision, to examine how Shakespeare, beginning at first with inherited dramatic forms and a conventional morality, learned to embody successive visions of human life in dramatic vehicles, each of which provides the emotional equivalent of an intellectual statement. This statement all of

---

[1] The moral vision in Shakespearian tragedy has been argued by D. G. James, *The Dream of Learning* (Oxford, 1951); Arthur Sewell, *Character and Society in Shakespeare* (Oxford, 1951); and Geoffrey Bush, *Shakespeare and the Natural Condition* (Cambridge, Mass., 1956). These writers, however, have denied the kinship of the moral vision to the religious vision. William G. McCollom, *Tragedy* (New York, 1957), p. 8, holds also that 'tragedy presents a poetic cosmology and is committed to a metaphysical attitude'. See also Herbert Weisinger, *Tragedy and the Paradox of the Fortunate Fall* (East Lansing, Mich., 1953); T. R. Henn, *The Harvest of Tragedy* (London, 1956).

the elements of drama – action, character and poetry – are designed
to support.

This is not to say that Shakespeare began each play with an
abstract idea. He began probably with a dramatic situation, but it
was one he chose because he saw implicit in it an idea with which
he was concerned. This situation he analysed and explored, combined it with other situations from various sources, so that it could
better express the idea whose germ within it he had initially perceived. As he shaped situation and idea, characters were envisaged
to perform specific thematic functions. We are not concerned with
Shakespeare's process of composition, if indeed we ever could
determine it, but with the fusion of theme, action, character and
language into a total unity which is the final aesthetic object.

Nor would I deny the realism of Shakespeare's art which so
many critics have affirmed. Shakespeare's dramatic method combined a realistic technique with a symbolic one, for the greatest of
art must attain a symbolic dimension.[1] So convincing is Shakespeare's realism that romantic critics often have been carried away
by the illusion of reality in his characters and have neglected their
symbolic functions within the total play. If idea implicit in character appears at times to be overstressed in the pages which follow,
this is not to deny the illusion of reality. Medieval and Renaissance allegory always couched its symbolism in realistic terms,
as *Piers Plowman*, *The Faerie Queene* or *Pilgrim's Progress* may
illustrate.

Dramatic illusion requires that the audience accept the author's
creations as fellow human beings for the duration of the play, and
that what these characters do seems reasonable in terms of emotions which the audience can itself experience. In the art of such
illusion Shakespeare was a master; it will not be my purpose to
demonstrate what generations of commentators and theatre audiences have made obvious. What must be stressed is that this appearance is merely an illusion, maintained in part by the rapid
movement of the action and by the willingness of the audience to
believe. There need be no conflict between the demands of realism
and symbol. It is, nevertheless, observable that as Shakespeare
became more and more absorbed in the religious and ethical

---

[1] This has been well argued by W. B. C. Watkins, *Shakespeare and Spenser* (Princeton, 1950), particularly pp. 75-110, and by S. L. Bethell, *Shakespeare and the Popular
Dramatic Tradition* (London, 1944).

dimensions of tragedy he concentrated more and more on the development of symbol, with a corollary unconcern for character consistency. This becomes evident as we move from *Hamlet* to *Othello*, and it is particularly clear in the final Roman plays, where characters such as Cleopatra and Aufidius are rendered psychologically inconsistent by the conflicting symbolic functions which the total plan requires that they perform.

The theatrical tradition in which Shakespeare worked was different from the nineteenth-century naturalist theatre which has so profoundly affected the drama of our own time. A weakness of Bradley's work,[1] great and perceptive as it undoubtedly was, was that he read Shakespeare's tragedies in terms of such a naturalist stage. Bradley recognized the philosophical dimension of tragedy, and he sought for a moral order in Shakespeare's tragedies. If no such order emerges from his study, it may be largely because he sought for Shakespeare's thematic content not in the total complex of each play, but in the operations of dramatic character realistically appraised. Such analysis could lead only to unanswerable mystery, for stage creations analysed as though they were human beings could reflect only the mystery and seeming indirection of human life. Bradley could lead his readers only to a Shakespeare without positive belief, to a conception of tragedy merely as the posing of unanswerable questions, and to a moral system in the plays which is upon close analysis not moral at all.[2] Such a tragedy as Bradley found in Shakespeare could have been written only in the secular Renaissance of nineteenth-century historians, and not in the Renaissance which more recent scholarship has revealed to us.

[1] *Shakespearean Tragedy* (London, 1949). Among Bradley's most judicious defenders in recent years have been Herbert Weisinger, 'The Study of Shakespearian Tragedy Since Bradley', *SQ*, VI (1955), 387-96, and J. I. M. Stewart, *Character and Motive in Shakespeare* (London, 1949). The methods of G. Wilson Knight are not so far removed from those of Bradley as some have supposed, and Knight himself in the preface to the 1949 edition of *The Wheel of Fire* acknowledged his profound indebtedness.

[2] See Lily B. Campbell, 'Concerning Bradley's *Shakespearean Tragedy*', *HLQ*, VII (1949), 1-18, reprinted in *Shakespeare's Tragic Heroes* (New York, 1952). Peter Alexander, *Hamlet, Father and Son* (Oxford, 1955), p. 53, writes that 'Bradley, in his zeal to reconcile us to the facts of tragedy, offers us a conclusion to which only a profound pessimism could reconcile us'. The limitations of Bradley's concentration on character have been stressed from different points of view by L. C. Knights, 'How Many Children Had Lady Macbeth?' in *Explorations* (New York, 1947), and Robert Langbaum, 'Character Versus Action in Shakespeare', *SQ*, VIII (1957), 57-69.

The historical critics who succeeded Bradley[1] have taught us that drama is not life; it is an artificial construct controlled by the restrictions of the stage-audience relation, and in order for it to exist at all it must violate physical reality. A dramatic character is governed by the over-all design and purpose of the total play to which he contributes. Violations of physical and psychological reality may be the very means by which tragedy is rendered profound and moving, for by distorting reality to support the order and design he imposes upon the materials of life, the dramatist gives meaning to what in real life may be a haphazard and insignificant event.

There is a wide gulf between the naturalist drama of the nineteenth century and the conventional drama of the Elizabethans, with its continuity from the Middle Ages and its symbolic content. Drama is built out of individual character and event; the tragic hero must be a free, conscious agent, capable of deliberate moral choice. But the individual may also be a symbol of mankind, and the problem he faces may be that which all men face. Shakespeare's interest is in mankind more than in individuals. He endows his characters with a convincing illusion of reality, but through them he explores issues of wider significance than the psychological problems of any individual personality.

The chapters which follow assume the continuity of Shakespeare's theatre with that of the Middle Ages, that Shakespearian tragedy is marked by symbolic features more closely associated with medieval art than with modern. This does not mean that Shakespeare's tragedies are to be regarded as mere *exempla* designed to teach a medieval doctrine of *de contemptu mundi*, or that the pattern of *de casibus* legend is synonymous with that of Renaissance tragedy. The most significant result of medieval studies in relation to Shakespeare[2] has been the renewed awareness they have given us that Elizabethan tragedy was the culmination of a popular dramatic tradition which has its roots securely in medieval life.

The Elizabethan stage was not primarily a realistic one. It was,

---

[1] I refer particularly to Levin Schücking, *Character Problems in Shakespeare's Plays* (London, 1922), and E. E. Stoll, whose principal writings include *Shakespeare Studies* (New York, 1927), *Poets and Playwrights* (Minneapolis, 1930), *Art and Artifice in Shakespeare* (Cambridge, 1933), *Shakespeare's Young Lovers* (London, 1937).

[2] See particularly Willard Farnham, *The Medieval Heritage of Elizabethan Tragedy* (Oxford, 1956); Howard Baker, *Induction to Tragedy* (Baton Rouge, 1936); Theodore Spencer, *Death and Elizabethan Tragedy* (Cambridge, Mass., 1936).

as Francis Fergusson has written, 'like older forms of Medieval art, popular, traditional and ritualistic'.[1] The continuity of tradition which links Shakespeare's theatre to its medieval forerunners reminds us that, like so many medieval art forms, the drama could be symbolic of life itself. The Globe theatre, with its starry firmament for a ceiling, the signs of the zodiac printed above its platform stage, was designed to represent the world, and figures who walked across its boards were often symbols of humanity in the large.

Medieval art was largely allegorical. Its impulse was didactic, and it relied upon specific symbol to depict universal truth. This was the method of Dante's *Divine Comedy*, which Fergusson has seen as the prototype of the drama of Western Europe. To effect its philosophical ends, Shakespeare's theatre used specific myths which had themselves evolved as symbols of human experience. In dealing with Shakespearian tragedy we must recognize the role which myth has served in man's unceasing endeavour to embody in specific symbolic terms the philosophical abstractions by which he lives. The medieval origins of Shakespearian tragedy reveal to us the inherent symbolism of Shakespeare's dramatic genre, and its capacity for philosophical statement.

Drama, more than any other art form, is dependent upon convention and tradition. The medieval heritage is important because many of the traditional complexes of character and event which comprise Elizabethan and Jacobean tragedy were shaped in the Middle Ages as vehicles for peculiarly medieval views of life. This is not to say that Elizabethan tragedy is medieval, that the differences are not enormous. Dramatic forms themselves distinctly Elizabethan, however, may be developments from medieval archetypes, of which the morality play may serve as a significant example. We cannot adequately understand Elizabethan tragedy unless we understand both the artistic and the intellectual milieu out of which it grew and developed. But at the same time we must not underestimate the considerable evolution through which the drama had passed, with the leavening influence of classical tradition, before Shakespeare approached it.

Shakespeare has survived and is significant today because of certain qualities not confined by the limited perspective of the Elizabethan age or of any age. To understand his plays, however,

[1] *The Idea of a Theatre* (Princeton, 1949), p. 3.

B

we must recognize the wide divergences between the author's age and our own. The attempt to see Shakespeare in terms of his own time has been pursued in many directions. We have had voluminous studies of every aspect of Elizabethan England: its science and cosmology, its psychology and moral philosophy, its astronomy and theology, its political theory and political problems, its literary criticism. The application of such historical scholarship to Shakespeare's plays has been under constant attack in recent years[1] and many of the objections have been well founded. It has sometimes been forgotten that if Shakespeare were merely an ordinary Elizabethan we would be not much concerned with him today. The excesses of some critics, however, should not blind us to the basic truth that Shakespeare was a product of his age. We must begin with this premise, but we must remember also that the creative artist knows how to analyse, question and reinterpret the cultural milieu in which he lives. In his very analysis of traditional ideas the greatness of his achievement often lies. We must use the new knowledge which historical scholarship has given us, but we must not bury the creative mind in the commonplaces of the world out of which he grows.

The kind of historical criticism which has laid itself most open to attack has based its conclusions on limited data and unwarranted assumptions; thus it has been essentially unhistorical. In the realm of Elizabethan speculative ideas historical scholarship must tread with a particular wariness. There are very few intellectual concepts about which we can say with real certainty that there was an 'Elizabethan view'. The Renaissance was an age of intellectual change and contradiction, with medieval and classical notions often in sharp conflict with one another. It is inevitable that there should have been such conflict, as there has been in every age, for a static idea of anything is a contradiction in terms. Ideas are always coming into being in opposition to older ideas or maintaining themselves in opposition to newer ones. In politics and religion there were heretical notions which censorship barred from print, but which we cannot doubt were much alive in men's minds. The creative artist chooses from among the great diversity of his age's ideas according to his own peculiar intellectual bent. The intellectual content of a Shakespearian tragedy, moreover, in-

---

[1] See, for instance, L. C. Knights, 'On Historical Scholarship and the Interpretation of Shakespeare', *Sewanee Review*, LXIII (1955), 223-40.

volves not the mere statement of ideas, Elizabethan or otherwise, but the exploration of ideas, examination both of ideas and their contraries in terms of human life. The play applies imaginative criteria to intellectual concepts. Out of this, if the dramatist is a great one, must emerge some affirmation which may be partly traditional or entirely new.

If it is doubtful that the obscure psychological treatises of Shakespeare's contemporaries will throw much light upon his plays, it is also true that there is a fundamental difference between a view of individual man derived from an erroneous conception of human physiology and a view of mankind based upon a cosmology which is philosophical rather than scientific, whose ultimate authority is in a view of God and not in the limited data of a still inadequate scientific method. This is why the great system of order and correspondences in the universe which is embodied in Richard Hooker's *Of the Laws of Ecclesiastical Polity* can have a validity such as the pseudo-scientific treatises of a Timothy Bright can not. A knowledge of the ordered universe which Renaissance Christian humanism carried on from the Middle Ages[1] is essential to an understanding of Shakespeare's tragedies. Such a conception of the universe is not a universal 'Elizabethan view'; we must recognize that it was being consistently challenged throughout Shakespeare's lifetime. But it is exactly the kind of view which tragedy, with its search for moral order, seeks to find, and a close reading of Shakespeare's plays – and not necessarily of the obscure treatises of his contemporaries – reveals that it was a view which Shakespeare deliberately espoused. Such a cosmology is rooted in the theological principles of the Anglican church, which it was Hooker's purpose to defend.

There is scepticism in Shakespeare's age, and there is constant exploration of traditional values, but there is also faith in a perfection rooted in divine purpose, and it is to this faith that Shakespearian tragedy directs its appeal. We need not ourselves accept Shakespeare's religious postulates in order to enjoy his plays. The only necessity is that they be believable and that the dramatist by the power of his art enable us to entertain their possibility. As we

[1] See Hardin Craig, *The Enchanted Glass* (New York, 1936); E. M. W. Tillyard, *The Elizabethan World Picture* (London, 1943); Theodore Spencer, *Shakespeare and the Nature of Man* (New York, 1949), pp. 1-20; J. F. Danby, *Shakespeare's Doctrine of Nature: A Study of King Lear* (London, 1949), pp. 20-53.

watch *Macbeth*, for instance, we assume with the author the possibility of human damnation, whether or not we so believe outside the theatre. We need not be Christians to appreciate Shakespeare, but we do need to share certain moral premises which have been the property of thinking men throughout history: the ethical primacy of love, justice, loyalty, and a belief in the distinction between good and evil.

Although its particular scientific details may be antiquated, Elizabethan cosmology, with its religious and philosophical emphasis upon order and degree, furnished the background against which Shakespeare's tragedies were conceived. We must realize also, however, that the scepticism of Bruno, Machiavelli and Montaigne had deeply penetrated the Elizabethan intellectual milieu. The very challenging of traditional beliefs in Shakespeare's age made necessary their constant reaffirmation, and such challenging, to a large extent, made tragedy possible. The very element of doubt gives rise to the tragic emotions. As the audience watches the hero suffering and dying, it wonders with him if the universe is indeed so ordered and just as man's most basic impulses compel him to believe. In the relief of this doubt lies the exultation and the renewed acceptance of life for which man goes to the theatre to witness the suffering and death of another. Tragedy can exist only where there is both faith and scepticism. The Middle Ages could not create it without scepticism, and the twentieth century cannot create it without faith.

When Shakespeare writes tragedy he is an artist imposing an order and form upon the raw materials of experience. Each of his characters is carefully moulded to fit an intellectual conception which the play in its totality is designed to embody. Every one of the tragedies is a separate attempt, if not finally to answer the great problem of man's relation to the forces of evil in the world, at least to pose it in such a way that new facets may be freshly illuminated in terms of human experience. If no two tragedies are exactly alike, it is because the questions with which they deal are themselves so complex and many-sided, and because Shakespeare's insight into human experience is of infinite range. He approaches the great issues of human life from many angles, with different hypotheses, and we have a resulting diversity in his plays. His primary purpose is not accurate depiction of life, and realistic as his technique may be, both character and event are distorted from reality when the total thematic design of a tragedy demands such distortion.

Shakespearian tragedy translates a moral vision into dramatic form, and thus it is a way of knowing.[1] That this way is different from that of science is obvious, for tragedy deals with things of the imagination, and its kind of truth must be emotionally experienced. But the experience of tragedy may bear a closer relation to that of religion than usually has been recognized. Different as the method of tragedy may be from that of religion, both pursue the same kind of knowledge. Tragedy and religion seek by different means the same affirmation of order, and in each there is a large emotional component which can never be in science. A vision which comprehended no order or meaning in the universe could not be tragedy at all. It would be mere calamity such as we read about in the newspapers every day, without dramatic significance. Tragedy must impose upon the raw material of human experience a pattern in which the relation of human suffering to human joy becomes apparent, and out of this must come the feeling of reconciliation with which every one of Shakespeare's tragedies ends, and which critics of the most divergent views have recognized.

This common goal allies tragedy to religion. Historically, we have always known that tragedy, both in ancient Greece and Western Europe, emerged out of religious ritual, but we have generally ignored the close relation which tragedy has maintained to the religious experience, both in Greece and in Shakespeare's England. Like the Christian paradox of the fortunate fall, tragedy searches for order and purpose in apparent disaster, and in doing so it reinforces a system of belief which essentially is religious.

To assert the intellectual content of tragedy is not to say that a Shakespearian play can ever be paraphrased as a simple philosophical statement. The intellectual end is cast in terms of specific

---

[1] This has been recognized in the recent books by D. G. James, Arthur Sewell and Geoffrey Bush. They have reasserted the cognitive function of tragedy, and they have argued that its way of knowing is different both from that of science and that of religion. In denying the common ends of tragedy and religion, these newer writers have again asserted a secular Shakespeare like Bradley's, one without positive belief, whose works must be read outside of the Christian milieu in which they were written. The Christian element in Shakespearian tragedy, on the other hand, has been recognized by S. L. Bethell; by J. F. Danby in his important study of *King Lear*; by Paul N. Siegel, *Shakespearean Tragedy and the Elizabethan Compromise* (New York, 1957); by H. S. Wilson, *On the Design of Shakespearian Tragedy* (Toronto, 1957); and by John Vyvyan, *The Shakespearean Ethic* (London, 1959).

characters and specific action, and it is communicated in poetry. The characters are not real people, but part of Shakespeare's artistry lies in his ability to create the illusion that they are, and the theatre audience is able emotionally to identify with them. Ultimately their functions are symbolic ones dictated by the over-all intellectual concerns of the play; they are embodiments of specific ideas and moral positions, but these are given 'a local habitation and a name'. Shakespeare as an artist goes beyond the philosopher in that his abstract ideas are tested in the imaginative setting of real-life situation. They are given emotional contexts, and the effect of his tragedy is to create a kind of tension between feeling and idea, between our emotional involvement in a specific situation and our rational contemplation of its meaning.

When we recognize the affinity of tragedy to the religious ex-perience, we see why a cardinal element in the tragedy of the Christian Renaissance is the possibility of man's redemption from evil. Just as Adam, in spite of his fall from Paradise, had, by the grace of God, been given the knowledge by means of which he might eventually overcome evil, the Shakespearian tragic hero through the process of his destruction may learn the nature of evil and thus attain a spiritual victory in spite of death. This does not mean that all of Shakespeare's tragic heroes attain salvation, for they do not, and it is not necessary that they should. Hamlet or Lear may undergo redemption, but Richard III or Macbeth is unequivocally damned, and the reconciliation experienced by the audience need be no less complete. Tragedy is a social art-form, and reconciliation must take place within the audience and not within the actors. The damnation of Macbeth, no less than the salvation of Lear, may serve to affirm the feeling of moral order in a purposive universe upon which tragic reconciliation depends. In spite of the fate of the tragic hero, society at the end of each tragedy must undergo a symbolic rebirth; there is always a Fortin-bras, Edgar or Malcolm ready to begin life with a renewed hope in the future, and in this hope the audience imaginatively partici-pates. This final sense of reconciliation is an essential ingredient of tragedy, of the Greek no less than the Elizabethan, and it was probably what Aristotle meant by *katharsis*.

The Aristotelian principle of *hamartia*, or the tragic flaw, a con-cept exceedingly vague and ill-defined in Aristotle himself, is very difficult to apply at all to a tragedy like Shakespeare's, based more closely as it is on the Christian notion of sin than on the Greek idea of *nemesis*. Bradley's particular use of *hamartia* led him to a static conception of Shakespearian tragedy. He measured Shakespeare's plays against a single dramatic formula which he could find exemplified only in *Hamlet*, *Othello*, *Lear* and *Macbeth*. But Shakespearian tragedy is not a static phenomenon. To exclude such plays as *Romeo and Juliet* and *Titus Andronicus* because they are early work, or such plays as *Richard III* and *Julius Caesar* because they deal with historical matter (as, incidentally, Renaissance theory held that all tragedy should) is an evasion of the issue.

We must assume, on the contrary, that there is no one formula – Aristotelian, Hegelian, or otherwise – to which all of the tragedies conform. Like every other artist, Shakespeare grew and developed as he worked. He experimented with various complexes of human character and situation, sometimes successfully and sometimes not. There are many patterns of action, changing from play to play, as Shakespeare experiments with traditional forms, changes and augments them, probing always into varying aspects of the great questions with which he is concerned. With this principle in mind, we will have no need to force such diverse plays as *Romeo and Juliet*, *Lear* or *Antony and Cleopatra* into rigidly preconceived conceptions of tragedy into which they cannot fit. Shakespearian tragedy must be approached as a dynamic and not a static phenomenon, one which shows growth and change and is full of variety.

With these considerations in view, the following chapters will attempt to trace Shakespeare's growth and development as a writer of tragedy from his early experiments in the last decade of the sixteenth century through his great triumphs of the Jacobean era. The treatment of the plays will be in an order as close to that of their composition as can be determined, so that Shakespeare's progression from play to play may be observed. *Troilus and Cressida* will not be included, for although there is strong bibliographical evidence that Shakespeare and his contemporaries regarded it as a tragedy, this evidence is far from conclusive. If it was designed as a tragedy, it is certainly so different from the others as to require separate treatment.

The discussion of the earlier plays will be devoted largely to Shakespeare's adaptation of traditional material, both of dramatic form and of philosophical substance. In *Titus Andronicus*, *Richard*

III and *Romeo and Juliet* Shakespeare is learning his craft and has not yet learned fully to make of tragedy a vehicle for intellectual statement. As each succeeding play grows richer in moral and intellectual vision, the emphasis of the chapters will be upon Shakespeare's conscious ordering of character and action into a total dramatic unity designed to embody intellectual content in specific emotional terms. An historical perspective, which evaluates the traditional forms of tragedy which Shakespeare inherited, must be tempered by a concentration upon the philosophical ends of tragedy, and upon the symbolic function of character, action and poetry within a larger unity not confined by the limits of a psychological verisimilitude, and thus in the manner of the conventional and symbolic Elizabethan theatre which historical scholarship has revealed to us. If there is little stress upon Shakespeare's poetic imagery in the following chapters, it is not because this is unimportant, but because imagery has been sufficiently treated in recent criticism.

It will be seen that in his earliest tragedies Shakespeare adapted certain traditional devices from the past and made changes in them largely so that they might better reflect certain moral ideas. These are highly imitative works, and as tragedy none is entirely successful. The dramatist is still unable completely to escape the limitations of his sources. They are important, however, in that they indicate, faintly in *Titus Andronicus* and *Richard III*, and more clearly in *Romeo and Juliet*, the direction in which Shakespeare is moving. After *Romeo and Juliet* Shakespeare turned to historical tragedy, learning more surely in each of the plays from *King John* through *Julius Caesar* to embody political as well as ethical ideas in dramatic form. Through his treatment of the relative certainties of political doctrine, Shakespeare probably learned to handle ideas more effectively, and from politics he passed to the more profound abstractions of the great ethical tragedies which followed. In *Hamlet* we see the finished artist in tragedy emerging, and with *Othello* his mastery is complete.

Out of Shakespeare's three earliest experiments we find emerging three basic patterns of tragic action, each one of which could be used to illuminate a different facet of the life-journey of man in conflict with evil. To these patterns Shakespeare returned again and again as he grew and developed, changing and expanding them as he learned to ask more profound and all-embracing questions with each succeeding play, until in *King Lear* and *Macbeth* he could approach the vastest mysteries of all and offer answers in imaginative terms which might reaffirm most forcefully the belief in an ordered purposive universe towards which all his tragedies tend. After this his relentless probing could lead him only to the paradox implicit in his two final Roman plays.

CHAPTER TWO

Senecan Beginnings: *Titus Andronicus* *Richard III, Romeo and Juliet*

————— ❧❀✦❀❧ —————

In Shakespeare's three earliest tragedies, *Titus Andronicus*, *Richard III* and *Romeo and Juliet*, we find him learning his craft, adapting and changing the traditional Senecan devices of the late 1580's, and in each instance creating at least something which is entirely new. The dominant mode of English tragedy when Shakespeare began to write was the popularized Senecanism of Thomas Kyd. *Titus Andronicus*, probably the earliest of the three plays, is the most imitative, and yet Shakespeare goes beyond the stock formulas of the Kydian revenge play. In this crude work Shakespeare already is concerned with the meaning of human destruction, as Kyd never was; he is groping towards a dramatic formula which may express significant truth about the relation of mankind to the forces of evil in the world.

In *Richard III* Shakespeare finds himself with a tragic hero who has already been cast for him in conventional Senecan terms by several generations of writers. He is not, however, satisfied with what literary tradition has bequeathed to him. Out of his deliberation emerges a Senecan villain-hero who is not entirely like his forebears, who is involved in a complex of events unlike that of *Titus Andronicus*, the play in its entirety exposing a different facet of the great problem of man's relation to the forces which may destroy him. Finally in *Romeo and Juliet* Shakespeare is able to take an inherited Senecan formula and out of it shape a vehicle for tragedy which is distinctly his own. The three plays reveal three distinctive patterns of tragic action, to each of which Shakespeare is later to return with a surer mastery.

II

When Ben Jonson in 1614 wrote in his Induction to *Bartholomew Fair* that 'Hee that will sweare, *Ieronimo* [Kyd's *Spanish Tragedy* or] *Andronicus* are the best playes, yet shall passe vnexcepted at, heere, as a man whose Iudgement shews it is constant, and hath stood still, these fiue and twentie, or thirtie yeeres,' he may not have been concerned with dating precisely the plays he was deriding,[1] but his statement does show that he thought of Kyd's *Spanish Tragedy* and Shakespeare's *Titus Andronicus* as belonging to the same era and as exemplifying the same outmoded style of tragedy. *The Spanish Tragedy*, written probably sometime between 1585 and 1589,[2] introduced to the English stage a peculiarly Elizabethan adaptation of Senecan revenge tragedy to the needs of a popular theatre. For at least a decade Kyd's influence dominated the English stage, and under this influence Shakespeare's first tragedy was conceived.

The action and interest of the Kydian revenge play are sustained by the unsuccessful attempts of the hero to avenge some ghastly crime committed by a diabolical villain. The revenge finally comes as the result of a clever stratagem at the end of the play, but until it does the avenger berates himself for his failure to accomplish his purpose; he goes temporarily mad; a ghost urges him on. His self-abuse and his madness serve only to delay his revenge and heighten the suspense. He has formidable obstacles. He must convince himself of the villain's guilt, and he usually requires an inordinate amount of proof. The villain is wily and strong, and he intrigues against the avenger as fully as he is intrigued against. The final revenge is of a particularly bloody sort, and it usually comes after the avenger has pretended a reconciliation with the villain in order to win his confidence.

The soul of the villain must be sent to hell, but the soul of the avenger must go there as well. The Kydian revenge play always ends with either the murder or suicide of the avenger, and incidentally the deaths of all the other principal characters in the play.

---

[1] That *Titus* is entirely by Shakespeare has been well argued by H. T. Price, 'The Authorship of *Titus Andronicus*', *JEGP*, XLII (1943), 45-81, and *Construction in Shakespeare* (Ann Arbor, Mich., 1951), pp. 37-41. R. F. Hill, 'The Composition of *Titus Andronicus*', *Shakespeare Survey 10* (Cambridge, 1957), pp. 60-70, concludes that it must have been written in 1589 or 1590. See also *Titus Andronicus*, ed. J. C. Maxwell (London, 1953), pp. xxiv-xxxiv.

[2] E. K. Chambers, *The Elizabethan Stage* (Oxford, 1923), III, 397.

By the excess of his vengeance and the villainy with which it is executed – and because vengeance itself is a violation of the law of God – the avenger damns his own soul as well as that of his victim.[1]

The primary interest of the Kydian revenge play is in action. It holds its audience by a crude sensationalism, by an artificially stimulated suspense, and by the shocking nature of the events it depicts. Such plays have little moral significance other than as illustration of the degradation of a man who places his faith in personal revenge rather than in the justice of God – a common Elizabethan doctrine. And this moral doctrine is rarely stressed. The Kydian revenge play does not really explore the question of human suffering; it is essentially melodrama and not tragedy at all.

In terms of dramatic craftsmanship alone, *Titus Andronicus* is superior to *The Spanish Tragedy*. It does not have the divided action of Kyd's play, with the ghost of Andrea at the beginning calling for revenge and then quite forgotten while the action shifts to Hieronimo and his scarcely related affairs. In spite of its obvious shortcomings, *Titus Andronicus* in poetry and in characterization is superior to any play written before it. This usually has been recognized, but *Titus Andronicus* has been called a failure because 'it lacks a sense of morality, seriousness and consistency'.[2] But it is the very sense of morality and the serious purpose with which Shakespeare approached his crude unpalatable material which, above all else, make *Titus Andronicus* so much greater than *The Spanish Tragedy*.

Shakespeare shaped what he found in his source[3] to fit the general pattern of the Kydian revenge play, but he made significant changes from his source, and these tend to make *Titus Andronicus* somewhat different from *The Spanish Tragedy*. Shakespeare's play is profoundly influenced, moreover, by his reading of Ovid, not only by the story of Philomela which he borrowed, but by the entire *Metamorphoses*, with its emphasis upon the trans-

---

[1] See F. T. Bowers, *Elizabethan Revenge Tragedy* (Princeton, 1940).

[2] G. B. Harrison, *Shakespeare's Tragedies* (London, 1951), p. 45.

[3] The source of this play was long disputed, but it now seems certain that Shakespeare used a prose *History of Titus Andronicus* extant today only in an eighteenth-century chapbook which appears to be a direct reprint of a lost sixteenth-century one. It is preserved in the Folger Shakespeare Library, Washington, D.C. Shakespeare's play has been carefully compared with this source by Ralph M. Sargent, 'The Source of *Titus Andronicus*', *SP*, XLVI (1949), 167-83.

formation of man into beast through excess of passion.[1] This transformation of Titus is set within a specific moral system which the play in its totality affirms.

Almost the entire first act is Shakespeare's invention,[2] his most significant addition to the story being the sacrifice of Alarbus. He shapes the character of Aaron as an independent force of evil, rather than as a mere agent of the queen. He introduces the parallel with Ovid's tale of Philomela, and he adds the final triumph of justice and order with the return of Lucius to Rome, in spite of the inconsistency which this involves, for there is no reason for a Goth army to serve Lucius against their own queen. Shakespeare also makes of Marcus a virtual chorus to comment upon the action as the play unfolds.

His most important innovation is in his conception of the principal characters and their relations to one another. Titus Andronicus is a commanding figure. He is a great and initially virtuous man, the first of Shakespeare's heroic figures whose very virtues are the source of their sins. In many ways he is a forerunner of Coriolanus. Titus embodies all the ancient Roman virtues: 'A nobler man, a braver warrior, / Lives not this day within the city walls' (I.i.25-26). He has given his life and his sons unselfishly in the cause of his country. He might now be emperor, but he respects hereditary right and chooses Saturninus instead. He is stern and he is proud, the master of his family, the last of the ancient Romans.

Titus is a superman, but being human he must, like all men, face the forces of evil in the world. In his encounter with evil Titus fails. He rejects the way of redemption which is offered him in the choral commentary of his brother, Marcus, and he moves towards inevitable damnation. By the life journey of his hero, Shakespeare explores in imaginative terms the universal way of damnation, for Titus becomes a prototype of erring humanity. In this early tragedy Shakespeare already is trying to shape his tragic hero as a symbol of mankind, and in the description of his fall to pose not so much the problem of an individual as that of humanity at large. This intellectual range, alien to the work of his

---

[1] See E. M. Waith, 'The Metamorphosis of Violence in *Titus Andronicus*', *Shakespeare Survey 10* (Cambridge, 1957), pp. 39-49.

[2] That this act could be the work of George Peele, as argued by J. D. Wilson in his new Cambridge edition (1949), pp. xxv-xxvi, H. T. Price has shown to be very unlikely. See *Construction in Shakespeare*, pp. 38-40.

contemporaries, he is to achieve in the great tragedies of his maturity.

Although Shakespeare makes his audience acutely aware of the hero's blindness, he causes them also to hope to the very end that he will learn the way of redemption before it is too late. So as not entirely to alienate his audience from Titus, while he depicts the moral degeneration which will lead to the final crime against nature, Shakespeare uses the pathos of Lavinia and the *naïveté* of Titus' grandchild. In the source Titus kills the emperor, but Shakespeare spares his hero the additional taint of regicide. The kissing of the dead body of Titus is another such attempt to win sympathy for him, crude as it may be, for the audience is invited to participate emotionally in the sorrow of his death.

Shakespeare tries also to place the fall of Titus within a larger framework in which evil too is destroyed, so that the audience, while lamenting the damnation of one soul, may have a renewed awareness of the perfection of God's order and of the operation of justice in the world. Marcus points out the path which Titus might have taken, and Lucius brings about a reconciliation when the forces both of good and evil lie dead upon the stage and the world is ready for rebirth. In the portrait of the degeneration and damnation of a noble figure because of weaknesses which spring from those very traits in him which the audience admires, and in the reconciliation which comes from the destruction of evil in spite of his fall, we have a formula for tragedy which postulates the reality of evil, man's free moral choice in spite of it, and divine justice in a harmonious moral order.

In *Titus Andronicus* the forces of good and evil are neatly arranged against one another. Of all the evil characters, Aaron is not only the most fully developed but also the manipulator of the evil action, the specific author of Titus' misfortunes. He may be regarded as a symbol of evil itself. He is black, the traditional colour of the devil (and more specifically of lechery), and like the devil he can never know remorse or penance. He remains defiant to the very end:

> Ten thousand worse than ever yet I did
> Would I perform, if I might have my will:
> If one good deed in all my life I did,
> I do repent it from my very soul.

> (V.iii.186-9)

Shakespeare's contemporaries commonly believed that the devil had power to infuse himself into the bodies of men and govern their actions. The devil may be tortured as Aaron is, but he can never be penitent, a suggestion Shakespeare was further to develop in Iago. As a dramatic embodiment of a specific vice, the lechery which governs Tamora, Aaron affords the first clear example of the symbolic use of character which is to be so marked a feature of the great plays of Shakespeare's maturity. Evil in *Titus Andronicus* is already envisaged as a motiveless force which operates through deception, and Shakespeare has learned to express its mode of operation in the appearance and action of a dramatic character.

Evil is always present in the world, but Titus brings it upon himself. To make this clear Shakespeare created the incidents of the first act, in which Titus gives himself to evil by three specific deeds: the sacrifice of Alarbus, the violation of Lavinia's betrothal to Bassianus, and the slaying of Mutius. Each of these acts proceeds out of a virtue corrupted into vice.

The ancient Roman code demanded that a captive enemy be sacrificed to appease the souls of those who have died in battle. There is a stern virtue in Titus' respect for this decree, a reverence for a primitive type of justice. There is no rancour in his reply to Tamora:

> Patient yourself, madam, and pardon me.
> These are their brethren, whom you Goths beheld
> Alive and dead, and for their brethren slain
> Religiously they ask a sacrifice:
> To this your son is mark'd, and die he must,
> To appease their groaning shadows that are gone.
>
> (I.i.121-6)

Allegiance to the ancient ideal of justice, however, blinds Titus to the greater good of mercy. Shakespeare's audience saw the play not in terms of a Roman morality but in terms of an Elizabethan one which upheld mercy as a greater ideal than justice, and which would have agreed entirely with Tamora's argument:

> But must my sons be slaughter'd in the streets,
> For valiant doings in their country's cause?
> O, if to fight for king and commonweal
> Were piety in thine, it is in these.

. . . .

Wilt thou draw near the nature of the gods?
Draw near them then in being merciful:
Sweet mercy is nobility's true badge.

(I.i.112-19)

Shakespeare poses the problem which is to occupy him in *The Merchant of Venice* and *Measure for Measure*: the relation of mercy to justice. Titus, like a later Shylock or Angelo, makes a wrong moral choice; his sin is in adherence to a Roman code of justice to the dead, in spite of the pleas of a Christian ideal of mercy and of the Renaissance creed that those who fight bravely for their country must be honoured even in defeat.

Elizabethans generally would have approved of Titus' refusal of the throne and of his choice of Saturninus over Bassianus, for he is the elder brother who claims the throne by just and lawful succession. There is virtue also in the intense family pride of Titus and in his loyalty to his emperor. It is only fitting that his daughter be a queen, and when Saturninus claims Lavinia as his bride, Titus readily agrees to the union as proper. Further, his emperor wills it, and the loyal subject must obey. This loyalty, this family pride, this respect for his own position and merits, and the sense of the honour which his emperor is offering him cause him to forget that Lavinia has already been betrothed to another. A betrothal in Elizabethan England was a binding contract with all of the force of law; to break it was to violate a woman's honour. Shakespeare's audience would have sided fully with the sons of Titus in their opposition to his decree. Similarly, an Elizabethan audience would have respected the position of Titus as master of his household; to his sons his word must be law, and for them to oppose him unthinkable. What Mutius stands for, however, is his sister's honour, and when Titus murders his son for his opposition, he is carrying the authority of the father to an excess in defiance of justice, honour and reason.

All of Titus' crimes proceed from perversions of virtuous instincts; in each instance Titus makes a wrong moral choice in which he sacrifices the greater good for the lesser one. This is a conventional definition of evil, which in Christian terms involved a blinding by pride which might cause a man to accept a lesser finite good rather than the greater infinite good of God's will.[1] By his attempt to be a God, Titus violates the law of God.

[1] See W. C. Curry, *Shakespeare's Philosophical Patterns* (Baton Rouge, 1937), p. 112.

Titus sins in the first act. In acts two and three we see Titus made to suffer by the evil forces which his own sins have unleashed upon him. By the second scene of the third act, Titus has begun to plot his revenge, and the rest of the play is concerned with its execution. This revenge is a rejection of the Christian way of redemption which called for a submission to the will of God in faith that God would protect man from evil, reward the virtuous and punish the guilty. The madness of Titus symbolizes the defect of reason which makes it impossible for him to see the Christian way out of his difficulties. Marcus counsels him, 'But yet let reason govern thy lament' (III.i.219). Reason here would mean an attuning of human will to divine will, with faith in the perfection of God's harmonious order. Titus, however, shoots arrows in defiance of the Gods. His damnation is inevitable.

In spite of the damnation of Titus, the audience is left not with a feeling of despair, but with a renewed acceptance of divine order and purpose. This feeling of reconciliation is supported by the destruction of evil, which in spite of Titus' damnation vindicates divine justice. The audience participates emotionally in the relief from suffering which comes to Lavinia and Titus, and in the promise of a new day for Rome with the coming of Lucius and his crowning as emperor:

> Thanks, gentle Romans: may I govern so,
> To heal Rome's harms, and wipe away her woe!
> (V.iii.147-8)

In spite of the crudity of style and the Senecan horrors which alienate modern readers, there is a controlling idea of tragedy behind *Titus Andronicus*, a conception of how evil operates in the world and may cause the destruction of a virtuous man by his own moral choice. This wrong moral choice is shown as the product of self-deception and pride, an adherence to an ideal of virtue which is not virtue at all. That evil operated through deception, disguised as good, is a basic Christian notion, going back to the story of Eve's seduction in the garden of Eden. It was at the heart of the medieval morality play, and Shakespeare was to use it again and again, most notably in *Othello*.

Shakespeare in *Titus Andronicus* already conceived of tragedy as an examination of man's relation to the forces of evil in the world, and he altered both his prose source and the dramatic tradition of

c

the Kydian revenge play so that he might express some such relation in a meaningful complex of events. Shakespeare was not yet
a great dramatist when he wrote *Titus Andronicus*, but he had a
greater awareness of the potentialities of tragedy than usually has
been allowed him.

III

When Shakespeare again turned to tragedy with *Richard III*,[1] he
was faced with a somewhat different problem, for the general lines
of his play were already laid out for him. Not only must he complete an historical tetralogy into which this play would fit as a final
unit, but the character of Richard III had already been cast for him
as that of the Senecan villain-hero by a long line of writers, from
Polydore Vergil and Sir Thomas More through the anonymous
author of *The True Tragedy of Richard III*.[2] Richard III had to be
treated as a 'scourge of God' who would castigate England for
her sins, but who while inflicting punishment upon others would
also damn his own soul.

Such a conception called for a simple pattern of dramatic action.
The entire play is centred about the rise and fall of a demonic hero
who is introduced as totally evil. He need make no sinful moral
choice through deception, for he bears the mark of the devil from
his very birth. He is a symbol of evil itself. This is emphasized in
his physical deformity, for Renaissance neo-Platonism saw the
body as the mirror of the soul. Richard begins his career fairly low
on fortune's ladder, but through the force of evil he is able to rise
in worldly power, infusing his own venom into society as he
moves upward. This corrupting power of evil is particularly evident in the wooing of Anne Neville, a symbolic portrait of virtue
undermined by sin. It is also implicit in the fall of Buckingham,
in the fate of all those whose noble instincts Richard is able to
subvert, and who are led to their own destruction along with him.

As Richard rises higher and higher in worldly power, he sinks
lower and lower into moral depravity, compounding sin upon sin,
atrocity upon atrocity. Finally when he is at the height of worldly
place, at the apex of fortune's wheel, and at the same time at the

---

[1] The play was written probably in 1592 or 1593. See Chambers, *William Shakespeare*, I, 270; J. Dover Wilson, ed., *Richard III* (Cambridge, 1954), pp. ix-xi.
[2] See G. B. Churchill, *Richard III up to Shakespeare* (Berlin, 1900). I have treated
these matters in *The English History Play in the Age of Shakespeare* (Princeton, 1957),
pp. 116-23.

lowest point of moral degradation, God intervenes, striking him suddenly from the top of fortune's wheel and damning him utterly in hell. For this purpose, God uses his own instrument, Henry of Richmond, an agent of divine grace who cleanses the social order, vindicates divine justice, and with the evil force of Richard destroyed, effects a rebirth of the good.

Here we have a pattern for tragedy unlike that of *Titus Andronicus*. In that play a noble soul is damned through deception and error, and the pattern of action is one of steady fall. In *Richard III* we have a pattern of rise and fall, with a sudden casting from the heights of a figure who is evil itself, who has challenged the moral fabric of society deliberately and knowingly because it is his very nature to do so. Both plays explore the way of damnation, and in both we have at the end a cleansing of the social order and a vindication of divine justice. This is even more markedly so in *Richard III* than in *Titus Andronicus*, for Richard's career from the very first – within the scope of the tetralogy of which this play is but a part – is part of a great providential scheme, God's plan to free England from sin and to unite her finally under the rule of the Tudors. Richard's very challenging of God's order is, like Satan's, a furthering of God's purposes. His evil in the larger view is part of a greater totality which is good.

In *Richard III* Shakespeare for the first time accomplished in a single play the ends of tragedy and of history. On the personal level we have an exploration of the way of damnation, of how a scourge of God may destroy God's enemies and in doing so damn his own soul. On the political level, the hero of *Richard III* is also England. Until the final act Richard is the symbol of England, and she suffers the degradation which her king's devotion to evil entails. In the final act Henry of Richmond becomes the new symbol of England, and in his virtue England undergoes redemption for her sins; she is restored to political health, just as a human soul may achieve salvation.

In *Richard III* Shakespeare has not yet learned to humanize his political symbol so fully as he is to do in *Richard II*, but we nevertheless can perceive some movement in this direction. As a symbol of evil, Richard might have been a wooden, lifeless figure, but Shakespeare has created in him the illusion of an intriguing individuality. Richard is more than the stock villain-hero of Senecan revenge drama. We see this in the remorse of conscience which he suffers on the evening before Bosworth Field and in the valour with which he goes forth to meet his death. Richard is humanized – as Aaron never is – and thus the statement about God's manner of operation, which the play in its entirety embodies, is cast in specific emotional and imaginative terms in which the audience actively can participate. There is an attractive side to Richard, and we retain to the end some measure of sympathy for him. Unlike the later Richard II, however, he undergoes no personal regeneration. His final courage is a perseverance in evil for which he must be damned, and his damnation sets off the contrasting salvation of England under Henry of Richmond. As tragedy the play might have been more effective with a Richard at the end reaching a self-knowledge and a willingness to expiate his sins. Such a resolution, however, Shakespeare's historical purpose made impossible, for Richard III could not be exhibited on the Tudor stage as other than totally evil. Upon his unredeemed depravity rested in large measure the claim of the Tudors to the throne.

By the ritual action of *Richard III* Shakespeare comments chorally upon the theme of his play. In the wooing of Anne Neville, for instance, he is not interested in presenting historical or psychological truth; that such a wooing ever could have occurred is unlikely. Shakespeare here is portraying symbolically the corrupting force of evil, and to do so he uses a technique which is deliberately unreal. The great choral scenes of lamentation, the curses of old Queen Margaret, the dream of Clarence and his penitential lament, are all ritual scenes which perform specific thematic functions. And the ritualism is emphasized by the neat and formal balance of the stichomythic dialogue, a Senecan device which is not nearly so prevalent in *Titus Andronicus* as it is in *Richard III*, and by such neat parallels as that of the twin speeches of Richard and Richmond on the eve of battle.

This ritual technique Shakespeare learned probably in the *Henry VI* plays with their strong didacticism, supported by the symbolic tradition of the native English morality plays.[1] In *Titus Andronicus* there is a suggestion of ritual in such minor scenes as that of Titus' shooting at the Gods. In later plays Shakespeare is to continue to use a ritual technique, but it will be more fully worked into

[1] See E. M. W. Tillyard, *Shakespeare's History Plays* (New York, 1947), pp. 208-9; A. P. Rossiter, 'The Structure of *Richard III*', *Durham University Journal*, xxxi (1938), 44-75.

the literal level of the action. When Hamlet spares the praying Claudius, for instance, we have a ritual statement of man's inability to destroy another's soul, but at the same time the literal action of the play is forwarded.

In *Richard III* Shakespeare learned to enrich his Senecan matter with symbolic elements, and to do so he fell back upon the native English stage tradition. He was thus able to emphasize the universal significance of his dramatic action more effectively than he could in *Titus Andronicus*. And, perhaps most significantly, he shaped out of traditional devices a type of tragic protagonist unlike that of *Titus Andronicus*, one whose career could expose a different aspect of man's relation to evil. To this distinctive pattern of tragic action he was to return many years later in *Macbeth*.

IV

The patterns for tragedy which Shakespeare developed in *Titus Andronicus* and *Richard III* each reflected the stern morality of Seneca, who saw destruction as the price of sin in a world governed by an inexorable *nemesis*. These are tragedies of damnation, with no hope for the fallen sinner, although Shakespeare strives to create a sense of reconciliation by vindicating divine justice and by a cleansing and redemption of the cosmos. The hero's damnation helps to effect the salvation of the whole. In *Romeo and Juliet*, written probably in 1595, Shakespeare forged a tragedy of a different kind. Again he returned to a Senecan tradition, but he so altered it that what emerged is a tragedy in which man is not destroyed by evil; in spite of his own weak and fallible nature he is able to learn the means of overcoming it and thus attain a victory in death, the tragic price of such knowledge. *Romeo and Juliet* is a play about growth and victory.

Shakespeare derived the story from Arthur Brooke's highly moralistic *Romeus and Juliet* of 1562. How Brooke regarded the tragedy is made clear in his short preface:

> And to this end, good Reader, is this tragical matter written, to describe unto thee a couple of unfortunate lovers, thralling themselves to unhonest desire; neglecting the authority and advice of parents and friends; conferring their principal counsels with drunken gossips and superstitious friars (the naturally fit instruments of unchastity); attempting all adventures of peril for th'attaining of their wicked lust; using auricular confession, the key of whoredom and

treason, for furtherance of their purpose; abusing the honourable name of lawful marriage to cloak the shame of stolen contracts; finally by all means of unhonest life hasting to most unhappy death.[1]

If Brooke sees any tragic meaning in the events of his story it is a simple one of retribution for sin. Romeus and Juliet are guilty of the long list of sins he enumerates; for this they suffer and die. God's providence decrees that sins must be punished, and fortune is merely the agent which executes this decree. No matter how the lovers may struggle against it, fortune betrays and frustrates them at every turn.

Fortune is a dominant motif in Brooke's version of the story. The poem is dotted with conventional lamentations on the cruelty of fortune, and Friar Lawrence in his final summation calls the tragedy, 'the wreak of frantic Fortune's rage'. This emphasis upon fortune was a major carry-over from Senecan drama. Shakespeare inherited a story already cast for him in a tragic pattern: that of two young lovers who move to an inevitable doom which fate has decreed, but who in their progress towards destruction commit sins which make their deaths the result of their own conduct. This is a Senecan formula, differing alone in that its subjects are not kings or princes but ordinary people. This was the extension of Seneca made popular in Italy by Giraldi Cinthio.[2]

Shakespeare's *Romeo and Juliet* usually has been regarded as just such a Senecan tragedy of inexorable fate[3]; some have emphasized the sinfulness of the young lovers.[4] We cannot deny the role of fate in Shakespeare's play; it is established in the prologue and it runs as a constant theme through all five acts. The fate which destroys Romeo and Juliet, however, is not an arbitrary, capricious force, any more than it is the inexorable agent of *nemesis* which in Senecan tragedy executed retribution for sin. The 'greater power than we can contradict' (V.iii.153) is divine providence, guiding the affairs of men in accordance with a plan which is merciful as well as just. Out of the evil of the family feud – a corruption of God's harmonious order – must come a rebirth of love, and the

---

[1] I use the edition by J. J. Monro (New York, 1908).

[2] See H. B. Charlton, *Shakespearian Tragedy* (Cambridge, 1948), p. 49.

[3] See, for instance, G. I. Duthie, ed., *Romeo and Juliet* (Cambridge, 1955), pp. xvii–xxiv; Charlton, pp. 49–63; H. S. Wilson, *On the Design of Shakespearian Tragedy* (Toronto, 1957), pp. 19–37.

[4] Most recently, Franklin M. Dickey, *Not Wisely But Too Well. Shakespeare's Love Tragedies* (San Marino, Calif., 1957), pp. 63–117.

lives of Romeo and Juliet are directed and controlled so that by their deaths the social order will be cleansed and restored to harmony. God's plan is merciful, but it is also just. The elders must pay for their sins with the lives of their children.

Shakespeare uses the story of the lovers to explore the operation of divine providence, the meaning of a fate which in the ordinary affairs of life will sometimes frustrate our most careful plans. Shakespeare's play attains a cosmic scope such as no telling of the story had ever had before, and in its totality it affirms the justice and the mercy of God. Romeo and Juliet are not mere pawns in the larger cosmic scheme, their death a necessary sacrifice for the greater social good. The lovers, in spite of their death, attain a victory in their own right which reflects the restoration to health of the world they leave. Romeo, upon whom Shakespeare concentrates, learns to overcome evil by a process of growth which culminates in his recognition of the harmonious order of God, and his acceptance of death as the necessary end of life within God's perfect plan. There is no retribution for sin in *Romeo and Juliet* so far as the lovers are concerned, for there is no sin. Shakespeare deliberately changed the story so as to minimize the responsibility of the lovers for their fate. In Shakespeare's departure from the Senecan tradition he inherited, lies the significance of *Romeo and Juliet* as tragedy.

In the emphasis upon youth which runs through the play we may find a clue to the new pattern which Shakespeare imposed upon Senecan tradition. Romeo and Juliet are children born into a world already full of an ancient evil not of their own making. The feud is emphasized in the opening lines of the prologue, and in the first scene of the play – before hero or heroine is introduced – the feud is portrayed in all of its ramifications, corrupting the social order from the lowliest servant up to the prince himself.

Romeo and Juliet epitomize the role in life of all men and women; for every being is born into a world in which evil already waits to destroy him, and he marches steadily towards an inexorable death which he cannot avoid. It is a world in which his plans, no matter how virtuous, may be frustrated by a seemingly malignant fate. It is this universality which gives the play its stature as tragedy, for Romeo and Juliet emerge as prototypes of everyman and everywoman. They attempt to find happiness in a world full of evil, to destroy evil by means of love, for with Friar Lawrence they see their marriage as the termination of the feud, but evil in the world cannot be destroyed; their fate cannot be escaped, and thus like all men and women they suffer and die. This is the human life journey, but man need not despair, for he is a creature of reason with the grace of God to guide him, and through his encounter with evil he may learn the nature of evil and discover what it means to be a man.

Shakespeare saw in the legend of Romeo and Juliet a story which illustrated neither retribution for sin nor the working out of a blind inexorable Senecan fatalism. He saw a story which might be used to affirm the providence of God, and at the same time to portray the maturing of youth through suffering and death. *Romeo and Juliet* may be called an 'education' play, drawing upon the morality tradition of such plays as *Nice Wanton* and *Lusty Juventus*. Romeo and Juliet learn the fundamental lessons of tragedy; the meaning of life and death. Their education can only culminate in death and then rebirth where evil has no place. Shakespeare in this play combined a story already cast for him in Senecan mould with an alien dramatic tradition based upon peculiarly Christian assumptions.

Romeo and Juliet are foolish; they are hasty and precipitous, and they make many mistakes; but to speak of a 'tragic flaw' in either of them is absurd. The impetuosity, haste, carelessness of the lovers are the normal attributes of youth. Their very shortcomings are what make them ordinary representatives of humanity. Their errors are all committed with a virtuous end in view, the same end which leads the wise and mature Friar Lawrence to marry them in spite of the dangers he clearly sees. They seek always after good. They are not deliberate or even unknowing sinners.

Shakespeare in *Romeo and Juliet* poses the question of how man may live in a world in which evil lurks about him and in which the inevitable end of all worldly aspirations must be death. Elizabethan Christian humanism held that although good and evil are in the world together, the entire universe is ruled by a benevolent God whose plan is purposive and just. The paradox of the fortunate fall taught that evil itself might contribute to this plan. Man, bearing the burden of original sin, had evil within him, but as the chosen creature of God he had good also. When evil predominated he was ruled by passion, but he had reason which could keep passion under control, and reason was an acceptance of the will of God. This doctrine is expressed by Friar Lawrence:

> For nought so vile that on the earth doth live
> But to the earth some special good doth give,
> Nor aught so good but strain'd from that fair use
> Revolts from true birth, stumbling on abuse:
>
> .   .   .   .
>
> Two such opposed kings encamp them still
> In man as well as herbs, grace and rude will;
> And where the worser is predominant,
> Full soon the canker death eats up that plant.
>
> (II.iii.17-30)

Grace is reason, and rude will is passion. Man may live happily in the world if he allows his reason to guide his actions, to show him that evil itself is designed to further the ends of a divine purpose. With reason thus guiding him, man may become impervious to the blows of fortune. He will accept his fate, whatever it may be, as contributing to a harmonious plan beyond his comprehension but good and just. Through his encounter with evil Romeo learns to accept his fate in such a manner.

We first meet Romeo assuming the conventional role of the melancholy lover, playing a game of courting a Capulet girl who he knows can never accede to his suit. This is the boy Romeo, not yet ready to face the responsibilities of life, unaware of the real sorrows which are the lot of man, but playing with a make-believe sorrow which he enjoys to the fullest. We usually think that at his first sight of Juliet he abandons this childish pose and experiences true love. This may be so, for the dramatist is forced to work rapidly even at the expense of character consistency, but it is not really the sight of Juliet which causes him to change. It is his own precipitous act of leaping out from the dark beneath her window with his

> I take thee at thy word:
> Call me but love, and I'll be new baptized;
> Henceforth I never will be Romeo.
>
> (II.ii.49-51)

With this speech, the game of make-believe love becomes no longer possible. The hasty act of impetuous youth is the means to maturity, a seeming paradox, for out of the errors of youth comes

the wisdom of age. Romeo must now face the reality of life with
all of its consequences both for good and evil. There may be a
double meaning in that final line. Never again will he be the same
Romeo who had pined for Rosaline. Juliet too can no longer be
the same once she has poured her heart out into the night. She too
must now face the world as it is. Her unpremeditated outpouring
of her love parallels the precipitous speech of Romeo.

Romeo and Juliet are uncertain and hasty in their first encoun-
ters with the problems of reality. Their plans at best are foolish
ones. Whether or not there was need for the immediate marriage
may be debated, but it is nevertheless concluded and the future is
awaited. The force of evil had already intruded into their world
immediately following Romeo's first sight of Juliet. His first
poetic rapture (I.v.46-55) had been echoed by the harsh voice of
Tybalt:

> This, by his voice, should be a Montague.
> Fetch me my rapier, boy.
>
> (I.v.56-57)

This is Shakespeare's poetic way of showing the ever-present
juxtaposition of love and hate, good and evil. Before the marriage
may be consummated Romeo must now face this evil force. He is
not yet, however, able to face it as he should. When Tybalt lies
dead at his feet, and a full awareness of his situation comes upon
him, Romeo cries out in despair:

> O, I am fortune's fool!
>
> (III.i.141)

This is a crucial line, and all of its implications must be under-
stood. 'Fool' had two common meanings in Shakespeare's age.
On the one hand it had the connotation of 'dupe' or 'plaything',
and thus the word usually is glossed. On the other hand it was a
common term for 'child'. The New Cambridge editors (p. 231)
indicate three other places in the play where it is used with that
meaning. When Romeo calls himself the 'dupe' or 'plaything' of
fortune, he is asserting a capricious, lawless fortune, and thus he
is denying the providence of God, of which in the Christian view
fortune is merely the agent. Romeo is proclaiming a view of God
similar to that which the blind Gloucester, in his delusion and
despair, is to utter in King Lear:

> As flies to wanton boys, are we to the gods,
> They kill us for their sport.   (IV.i.38-39)

This is the philosophy of despair; it sees the universe as a mindless chaos, without guiding plan.

With this view of life the secondary meaning of 'fool' is in complete accord. As long as man sees fortune as capricious and the universe as without plan, he must be the slave of fortune. Romeo is the child of fortune at this point because he is governed by it as the child is governed by its father. He is constrained to blind obedience. He has not yet learned the way of acceptance by which the control of fortune may be thrown off. When Romeo's own will is in accord with the universal plan of God, he will no longer be the child of fortune in this sense. He will be the master of fortune in that it can never direct him contrary to his own will. In this sense of 'child' there is also the secondary implication that Romeo is more fortunate than he himself perceives, that he is protected as the child is by his father. The divine providence whose 'fool' he is will lead him, in spite of his present ignorance, to a self-mastery and wisdom, and it will use his present seeming misfortune to restore harmony and order to the world.

From this low point Romeo must make his slow journey to maturity. Shakespeare shows his progression in three stages. First we find him in the Friar's cell, weeping and wailing, beating his head upon the ground and offering to kill himself. This abject surrender to passion is the behaviour not of a rational man but of a beast, as the Friar declares:

> Hold thy desperate hand:
> Art thou a man? thy form cries out thou art:
> Thy tears are womanish; thy wild acts denote
> The unreasonable fury of a beast.
>
>   (III.iii.108-11)

Romeo's education now begins at the hands of Friar Lawrence who, in a lengthy speech (III.iii.118-44) teaches him to make a virtue of necessity, that to rail on fortune is fruitless, that reason will demonstrate to him that he is more fortunate than he thinks he is. When, rather than kill himself, he stops his weeping and goes to comfort Juliet, he has taken the first step towards maturity.

That his growth is a steady one from that point forward we may perceive from a bare hint as Romeo climbs from Juliet's window to be off for Mantua. 'O, think'st thou we shall ever meet again?' asks Juliet, and Romeo replies:

> I doubt it not; and all these woes shall serve
> For sweet discourses in our time to come.
>
> (III.v.51-53)

What is significant here is that Romeo has thrown off despair and can face the future with some degree of hope in an ultimate providence. It is but the barest hint of a change in him, and we see no more of him until the beginning of Act V where in Mantua we perceive by his first words that he is a new man entirely. All of Act IV had been devoted to Juliet. The dramatist has not had time to show in detail the growth of Romeo although he has indicated it in part by the changing imagery of Romeo's speeches, growing as they do from the conventional rhetorical display of the first act to a more spontaneous and natural mode of expression which betokens true feeling and sincerity.[1] The change must be made clear in Romeo's first speech and it must be accepted by the audience as an accomplished fact. We immediately sense a new serenity about him as he walks upon the stage at the beginning of Act V:

> If I may trust the flattering truth of sleep,
> My dreams presage some joyful news at hand:
> My bosom's lord sits lightly in his throne;
> And all this day an unaccustom'd spirit
> Lifts me above the ground with cheerful thoughts.
>
> (V.i.1-5)

He expects joyful tidings, but the news which Balthazar brings is the most horrible of which he can conceive. Shakespeare gives this opening speech to Romeo so that it may set off the shock of the news of Juliet's supposed death coming when happy news is expected, and in the face of this shock to illustrate the manner in which the new Romeo can receive the severest blow of which fortune is capable.

To this dread report, Romeo replies with the simple but crucial line:

> Is it in so? then I denie you starres[2]

[1] See W. H. Clemen, *The Development of Shakespeare's Imagery* (Cambridge, Mass., 1951), p. 79.

[2] I have argued for this Q² reading in *Studies in The English Renaissance Drama*, ed. Bennett, Cargill and Hall (New York, 1959), pp. 269-86.

In denying fortune Romeo is asserting his independence of it, casting off its control as the child may cast off that of its father. There may be a subtle recollection here of the secondary meaning of 'child' in that other crucial line, 'O, I am fortune's fool'. The fool, or child, of fortune has now thrown off the control of fortune. In terms of Renaissance Christian stoicism there was but one means by which this might be accomplished: by a recognition of the way of the world as the will of God, and by a calm, fearless acceptance of death as the necessary end of man which releases him from earthly evil and assures him of a true felicity in heaven. For Romeo this will be reunion with Juliet.

The suicide of the lovers was difficult for Shakespeare to reconcile with the Christian framework he imposed upon his story. In the Senecan tradition in which the legend came down to Shakespeare, there was approval of suicide as a heroic means of release from a world full of pain and as a way of expiation for complicity in the death of a loved one. In spite of the Christian injunction against self-destruction, the Elizabethan drama carried on the tradition of suicide as noble and heroic, and Shakespeare could depend upon his audience naturally to think of the deaths of Romeo and Juliet in these terms. Their suicide is not to be taken – as some recent critics have taken it – as evidence of their damnation. Their manner of death was inherited by Shakespeare as an essential part of the story. It is imperfectly integrated into the new pattern which Shakespeare imposed upon his alien source, but if it has any meaning in this pattern it must be as a symbolic act of acceptance of inevitable death. Dramatically it is the most effective means by which such acceptance might be portrayed. The results of this act are not damnation, but instead the destruction of evil. Out of the self-inflicted deaths of Romeo and Juliet comes a rebirth of good; the audience experiences a sense of reconciliation which would be impossible were the lovers to be regarded as damned. For them to suffer damnation for no greater sin than the ordinary attributes of youth, or as a necessary sacrifice to the regeneration of the social whole, would be to deny the mercy and justice of God which the total structure of the play was so carefully designed to support.

The doctrine of Shakespearian tragedy is not expressed by the method of logic; Shakespeare aims at a total poetic impression whose intellectual statement is emotionally experienced. A true Christian might not have committed suicide, but we cannot apply

to poetic drama the criteria of philosophic discourse. The simple
point which Shakespeare wishes to make is that Romeo has grown
to maturity, has learned to accept the order of the universe with
all it may entail, that he is ready for death, and that he can accept
it bravely and calmly as the necessary means towards the greater
good of reunion with Juliet. He will, as he puts it:

> shake the yoke of inauspicious stars
> From this world-wearied flesh.
>
> (V.iii.111-12)

When Paris says to him in the graveyard, 'for thou must die', it is
not merely to Paris that Romeo replies:

> I must indeed; and therefore came I hither.
>
> (V.iii.57-58)

In that simple line is a summation of Romeo's development. He
has come willingly to embrace the necessary end of life's journey.

The world of *Romeo and Juliet* is a sombre, realistic one in which
youth is born into evil and must struggle against it ceaselessly
until the conflict is ended by death. But Shakespeare's tragic vision
is not one of resignation or despair; it is one of defiance and hope,
of pride in those qualities of man which enable him to survive and
achieve victory in such a world. A Christian view of man's position in the universe provides a design for tragedy in this early
play. This design, character and event are patterned by the artist
to support. There are inconsistencies. Shakespeare has not yet
been able entirely to escape the limitations imposed by his sources.
We can nevertheless perceive governing and shaping the matter
which Shakespeare took from Arthur Brooke the idea of tragedy
as a portrait of man's journey from youth to maturity, encounter-
ing the evil in the world, learning to live with it, and achieving
victory over it by death. Shakespeare deliberately alters his source
to support his statement that the ultimate plan of the universe is
good, for there is no mention at the end of Brooke's version of
either the parents or the feud, whereas in Shakespeare's play we
are made to see that through the suffering of individuals the social
order is cleansed of evil; the deep-rooted family feud is finally
brought to an end. In the governing design of *Romeo and Juliet* we
have an important milestone in Shakespeare's career. He had developed out of traditional devices a new formula for tragedy, and

to this formula, so unlike that of *Titus Andronicus* or *Richard III*, he was to return with greater power in *Hamlet*.

V

In the three early plays which we have considered, there is an epitome of the patterns for tragedy which are to occupy Shakespeare throughout his career. Here already are the three basic forms which Shakespeare is to extend and develop in his later plays. There is the tragedy of the virtuous man's fall through deception in *Titus Andronicus*, of the deliberately evil man's rise and fall in *Richard III*, and of the ordinary man's growth to maturity in *Romeo and Juliet*. All have their origins in the English Senecanism of the 1580's, but all go beyond inherited dramatic tradition, for with each progressive experiment, Shakespeare makes his changes and extensions, mingling with his Senecan matter other traditions of the popular Elizabethan stage, and seasoning all with the unique quality of his own artistic imagination.

In these early plays we can see also that Shakespeare is no mere imitator of his contemporaries, that for him tragedy is more than sensationalism or stagecraft. Each play in its own way is a serious exploration of man's place in the universe, and in each play there is implicit a positive statement which affirms justice in the universe and the benevolence of God. Shakespeare is not yet the dramatist he was to become, but we can nevertheless see how such statement controls and shapes character and action into a meaningful pattern.

Historical Tragedy: *King John* *Richard II, Julius Caesar*

Following *Romeo and Juliet*, Shakespeare appears to have devoted himself for some five or six years to romantic comedy and to the English historical drama he had begun with the *Henry VI* plays and *Richard III*, and which was to culminate in the tetralogy of plays from *Richard II* to *Henry V*. Probably soon after *Richard III* Shakespeare had also produced *King John*, perhaps the most difficult to date of all his plays, although the meagre evidence seems to indicate sometime between 1592 and 1594 as most likely.[1] The concern with English history may have led to Roman history, for *Julius Caesar* was probably written in 1599, hard upon the completion of *Henry V*.

There is a tradition slow in dying among Shakespearian critics which would separate the history plays from the mainstream of Shakespearian tragedy, as though a concern with history precluded involvement in the ethical questions which are the province of tragedy. Such a separation, as I have elsewhere argued,[2] is meaningless and unnecessary. Shakespeare's contemporaries made no distinction between history and tragedy; it was, in fact, a commonplace of Renaissance neo-classicism that history was the most suitable subject matter for tragedy, a doctrine which Ben Jonson very notably expressed when in the preface to the 1605 edition of *Sejanus* he pointed to his 'truth of argument' as evidence that he had 'discharged the other offices of a tragic writer'.

---

[1] See J. D. Wilson, ed., *King John* (Cambridge, 1936), p. lvii. Chambers' date of 1596-7 (*William Shakespeare*, I, 270) has little to support it, and E. A. J. Honigmann's elaborate argument for 1590-1 in his New Arden edition (London, 1954) is hardly convincing. See the refutation by R. A. Law, 'On the Date of *King John*', *SP*, LIV (1957), 119-27.

[2] *The English History Play in the Age of Shakespeare*, particularly pp. 28-30.

In *Richard III* Shakespeare framed a play to complete an historical tetralogy whose subject was the fate of England, and at the same time he created a tragedy in which the degradation of England and her salvation through purgation of evil within herself were mirrored in the life-journey of the tragic hero who was her king. Just as the story of Richard III had already been shaped by Shakespeare's predecessors into a vehicle for tragedy, that of King John had been given tragic potentialities in the two-part *Troublesome Reign of John* which was Shakespeare's source. In *Richard II* and *Julius Caesar*, we find Shakespeare approaching the matter of history with a surer hand, and out of it creating tragedy of singular power. In these plays he is learning lessons which are to have fruition in the great tragedies of the succeeding decade. After *Julius Caesar* we are ready for *Hamlet*.

But the very fact that these plays do accomplish the ends of the Tudor historian, that they use the past in order to teach political wisdom to the present, conditions their scope as tragedy. Like the other tragedies, these embody intellectual statements which character and action support, and which are particularly implicit in the pathways to destruction taken by the central figures. But the salvation of the body politic receives greater emphasis than that of the individual man. That the plays are histories conditions the symbolic function of character. The hero-king stands always for England, and the principle implicit in his life-journey is one of national destiny, although this may be related closely to his own damnation or salvation. The fate of Brutus or Caesar is secondary to that of Rome, and as tragic heroes they also reflect in specific human terms principles of general political conduct.

II

In *King John* Shakespeare is bound to some extent by the portrait of his hero which had been drawn before him by Protestant chroniclers. In these accounts King John emerged as a pre-Reformation hero, the only king before Henry VIII who had dared oppose the papacy. As one who had rallied the dissident barons to a defence of England against France and Austria who fought under the papal ensign, John had become a symbol of English nationalism. Having died finally at the hands of the evil monk, Simon of Swynsett – historically, John died of over-eating – he could be viewed as a royal martyr. The chronicles recorded, however, that

D

he failed in his struggle against the church of Rome, and that he
was poisoned after an ignominious capitulation. This failure usually was attributed to his own insufficiency, his sinful complicity
in the death of Prince Arthur, son of his elder brother, Geoffrey.
In such a concept of John there was a potential for tragedy, a view
of man frustrated in his striving for a noble end because of his
own sin which he regrets but cannot renounce, for the death of
Arthur was essential to John's own claim to the throne, and the
rule of the weak and effeminate boy, Arthur, would have been bad
for England. John's life-journey might be viewed as not unlike
that of a Titus Andronicus, who also, in spite of his noble aspirations, is doomed to destruction because of a commitment to evil
which proceeds from those very qualities which are the source of
his greatness.[1]

In *King John* Shakespeare returned to the pattern for tragedy he
had evolved in *Titus Andronicus*, but he now enlarged it into a
vehicle almost entirely new. By stressing John as a symbol of English nationalism, and by emphasizing his remorse for his crime,
Shakespeare effected a partial regeneration of his hero so that in
his downfall he might still achieve some victory. In this play
Shakespeare used for the first time that device of character parallelism which was to be brought to perfection in *Richard II* and
which was to mark his maturest tragedies. John and the Bastard
are foils to one another. Faulconbridge at first mirrors the strength
of John in his own weakness and later the weakness of John in
his own strength. When the play opens John is on top and the
Bastard below; when it closes the Bastard is on top and John has

---

[1] *King John* has been regarded as among the less successful of Shakespeare's plays,
lacking in structure, with no obvious hero, a loose succession of scenes, saved only
by the vitality of Faulconbridge and the poignancy of Constance. See Edward
Dowden, *Shakespeare, His Mind and Art* (New York, 1903), p. 153; E. M. W.
Tillyard, *Shakespeare's History Plays* (New York, 1947), pp. 232-3; L. B. Campbell,
Shakespeare's 'Histories' (San Marino, Calif., 1947), pp. 126-67; John Palmer, *Political
Characters in Shakespeare* (London, 1945), pp. 321-34; H. B. Charlton, *Shakespearian
Tragedy* (Cambridge, 1948), pp. 65-69. John Middleton Murry, *Shakespeare* (London,
1936), pp. 159-69, has seen the Bastard as the hero, with King John merely a foil to
set him off. Such a view removes the Bastard from his context in the total dramatic
structure and distorts the play as surely as does Miss Campbell's contrary notion
(pp. 166-7) that he is merely a chorus commenting from the outside upon the action
of a play in which he plays no integral part. That *King John* is a neatly unified dramatic
structure of which John is the hero has been argued by Adrian Bonjour, 'The Road
to Swinstead Abbey: A Study of the Sense and Structure of *King John*', *ELH*, XVIII
(1951), 253-74.

fallen. There are two parallel movements: as John descends the Bastard rises. This pattern of rise and fall had its roots in *de casibus* tragedy of the Middle Ages.

Shakespeare's *King John* is a unified dramatic structure which expresses a statement both political and ethical. John's life-journey affirms the inseparability of private and public morality, that only a good man can be a good king. At the same time the parallel progressions of John and Faulconbridge assert that England can be united only when her ruler learns to subordinate his private desires to the well-being of his country. This theme of national unity welds the stories of John and the Bastard into a consistent dramatic whole. In the attainment of English unity at the end of the play, with Faulconbridge surrendering his power to the new king, Henry III, the audience recognizes that the goal which John had sought has been realized in spite of his own suffering and death. The man John is destroyed, but John, the symbol of national unity, is triumphant.

In the conflict between John and Arthur for the English throne, a crucial issue of the first three acts, Shakespeare makes two points clear: that John is a usurper who holds the throne only by virtue of *de facto* possession, and that, in spite of this, he is to be preferred to Arthur who has a legitimate claim. In the fourth line of the play the French ambassador refers to John's 'borrow'd majesty', and when John claims the throne on the basis of 'our strong possession and our right' (I.i.39), his mother, Elinor, reminds the audience:

> Your strong possession much more than your right,
> Or else it must go wrong with you and me:
> So much my conscience whispers in your ear,
> Which none but heaven and you and I shall hear.
>
> (I.i.40-43)

That he is a good king for England Shakespeare emphasizes in John's victory over the French, his defiance of the Pope and his support of the English nationalism of which throughout the play he is both symbol and rallying point.

Arthur's inadequacy is emphasized in that, as surely as John stands for England and royal supremacy, Arthur represents the power of Rome and the hostile forces of France and Austria who stand opposed to English nationalism. Arthur, moreover, is a child, weak and powerless, the kind of ruler Tudor Englishmen

most feared, for they saw his type of rule mirrored in the disas-
trous reign of a similar child king, Henry VI. Arthur's insufficiency he himself sums up:

> Good my mother, peace!
> I would that I were low laid in my grave:
> I am not worth this coil that's made for me.
>
>   (II.i.163-5)

The opposing forces are clearly aligned at the play's opening:
England, royal supremacy, John and Faulconbridge stand opposed to France, Rome and Arthur. Shakespeare's political sympathies are obvious, but in his characteristic manner he tempers
the emotional commitment of his audience to the side of John by
his portrait of the cruel Queen Elinor, and he wins a large measure
of sympathy for the side of Arthur by his portrait of Constance.
This conditions the audience for the change of sympathies to
come when John commits his tragic error.

For the first two and a half acts John is a good and great king.
His initial strength appears in his answer to the French ambassador:

> Be thou as lightning in the eyes of France;
> For ere thou canst report I will be there,
> The thunder of my cannon shall be heard:
> So hence! Be thou the trumpet of our wrath
> And sullen presage of your own decay.   (I.i.24-28)

John is able to win Faulconbridge to his service and to defy the
Pope in unequivocal terms:

> What earthy name to interrogatories
> Can task the free breath of a sacred king?
> Thou canst not, cardinal, devise a name
> So slight, unworthy and ridiculous,
> To charge me to an answer, as the pope.
> Tell him this tale; and from the mouth of England
> Add thus much more, that no Italian priest
> Shall tithe or toll in our dominions;
> But as we, under heaven, are supreme head,
> So under Him that great supremacy,
> Where we do reign, we will alone uphold,
> Without the assistance of a mortal hand:
> So tell the pope, all reverence set apart
> To him and his usurp'd authority.   (III.i.147-60)

The culminating evidence of John's strength is his defeat of the French on the plain before Angier and his capture of Arthur. This brings us to the middle of the third act, with John at the peak of his glory, but when in III.iii he suborns Hubert to murder Arthur, he commits the sin which causes him to degenerate both as man and as king, and the rest of the play demonstrates his decline.

While John in these first three acts rides high on fortune's wheel, Faulconbridge is fairly low. He bears the moral stigma of his bastardy, which he proudly affirms to his mother's dishonour. He is a bluff, likeable character, but there is little moral distinction about him. The shameful league of France and England gives him a new respect for commodity:

> Since kings break faith upon commodity,
> Gain, be my lord, for I will worship thee.
>
> (II.i.597-8)

The cynicism of this 'commodity' speech reflects contempt for the Christian humanist notions of order and degree which were the bases of Elizabethan morality. The theme of the grasping adventurer is carried on in the relish with which the Bastard goes forth to ransack the English abbeys:

> Bell, book, and candle shall not drive me back,
> When gold and silver becks me to come on.
>
> (III.iii.12-13)

But Shakespeare will not entirely alienate the audience from the Bastard who is to rise in moral stature as John declines. With this rise Faulconbridge will assume the control of England's destiny which John forfeits.

No sooner has King John given his order to Hubert than in the following scene (III.iv) we see his defeated enemies beginning to recoup their forces against him. Shakespeare now uses the lamentations of Constance to wean his audience's sympathies away from John. This alienation is completed by the painful and pathetic scene (IV.i) in which Arthur pleads with Hubert for his eyes. In Hubert's inability to commit the crime to which he has been suborned – a defection from duty with which the audience is made to sympathize – we see the power of John beginning to crumble.

Now we are ready for a quick succession of blows which will topple John both as man and king. As he explains the need for a second coronation, John gives evidence of the fears which have begun to plague him (IV.ii.40-46). Then follow in succession the news that Arthur is dead, with the consternation among the nobles which this provokes, the news of the French army regrouped and ready to attack England, and finally the news that John's key support, Queen Elinor, is dead. King John in one scene is struck on the political plane, the military, and on that of personal family affection. He is able himself to see that these three blows which stagger both the private and the public man, proceed from his order for the death of Arthur. He knows at once why Salisbury and Pembroke are deserting him:

> They burn in indignation. I repent:
> There is no sure foundation set on blood,
> No certain life achieved by others' death.
>
> (IV.ii.103-5)

As his disasters begin to mount he turns upon Hubert and blames him for the deed:

> Why seek'st thou to possess me with these fears?
> Why urgest thou so oft young Arthur's death?
> Thy hand hath murder'd him: I had a mighty cause
> To wish him dead, but thou hadst none to kill him.
>
> (IV.ii.203-6)

And then his remorse breaks fully forth:

> O, when the last account 'twixt heaven and earth
> Is to be made, then shall this hand and seal
> Witness against us to damnation!
> How oft the sight of means to do ill deeds
> Make deeds ill done!
>
> (IV.ii.216-20)

The discord in his kingdom springs from Arthur's death:

> My nobles leave me; and my state is braved,
> Even at my gates, with ranks of foreign powers:
> Nay, in the body of this fleshly land,
> This kingdom, this confine of blood and breath,
> Hostility and civil tumult reigns
> Between my conscience and my cousin's death.
>
> (IV.ii.243-8)

This discord troubles both the state and John's own little world of man. He is overjoyed by Hubert's announcement that Arthur has not been killed (IV.ii.259-60), but in the very next scene (IV.iii) we behold the accidental death of Arthur in spite of all, and we know that John, no matter how great his remorse, must bear the guilt of it and that this guilt will destroy him.

The collapse of King John is now shown by the revolt of the lords and by his abject and ignominious submission to Pandulph, the Papal legate, with which the fifth act begins. Now there is nothing left for John but death. With the king's decline the Bastard Faulconbridge begins to rise in moral stature until he is ready to assume the guidance of England which John by his moral defection has relinquished. We see the Bastard's rise first in his castigation of Hubert for the death of Arthur (IV.iii.125-34) and then in his resolution of the conflict within himself: shall he serve John in spite of Arthur's death, or shall he join the rebellious lords in opposing him. He attains his full moral stature when he places the unity of England above all other considerations. In spite of everything, he urges John to a defence of England:

> But wherefore do you droop? why look you sad?
> Be great in act, as you have been in thought;
> Let not the world see fear and sad distrust
> Govern the motion of a kingly eye:
> Be stirring as the time; be fire with fire;
> Threaten the threatener and outface the brow
> Of bragging horror: so shall inferior eyes,
> That borrow their behaviours from the great,
> Grow great by your example and put on
> The dauntless spirit of resolution.
> Away, and glister like the god of war,
> When he intendeth to become the field:
> Show boldness and aspiring confidence.
> What, shall they seek the lion in his den,
> And fright him there? and make him tremble there?
> O, let it not be said: forage, and run
> To meet displeasure farther from the doors,
> And grapple with him ere he come so nigh.
>
> (V.i.44-61)

When John gives to him 'the ordering of this present time' (V.i. 77), Faulconbridge assumes the leadership of England. He proclaims to the French that John's 'royalty doth speak in me' (V.ii.

129). He is a symbol now of English unity, and as such he destroys the French invaders. The English lords are won back to the crown, and Faulconbridge is left to speak the great apostrophe to English unity with which the play closes (V.vii.110-18). Faulconbridge surrenders his power to the new king, Henry III, thus assuring a continuance of orderly legal government, with the rightful heir in place. In setting the good of England above his personal gain and glory, he mirrors the theme of the play.

In spite of John's fall, through the parallel rise of Faulconbridge England is able to attain salvation. But what of John, the man? He dies ignobly, poisoned by a treacherous monk, but Shakespeare suggests in the words of Faulconbridge that John too has attained salvation:

> Art thou gone so? I do but stay behind
> To do the office for thee of revenge,
> And then my soul shall wait on thee to heaven,
> As it on earth hath been thy servant still.
>
> (V.vii.70-73)

John's remorse for Arthur's death and the victory of England in spite of his sins win for him the expiation reflected in the eulogies of Faulconbridge and young Prince Henry.

We can thus discern in *King John* a pattern for tragedy which extends what Shakespeare had evolved in *Titus Andronicus*. As historical tragedy the play fuses the political and the ethical, with John as the mirror of both. At first he is great both as man and king. Then he commits a sin which is itself both political and ethical: he destroys his rival for the throne, and he causes the death of a child. England and its king degenerate together. The king dies in body, but he is saved in soul, just as England is saved in actuality. This regeneration is effected by Faulconbridge, who in his rise symbolizes both the political and the ethical ideals for which John strives but which he cannot attain. The Bastard's victory completes the pattern of a tragedy of salvation, both personal and political.

III

Richard II is the opening play of an historical tetralogy whose theme is the fall of England and her triumphant regeneration. The four-play sequence gives dramatic form to important political doctrine, expressing Shakespeare's answer to the great questions of his age: what is a perfect king and what are the limits of his power. In *Richard II* Shakespeare shows us the initial fall, upon which the house of Lancaster will rise and in its rise effect a redemption of England. As historical tragedy *Richard II* is concerned not only with the fall of a man, but with the fall also of the England he represents, and as in *King John* the statement of the play is ethical and political at once.[1]

With Richard and Henry Bolingbroke each the opposing mirror of the other's vices and virtues, strengths and weaknesses, Shakespeare repeats the technique of character parallelism he had developed in *King John*. As Richard falls, Henry rises, and in the deposition scene of the fourth act Richard gives to Henry the symbolic representation of England which is always in the title of the king. Shakespeare uses York to emphasize that with Henry's acceptance of the crown he is fully the king of England and is entitled to all the allegiance formerly due to Richard. This is underscored by York's pleading for the death of Aumerle, altered somewhat from Holinshed where he had more reason to demand his son's death. In the fifth act begins the regeneration of England under the rule of the house of Lancaster with which the three remaining plays will be concerned, and which will have its culmination in the glorious patriotic pageant of *Henry V*. We have, as in *King John*, the simultaneous fall of England and her royal symbol, and then the salvation of England through the office of the new symbol.

In these respects Shakespeare does not go beyond the tragic pattern he had developed in *King John*. But there is more in *Richard II* than this. With the fall of John and the rise of Faulconbridge, there had been a corresponding shift of sympathy from the declining to the ascending figure. In *Richard II* Shakespeare reverses this process. In the opening scenes of the play Richard is portrayed in the most unattractive of colours, whereas Bolingbroke is the wronged champion of England who in his quest for justice carries the sympathy of the audience with him. As the play progresses and Richard begins to fall, sympathy for him steadily mounts, while Bolingbroke becomes steadily less attractive. Shakespeare infuses into his political tragedy a human element which is lacking in *King John*, where any pathos the audience is likely to feel over the king's death is lost in the triumphant celebration of Eng-

---

[1] It was probably written in 1595 or 1596. See Chambers, *William Shakespeare*, I, 271; Peter Ure, ed., *Richard II* (London, 1956), pp. xxix-xxx.

land's final victory. This human element is perfectly fused with the political, for although Shakespeare recognizes the necessity of Bolingbroke's rule for the preservation of England, he nevertheless censures his means of attaining the crown. Henry IV's triumph as King of England is at the same time Henry Bolingbroke's moral downfall as a man. In the same manner Richard's downfall as a king leads to his regeneration as a man.

In the Bishop of Carlisle's speech (IV.i.114-49), there are forebodings of the trouble to come, but nevertheless, with Henry's offer to 'make a voyage to the Holy Land, / To wash this blood off from my guilty hand' (V.vi.49-50), England for the moment is triumphant. She now has a king who has given evidence in his handling of the conflict between Aumerle and Bagot and in his treatment of Aumerle's abortive insurrection, that he will remedy the evils of Richard's reign. But it is not by this political triumph that the audience is most affected. It is caught up rather with the spectacle of Richard in his cell at Pomfret, entertaining his groom with a new humility, and striking back with a last vain effort at the cruel figure who comes to murder him.

Richard has been called a play actor, a sentimentalist, one enchanted with his own appearance and the sound of his own voice. But these qualities are no more the causes of his destruction than the haste and impetuosity of youth could cause the destruction of Romeo. *Richard II* is a history play, and Richard's downfall is cast in political terms. He is unable to perform the duties of kingship for which his birth has made him responsible. He has redeeming qualities as a man, but he is placed in a position where he must wield a political power of which he is not capable. This is the cause of his tragedy.

Bolingbroke is an adversary with those very public qualities which Richard lacks. The two men confront one another in the opening scene, and already we see that Bolingbroke stands for strength and justice, while Richard stands for the reverse. Shakespeare depends upon his audience's knowledge of the events leading to the murder at Calais of Richard's uncle, Thomas of Woodstock, Duke of Gloucester. The audience knows that Richard himself has ordered his uncle's death and that Bolingbroke in accusing Mowbray is in effect accusing the king in whose service Mowbray had acted. Richard's weakness in this situation is reflected in his consent to the combat at arms (I.i.196-205). This is immediately followed by a short scene between John of Gaunt and the Duchess of Gloucester which reaffirms Richard's guilt. 'God's is the quarrel;' says Gaunt, 'for God's substitute, / His deputy anointed in His sight, / Hath caused his death' (I.ii.37-39). A weak and ineffective king tainted with moral guilt is opposed to a strong and effective challenger speaking in the cause of justice.

The tournament scene (I.iii), with the banishment of Mowbray and Bolingbroke, serves further to underscore Richard's effeminate wilfulness and political ineptitude. In Bolingbroke's brave acceptance of his unjust fate, we are prepared for the contrasting scene (I.iv) of Richard's thoughtless yet uneasy jocularity with his favourites, and then the avaricious cruelty with which he receives the news of his uncle Gaunt's approaching death:

> Now put it, God, in the physician's mind
> To help him to his grave immediately!
> The lining of his coffers shall make coats
> To deck our soldiers for these Irish wars.
> Come, gentlemen, let's all go visit him:
> Pray God we may make haste, and come too late!
> (I.iv.59-64)

In Gaunt's death scene (II.i) all the sins of Richard, both personal and political, are exhibited to the audience, and Richard reduces himself to his lowest moral level in the play. The sympathies of the audience at this point rest with Bolingbroke.

Then begins the slow reversal. To redirect audience sympathy Shakespeare uses Richard's queen. We have seen Richard at his most loathsome and rapacious as he prepared to loot the property of Gaunt to finance a vain and foolish Irish war. Now we begin to see another side of him in the Queen's words:

> To please the king I did; to please myself
> I cannot do it; yet I know no cause
> Why I should welcome such a guest as grief,
> Save bidding farewell to so sweet a guest
> As my sweet Richard.
> (II.ii.5-9)

Shakespeare draws for us, without regard for the chronicles, a gentle and pathetic queen whose sorrow we can share, and thus the harsh image we have gained of the man for whom she weeps begins to soften in our sympathetic participation in her grief. The

news of the rebellion comes to the audience not as a welcome
relief to Bolingbroke's wrongs, but as cause of sorrow for a weeping queen, and Worcester's breaking of his staff of office is viewed
not as justifiable partisanship, but as reprehensible perfidy.

By such means Shakespeare effects his reversal of sympathies.
The third act begins with Bolingbroke's condemnation of Bushy
and Green, and no matter how great their crimes, there is nothing
in Bolingbroke's curt 'My Lord Northumberland, see them dispatch'd' (III.i.35) to endear him to an audience. His cold-blooded
efficiency is contrasted in the next scene with the woeful inadequacy of Richard upon his return from Ireland. This scene (III.ii)
underscores the pathos of Richard's situation, and in spite of his
unkingly behaviour, it wins for him a large measure of audience
sympathy. Shakespeare's juxtaposition of cold-blooded efficiency
against pathetic but human inadequacy is continued in the scene
before Flint castle (III.iii). The garden episode (III.iv) contains
important political allegory, but it also serves to raise further the
audience's identification with Richard's cause. Richard's fall is
mirrored in the plight of his helpless queen, and the Gardener's
speech is Shakespeare's direction of audience sentiment:

> Poor queen! so that thy state might be no worse,
> I would my skill were subject to thy curse.
> Here did she fall a tear; here in this place
> I'll set a bank of rue, sour herb of grace:
> Rue, even for ruth, here shortly shall be seen,
> In the remembrance of a weeping queen.

> (III.iv.102-7)

On the other hand, Bolingbroke's 'In God's name, I'll ascend
the regal throne' (IV.i.113), coming as it does when our sympathies for 'plume-pluck'd Richard' have been fully awakened, serves
to turn the audience from him. He sinks lower and lower as a
man, while at the same time the fifth act establishes his greatness
as a king. Our final estimate of Bolingbroke the king is in York's
unswerving loyalty to him, for York throughout the play mirrors
the attitude of the ordinary Englishman which the audience is
expected to share. Bolingbroke the man sinks to the level of the
muttered wish which leads Pierce of Exton to commit the crime
his king desires but will not directly order.

The final act of *Richard II* is designed to accomplish two large objectives, the one political and the other personal. Through the affairs of Aumerle and York Shakespeare affirms that England now has a strong king who will restore her to the glory from which Richard's reign has brought her, and that in spite of his usurpation Henry IV is the lawful king of England in whom the hope of the future must reside. On the other hand this act shows us the final development of Richard the man. The pathos of his situation is again reflected as we see him through the eyes of the queen:

> But soft, but see, or rather do not see,
> My fair rose wither: yet look up, behold,
> That you in pity may dissolve to dew,
> And wash him fresh again with true-love tears.
> Ah, thou, the model where old Troy did stand,
> Thou map of honour, thou King Richard's tomb,
> And not King Richard; thou most beauteous inn,
> Why should hard-favour'd grief be lodged in thee,
> When triumph is become an alehouse guest?
>
> (V.i.7-15)

Since the cause of Richard's downfall has been political, it is impossible for Shakespeare to show a regeneration of Richard in the sense that he learns to overcome the fault which has led to his tragedy. Within the pattern of the total play this regeneration is implicit in the triumph of Bolingbroke, for the loss of Richard had been the loss of England, and in Henry IV this loss is recovered. We have a situation analogous to that at the end of *King John*. Shakespeare, however, does attempt to portray some personal regeneration of Richard. In his farewell to his queen we see a stoic resignation which enables him to accept his fate:

> Join not with grief, fair woman, do not so,
> To make my end too sudden: learn, good soul,
> To think our former state a happy dream;
> From which awaked, the truth of what we are
> Shows us but this: I am sworn brother, sweet,
> To grim necessity, and he and I
> Will keep a league till death.
>
> (V.i.16-22)

This may indicate the kind of growth we have seen in Romeo who also learned to accept the inevitable end of man. Richard's awareness of his brotherhood to 'grim necessity' may be regarded as the culminating evidence of a growth in self-knowledge which had begun with his first awareness of Bolingbroke's inevitable triumph. Richard has a surer grasp of political reality than his cousin, for Richard sees from the first what Bolingbroke apparently does not: that once the banished Duke has set foot again in England with an army to support him, it is impossible for him to turn back until he has not only usurped the crown but caused Richard's death. An absolute monarch cannot tolerate a lord who has forced him to make conditions, and a usurping monarch cannot leave alive a rival with a better claim to the throne; these are elementary maxims of Renaissance power politics. By his own act Bolingbroke becomes the creature of historical necessity.

It is Richard who first raises the question of deposition. There can be no doubt of the sinfulness of his abject submission to Bolingbroke without a struggle, his abandonment of his role as the hallowed agent of God on earth. Once this sin has been committed, Richard knows that its consequence must be his death. When Bolingbroke kneels before him in the base court at Flint castle and declares: 'My gracious lord, I come but for mine own', Richard's reply shows a full awareness of this reality: 'Your own is yours, and I am yours, and all' (III.iii.196-7). His sense of his own guilt is particularly evident in the deposition scene:

> Nay, if I turn mine eyes upon myself,
> I find myself a traitor with the rest;
> For I have given here my soul's consent
> To undeck the pompous body of a king;
> Made glory base and sovereignty a slave,
> Proud majesty a subject, state a peasant.
>
> (IV.i.247-52)

Richard in the course of his downfall becomes aware, more surely than Bolingbroke, not only of his own sin, the 'weaved-up folly' (IV.i.229) which has been his life, but also of the inevitable consequences of that sin which in his league with 'grim necessity' he learns fully to accept.

At Pomfret castle Richard shows a new power of introspection in his soliloquy (V.v.1-66) and a new humility in his conversation with the stable groom which follows immediately. In the last moments of his life Richard rises to a plane of action of which in

the days of his vain fascination with himself he was incapable.
'The devil take Henry of Lancaster and thee!' he cries out as he
beats his jailor, 'Patience is stale, and I am weary of it' (V.v.102-3).
He kills two of his assailants before Pierce of Exton strikes him
down, and in Richard's death-speech Shakespeare assures the
audience that although the king has lost his kingdom he has saved
his soul:

> Mount, mount, my soul! thy seat is up on high;
> Whilst my gross flesh sinks downward, here to die.
>
> (V.v.112-13)

Bolingbroke, on the other hand, although he has attained his
political triumph, bears the sin of Richard's murder. Yet much as
he declines in audience sympathy, Shakespeare never makes a
villain of him. The chronicles had branded him as a usurper, but
Shakespeare mutes the usurpation theme. Bolingbroke is made to
appear as a minion of fortune who rises to fill a position which
Richard vacates. Richard himself surrenders his throne; his deposition is the inevitable result of his own behaviour, and it is a
course which Richard chooses. On his landing in Wales Richard
offers Bolingbroke the crown before it has been asked of him:

> And yet not so, for what can we bequeath
> Save our deposed bodies to the ground?
> Our lands, our lives and all are Bolingbroke's.
>
> (III.ii.149-51)

That Richard is responsible for his own deposition is emphasized
in York's reaction to the king's seizure of Gaunt's estates:

> Take Hereford's rights away, and take from Time
> His charters and his customary rights;
> Let not to-morrow then ensue to-day;
> Be not thyself; for how art thou a king
> But by fair sequence and succession?
>
> (II.i.195-9)

Richard himself, as York makes clear, is denying the laws of
primogeniture upon which his own claim to kingship depends.
It is he, not Bolingbroke, who first disturbs God's harmonious
order, who first attacks the divinely sanctioned principles of 'fair

sequence and succession'. This theme of self-deposition is emphasized in the choric ritual of the deposition scene:

> Now mark me, how I will undo myself:
> I give this heavy weight from off my head
> And this unwieldy sceptre from my hand,
> The pride of kingly sway from out my heart;
> With mine own tears I wash away my balm,
> With mine own hands I give away my crown,
> With mine own tongue deny my sacred state,
> With mine own breath release all duteous oaths:
> All pomp and majesty I do forswear.
>
> (IV.i.203-11)

Richard's death is necessary to the safety of the state, and Henry
as a statesman wishes it, but he never directly orders it, and his
banishment of the murderer indicates his horror of the crime. The
audience knows that he will never make his voyage to the Holy
Land, that his son will bear the weight of this sin even on the day
of Agincourt, that it will be expiated only in another generation,
with the blood of his pathetic grandson, Henry VI. Of this the
Bishop of Carlisle had given warning. Shakespeare in his Lancas-
trian plays was forced to show the triumph of England through
the victory of a usurper and murderer. This was difficult to reconcile with a belief in private morality as an essential quality of kingship, and if Shakespeare's attempt to do so is not entirely successful, we must remember that the story with which he worked did
not easily lend itself to such treatment.

Richard II is an historical tragedy which, in its particular fusion
of political and ethical statement, recapitulates the pattern which
Shakespeare in *King John* had developed from its crude beginnings
in *Titus Andronicus*. Shakespeare now develops the personal side
of his tragedy beyond what he had attempted in *King John*, and he
sets the personal issues at variance with the political. Political victory is accompanied by moral guilt, and moral victory by political
surrender. There is some attempt at regeneration of the tragic
hero in both plays, but whereas in *King John* this had been through
a vindication of the political principles for which the hero had
stood, in *Richard II* this regeneration is without regard to political
issues. Shakespeare has learned to create personal human tragedy
while furthering the political concerns of the history play. In
Richard II history and tragedy are perfectly fused.

IV

In *Julius Caesar* Shakespeare experiments with a unique manipulation of two tragic situations within a single play.[1] The tragedies of Caesar and of Brutus are each both ethical and political, and each hero's career reflects a similar pattern of action. Both tragedies are combined by and subordinated to the larger theme which governs the play: the tragedy of Rome to which Caesar and Brutus each in his own way contributes.

In *Julius Caesar* Shakespeare further extended the pattern he had developed from *Titus Andronicus* through *Richard II*, to develop for the first time a full-scale tragedy of moral choice, drawing upon the tradition of the English morality play.[2] In such a tragedy the hero is faced with a choice between good and evil; through his own imperfections he makes a wrong choice, comes to see the error of his choice in his consequent suffering, and before his death renounces it. This progression is fully displayed in Brutus and partially in Caesar. Shakespeare dwells on the scope and terms of each moral choice itself, the forces militating for and against it, and the exact process by which the hero is led to commit his error. In *Julius Caesar* and the plays which follow it characters come more and more to represent particular moral positions.

Before we can understand *Julius Caesar* as tragedy, we must see clearly its political issues, and about these there has been wide disagreement.[3] We must recognize, to begin with, that Caesar is

---

[1] *Julius Caesar* was written almost certainly in 1599. See Chambers, *William Shakespeare*, I, 397; T. S. Dorsch, ed., *Julius Caesar* (London, 1955), pp. vii-viii. M. W. MacCallum, *Shakespeare's Roman Plays and Their Background* (London, 1910), p. 174, would date it in 1600 or 1601, but the evidence, well summarized by Dorsch, is all to the contrary.

[2] This has been well argued by Virgil K. Whitaker, *Shakespeare's Use of Learning* (San Marino, 1953), pp. 224-50, although we cannot accept the terms of Brutus' moral choice as Whitaker explains them, and he fails to perceive that Caesar undergoes a similar tragic progression.

[3] Many critics have argued that the play is without political implications at all, most recently Vernon Hall, Jr., in *Studies in The English Renaissance Drama*, pp. 106-24. Ernest Schanzer, 'The Problem of *Julius Caesar*', *SQ*, VI (1955), 297-308, has argued that Shakespeare was deliberately ambiguous in his political attitudes, creating a 'problem play'. Perhaps the most common view today is that first given wide currency by McCallum (pp. 212-27) and more recently repeated by Whitaker and J. E. Phillips, *The State in Shakespeare's Greek and Roman Plays* (New York, 1940), pp. 172-88. These writers see the play as a vindication of absolute monarchy, represented by Caesar, with Brutus as the tragic hero who falls into the tragic error of opposing the political system ordained by God. This view tends to slight the role

E

not a king and that at no place in the play does Shakespeare call
him a king. The very opposite is made clear in the second scene
when Cassius says:

> I had as lief not be as live to be
> In awe of such a thing as I myself.
> I was born free as Caesar; so were you.
>
> (I.ii.95-97)

A king was not like other men. He derived his power, according
to Tudor theory, because he was God's agent on earth, designated
by God through the legitimacy of his lineal descent. Caesar has no
such claim. He is an adventurer who, by force, has replaced another adventurer, Pompey, and he is now reaping the civil acclaim
which had been Pompey's, as the first scene makes clear. If Caesar
is to be crowned it will be by the mob. The people cheer in approval when Caesar refuses the crown at the Lupercal, as Casca
explains, but Casca makes it equally clear that this refusal is only
a temporary gesture and that the people are fickle and may be
brought easily by Caesar to accede to his will (I.ii.235-78). The
Senate in conferring the crown would be acceding merely to
Caesar's power seconded by the mob. It is wrong to regard *Julius
Caesar* as a play about a king who is murdered by rebellious citi-
zens. It is a play about a great general who aspires to be a king
and who is murdered on the eve of his success.

Plutarch had seen the desire for kingship as the cause of Caesar's
tragedy:

> But the chiefest cause that made him mortally hated was the cove-
> tous desire he had to be called king; which first gave the people just
> cause and next his secret enemies honest colour, to bear him ill will.[1]

Plutarch's view of Caesar is one of several which came down to
the Renaissance. One view, to be found in many Elizabethan tracts
in defence of monarchy, saw him as a great hero designated by
God to establish monarchy in a corrupt society, only to be struck
down by rebels who brought ruin to their country and damnation
to their souls. On the other hand, stemming from Plutarch and
repeated by a long line of Renaissance writers, is the view of

---

of Caesar in the play and to ignore the fact that he is not a king and that in no place
does Shakespeare call him one. I have treated the play's political issues at greater
length in *JEGP*, LVI (1957), 10-22.

[1] *Shakespeare's Plutarch*, ed. C. F. Tucker Brooke (New York, 1909), I, 90.

Caesar as a great hero who became so puffed up with pride and ambition that he destroyed the most noble edifice ever created by man, the Roman republic.[1] This view of Caesar, the would-be tyrant, is in every Renaissance Caesar play which has come down to us. Such a view lent itself readily to treatment in the popular manner of Renaissance Senecanism, and I would suggest that it is this view which Shakespeare explored in his own *Julius Caesar*.[2]

The charge of illogic so often levelled against Brutus stems from his Orchard soliloquy (II.i.9-34), in which he justifies his action against Caesar. There is illogic in the action of Brutus, but it is not in his decision that Caesar is a danger to Rome. The Orchard speech is not only logical; it focuses upon the basic question of the play, the usurpation of power. Caesar must be destroyed, as Brutus sees it, not because he has been a tyrant, but because he aspires to unlawful power, and such power must inevitably corrupt the most virtuous man and make a tyrant of him:

> But 'tis a common proof,
> That lowliness is young ambition's ladder,
> Whereto the climber-upward turns his face;
> But when he once attains the upmost round,
> He then unto the ladder turns his back,
> Looks in the clouds, scorning the base degrees
> By which he did ascend. So Caesar may.
> Then, lest he may, prevent.
>
> (II.i.21-28)

In terms of Tudor political doctrine these lines are not without logic.[3] Tudor theorists justified the absolutism of a lawful king on the grounds that, as an agent of God, he executed God's purposes. But an absolute ruler without God's sanction and thus without the check of responsibility to God – as Caesar would be

---

[1] T. J. B. Spencer, 'Shakespeare and the Elizabethan Romans', *Shakespeare Survey 10* (Cambridge, 1957), pp. 37-38, has shown that Caesar was a subject for wide discussion in Shakespeare's England, and that there were many conflicting views. There is no one view which we can call the typically Elizabethan one.

[2] That Shakespeare in earlier plays may have referred to Caesar in a more favourable light cannot influence our view of *Julius Caesar*, for as Schanzer has shown by an examination of all the Caesar references in the plays, Shakespeare's attitude towards Caesar apparently changed after his reading of Plutarch and his consideration of the matter in preparation for *Julius Caesar*. See *SQ*, VI (1955), 299-300.

[3] J. Dover Wilson, ed., *Julius Caesar* (Cambridge, 1949), p. xxxi, has been virtually alone among modern commentators in denying the illogic of these lines.

if he were crowned – would be a tyrant. An ordinary man, no matter how great, could not aspire to kingship; he could only aspire to tyranny, and this is precisely what Brutus fears. He estimates properly the political threat of Caesar. His sin is the manner in which he opposes that threat. To attain a public good he commits a private evil; his tragedy, like that of King John, affirms that public morality can be built only upon private virtue.

Brutus' fears, we must conclude, far from being foolish, are, in Tudor terms, well grounded, and they were probably Shakespeare's fears as well. The succession issue was perhaps the most vital political problem in England when *Julius Caesar* was written in 1599, and the possibility that a powerful general with no legitimate claim, but with the support of the rabble, might make a bid for the throne was a fear not lightly to be discounted. The abortive attempt of Essex some two years later attests to the ever-present possibility in 1599. If the history play used events of the past to mirror contemporary political problems, *Julius Caesar* is no exception.

There are, as I have suggested, two tragic heroes in *Julius Caesar*, Brutus and Caesar, although the one is treated more fully than the other. Each brings about his own destruction, and together they bring chaos to Rome. Each is among the greatest men the world has ever known, but each makes a wrong moral choice. The source of Caesar's tragedy Shakespeare found not primarily in Plutarch, but chiefly as part of the long tradition of Senecan Caesar plays which preceded his.[1] It was a tragic pride and ambition which became apparent upon his return to Rome after the defeat of Pompey's sons in Spain. It is touched upon only lightly by Plutarch, who concludes that Caesar 'reaped no fruit of all his reign and dominion, which he had so vehemently desired all his life, pursued with such extreme danger, but a vain name only, and a superficial glory that procured him the envy and hatred of his country' (I.105-6), but it is amplified in Renaissance accounts of which Montaigne's may furnish a convenient example:

> But all these noble inclinations were stifled and corrupted by that furious passion of ambition by which he was so forcibly carried away, that we may safely declare that it held the rudder and steered all his actions. . . .

[1] See H. M. Ayres, 'Shakespeare's *Julius Caesar* in the Light of Some Other Versions', *PMLA*, xxv (1910), 183-227.

To sum up, this single vice, in my opinion, destroyed in him the richest and most beautiful nature that ever was, and made his memory abominable to all good men, since it led him to seek his glory in the ruin of his country and the subversion of the most powerful and flourishing Republic the world will ever see.[1]

The greatest man in the world had risen so high that he was ripe for the inevitable fall. Above all else, Caesar wanted to be king, and to attain a power to which he was not entitled, he would accept the support of the mob. This inordinate desire for kingship is the height of Caesar's tragic folly, the *hubris* which will destroy him. On the day of his assassination he remains firm in his decision to remain at home until Decius Brutus offers him the prospect of a crown:

> the Senate have concluded
> To give this day a crown to mighty Caesar.
> If you shall send them word you will not come,
> Their minds may change.
>
> (II.ii.93-96)

This is the temptation which he cannot resist, and it is the immediate cause of his destruction. Shakespeare has carefully prepared his audience for the wrong moral choice which now follows.

That Caesar can never be a fitting king for Rome has been indicated in the second scene of the play. Caesar here turns to Antony preparing to run in the Lupercal:

> Forget not, in your speed, Antonius,
> To touch Calpurnia; for our elders say,
> The barren, touched in this holy chase,
> Shake off their sterile curse.
>
> (I.ii.6-9)

Shakespeare introduces Calpurnia's sterility to make clear to the audience that Caesar has no heirs, and that should he die as king, Rome would be left in that very state of civil chaos, without a lawful claimant to the throne, which Tudor Englishmen so feared would follow the death of their own Elizabeth.

Caesar's pride is shown in the pomposity of his boastful speeches:

[1] *The Essays*, trans. by E. J. Trechmann (New York, Modern Library, 1946), pp. 636-7.

> danger knows full well
> That Caesar is more dangerous than he:
> We are two lions litter'd in one day,
> And I the elder and more terrible.
>
> (II.ii.44-47)

An audience could not receive such lines as other than almost ludicrous posturing; Caesar is denying the limitations of his nature as a man. His pride is shown also in his refusal to heed the words of the soothsayer: 'He is a dreamer; let us leave him; pass' (I.ii.24). Elizabethans generally believed that prophecies were to be taken seriously, and certainly that no prudent statesman could run the risk of ignoring them. This is again stressed in Caesar's reaction to Calpurnia's dream (II.ii); here his folly is underscored dramatically by the audience's knowledge of how right Calpurnia actually is. Throughout the first three acts Shakespeare shows us a strutting, vainglorious Caesar, denying his kinship to humanity and claiming the qualities of a god. The pathetic irony of this tragic delusion Shakespeare indicates by ingenious little touches. When Caesar has proclaimed that he is impervious to the fears which might visit lesser men, this is followed immediately by a reminder that this god suffers, in fact, from one of the most human of afflictions: 'Come on my right hand, for this ear is deaf' (I.ii.213).

This technique is used again in the boastful vaunt which Caesar delivers just before his death:

> I could be well moved, if I were as you;
> If I could pray to move, prayers would move me:
> But I am constant as the northern star,
> Of whose true-fix'd and resting quality
> There is no fellow in the firmament.
> The skies are painted with unnumber'd sparks,
> They are all fire and every one doth shine,
> But there's but one in all doth hold his place:
> So in the world; 'tis furnish'd well with men,
> And men are flesh and blood, and apprehensive;
> Yet in the number I do know but one
> That unassailable holds on his rank,
> Unshaked of motion: and that I am he.
>
> (III.i.58-70)

In the flashing daggers of the conspirators we are shown the pathetic delusion in these lines, that no man is constant as the

Northern Star. Caesar cannot escape the limitations of his own flesh and blood; he is just a man after all, weak and subject to the fate of any man who would make himself a god. His death is an ironic commentary upon his own pretensions.

Caesar's wrong moral choice is his decision to go to the Senate to accept a crown to which he has no lawful claim. The traditional debate which in the earlier drama accompanied the choice of the morality play hero occupies the scene in which this choice is made, with Calpurnia filling the role of good angel and Decius Brutus that of bad. The temptation of Decius causes Caesar to deny the pleas of his wife. In the pattern of the total play, however, it is Marc Antony rather than Decius who performs the traditional role of the tempter, for Antony thrice offers Caesar the throne at the feast of the Lupercal. Antony after Caesar's death is used as a symbol of those very elements for which Caesar stood, and which Brutus because of his own sinful moral choice cannot destroy.

Antony must triumph, but that the triumph is one of evil rather than good is made implicit by Antony's own immorality, his ruthless manipulation of the mob for personal revenge at the expense of Rome, and particularly in the cold brutality of the proscription scene:

ANTONY: These many, then, shall die; their names are prick'd.
OCTAVIUS: Your brother too must die; consent you, Lepidus?
LEPIDUS: I do consent,—
OCTAVIUS: Prick him down, Antony.
LEPIDUS: Upon condition Publius shall not live,
  Who is your sister's son, Mark Antony.
ANTONY: He shall not live; look, with a spot I damn him.
                                                    (IV.i.1-6)

Caesar's spirit is victorious in spite of Brutus, and a cold-blooded exchange of kinsmen is the fruit of such victory.[1] From Antony's triumph emerge the very evils Brutus had vainly sought to stem. If there is any hope for Rome it is not in Antony, but in the young Octavius who, before the end of the play, we see emerging as the force which will put Antony down (V.i.19-20).

We have no evidence that Caesar ever becomes aware of the sin

[1] It is difficult to reconcile this scene with G. Wilson Knight's view that 'the murder of Caesar is a gash in the body of Rome, and this gash is healed by love', with Antony as the spirit of love bringing peace and order to a troubled world. See *The Imperial Theme* (London, 1951), p. 63.

which has led to his downfall. This form of recognition and regeneration Shakespeare reserves for his treatment of Brutus, in
whom he seems to have been more deeply interested. There are
two facets to the tragedy of Brutus, the one directly related to the
other. His failure to lead the conspiracy to success stems directly
from his other failure: to live up to his own ideals of conduct.
Brutus has been called an idealist philosopher, lacking in those
public virtues which the successful leader must have, unable to
cope with the crude realities of politics.[1] This inability springs
from the root of his tragedy, his own separation of public from
private morality. All of his tactical errors – his rejection of the
oath, his refusal to murder Antony, his insistence that Antony be
allowed to speak at Caesar's funeral – all spring from his unwillingness to accept the logical consequences of his own immoral act.
He argues from the standpoint of a morality which has already
been corrupted.

Cassius knows the logical consequences of Caesar's murder, that
once the immoral course has been taken, a reassertion of morality
can only spring from self-deception and lead to disaster. Of all the
conspirators, Cassius alone sees that Brutus has forfeited the moral
stature which made him at first the obvious choice for leader, and
he sees the folly of his attempt to reassert it. In this Cassius too
plays a tragic role, for in spite of his clear insight he allows Brutus
to prevail to the destruction of all. While Cassius is fully developed
as a complex personality, he is used to fill a thematic function in
the total play. Shakespeare needs a contrast to Brutus who will
logically accept the immorality of Caesar's death and who will
show the audience the self-deception of Brutus.

Under the leadership of Cassius, the conspirators might have
achieved an immediate success, but it could not have been a last-
ing one, for the conspiracy itself was evil, and even had it been
properly managed, it could have brought only disaster to Rome.
Great as Caesar's threat to Rome might have been, to oppose it
by conspiracy and murder was wrong. The death of Caesar may
have been as essential to the preservation of Rome as was the
death of Prince Arthur to the stability of England, but Shakespeare can no more condone Brutus' action than he can King
John's order for the death of Arthur. In order to attain a goal of
public good, Brutus commits a private crime: he murders his

[1] See John Palmer's analysis in *The Political Characters of Shakespeare*, pp. 1-64.

friend. This is his wrong moral choice and the source of his tragedy. The crime of Brutus, the virtuous murderer, is a violation of the closest bonds which tie man to man, bonds with which the audience instinctively identifies. We have a sharp dramatic anti-thesis between an abstract political ideal and the ordinary human goodness which it violates. Brutus is aware of this violation, and he is willing to face it.

Shakespeare censures Brutus not for his ends, but for the means he uses to attain those ends. There is never any question of the menace to Rome which Caesar represents. Brutus' means of op-posing it, however, Shakespeare unequivocally condemns. The dramatist is saying, in effect, that although immediate political success may be won by the amoral statesman like Marc Antony, good government must be based upon morality. Implicit in the destruction of Brutus is the Aristotelian principle that the final test of government is virtue and that public morality must be grounded firmly upon private morality. The tragedy of Brutus is that he does not realize this until it is too late.

The murder of Caesar is an evil act which, by its very nature, never can give rise to good. There is an irony and a pathos in Brutus' failure to perceive this truth, and this Shakespeare makes clear in the futile attempts of Brutus to raise the bloody murder of his friend to the status of a ritual, sacramental act.[1] Cassius knows that once the murder has been decided upon, the conspirators are committed to a course which can allow no moral scruples to stand in the way of their success; morality already has been abandoned. The death of Antony and of others is essential, as later events are to prove. But Brutus will not accept this:

> Our course will seem too bloody, Caius Cassius,
> To cut the head off and then hack the limbs,
> Like wrath in death and envy afterwards;
> For Antony is but a limb of Caesar:
> Let us be sacrificers, but not butchers, Caius.
> We all stand up against the spirit of Caesar;
> And in the spirit of men there is no blood:
> O, that we then could come by Caesar's spirit,
> And not dismember Caesar! But, alas,
> Caesar must bleed for it! And, gentle friends,

---

[1] See Brents Stirling, *Unity in Shakespearian Tragedy* (New York, 1956), pp. 40-54; and Ernest Schanzer, 'The Tragedy of Shakespeare's Brutus', *ELH*, xxii (1955), 1-16.

> Let's kill him boldly, but not wrathfully;
> Let's carve him as a dish fit for the gods,
> Not hew him as a carcass fit for hounds:
> And let our hearts, as subtle masters do,
> Stir up their servants to an act of rage,
> And after seem to chide 'em. This shall make
> Our purpose necessary and not envious:
> Which so appearing to the common eyes,
> We shall be call'd purgers, not murderers. (II.i.162-80)

Thus Brutus seeks to find in an evil act an element of noble sacrifice which is not in it. He would kill the spirit of Caesar, but the
sad lesson he must learn is that he has killed only the body of
Caesar and that the spirit will return to haunt him at Phillipi. This
dichotomy of blood and spirit is woven into the texture of the
play; it pervades the imagery, and the ghastly spectacle of Brutus
and his 'gentle friends' actually bathing their arms in Caesar's
blood after the murder (III.i.103-10)[1] symbolically reaffirms that
in spite of Brutus' protests the conspirators are committed utterly
to the bloody course, that they have indeed hewed Caesar as 'a
carcass fit for hounds', for the gods will not accept the sacrificial
rite of murder, and the spirit Brutus seeks has eluded him entirely.
Incantation and ritual are used as ironic commentary upon the
self-deception inherent in Brutus' moral choice.

Brutus, more than Caesar, carries on the dramatic tradition of
the morality play hero who must choose between good and evil
forces which vie for his soul, and in this scheme Cassius plays the
symbolic role of the seducer who makes clear for the audience
those very qualities which lead Brutus to make his fatal error.
But what Shakespeare castigates as Brutus' evil choice is not his
decision that Caesar is a threat to Rome, but rather his decision to
join Cassius in conspiracy and murder, and this is an important
distinction. As disasters begin to mount after Antony's funeral
oration, Brutus, like a morality hero, slowly becomes aware of the
error of his choice. This growing awareness Shakespeare makes
clear in the quarrel scene in the fourth act.

Cassius, as we have seen, has been committed all along to the
immoral consequences of the first sinful act, and he has argued
that they be accepted. He has always, however, given in to Brutus'

---

[1] See Leo Kirschbaum, 'Shakespeare's Stage Blood and its Critical Significance',
PMLA, LXIV (1949), 517-29; G. Wilson Knight, *The Imperial Theme*, pp. 45-52.

counter-arguments. This has been true in the matters of the oath (II.i.114-40) and of Antony's death. Now Cassius argues the necessity for a relatively slight immorality, that his bribe-taking officer, Lucius Pella, should not have been condemned. The pathetic irony of Brutus' self-deception breaks forth in all its vehemence:

> Remember March, the ides of March remember:
> Did not great Julius bleed for justice' sake?
> What villain touch'd his body, that did stab,
> And not for justice? What, shall one of us,
> That struck the foremost man of all this world
> But for supporting robbers, shall we now
> Contaminate our fingers with base bribes,
> And sell the mighty space of our large honours
> For so much trash as may be grasped thus?
> I had rather be a dog, and bay the moon,
> Than such a Roman.
>
> (IV.iii.18-28)

Through these lines comes the vain effort of a man trying to convince himself of the truth of what he already is beginning to know is false. The audience knows that every man but Brutus himself stabbed, 'and not for justice', and as Cassius persists in his demands, this truth must be brought home to Brutus with an overwhelming certainty. He accepts the renewed friendship of Cassius, but it is a despairing gesture, and his awareness of his error emerges finally in the simple line, 'You have done what you should be sorry for' (IV.iii.65).

The murder of Caesar is now upon his conscience all through the scenes before Phillipi, and he sees his own death as an atonement for his crime:

> Caesar, now be still:
> I kill'd not thee with half so good a will.
>
> (V.v.50-51)

That Brutus ever questions the political principles which have led him to join with Cassius, however, there is no suggestion. Although the error of his entry into the conspiracy has long been evident to him, to the very end he maintains the rightness of his cause:

> And I am Brutus, Marcus Brutus, I;
> Brutus, my country's friend; know me for Brutus!
>
> (V.iv.7-8)

Shakespeare in *Julius Caesar* was interested in two great figures from Roman history, and he treated both in accordance with the historical and literary tradition which he inherited: Caesar as the noble hero overthrown by his pride and ambition, and Brutus as the virtuous would-be saviour of his country who, through his own insufficiency, brings only greater tragedy to Rome. Of the two tragedies, that of Brutus more completely attracted his interest. As an historical dramatist, Shakespeare was fully aware of the political implications of his theme. He saw, on the one hand, a lesson in the civil chaos which results when a great and noble leader tries to overthrow long-established institutions and seeks with the support of the mob to attain a kingship to which he has no lawful claim. On the other hand, he saw the chaos which results when men of noble instincts violate their own natures and enter into evil so that political good may result.

I have dwelt upon the political issues in *Julius Caesar* because in this play these issues are at the root of the tragic conflict. The heroes of Roman history were viewed by Shakespeare's audience at a distance which blurred their human imperfections and made of them supermen such as the world had never again beheld. There is always a grandeur and magnificence about them, and it is thus easy for Shakespeare to envisage them as embodiments of moral principles. In *Julius Caesar* we find such characters, each embodying a specific moral attitude, subjected to imaginative exploration. There is a higher degree of intellectual symbolism in this play than in *King John* or *Richard II*, and Shakespeare can approach his subject with a higher and more impersonal degree of objectivity. He is not bound here by the peculiarly Tudor views of history, as he had been in the English historical tragedies. In *Julius Caesar* Shakespeare learned techniques which he was to apply in later plays. He could now, better than ever before, embody intellectual statement in dramatic character, and in character conflict expose the implications of clashing ideologies. These lessons he applied in *Hamlet*, a play in which he returned briefly to an early mode of tragedy, and when he came to write *Othello* the lessons learned in *Julius Caesar* came to a full measure of fruition.

CHAPTER FOUR

The Pattern of Growth: *Hamlet*

lthough Prince Hamlet is probably the most intriguing figure in the world's literature, Shakespeare did not create him primarily as an individual case study, for he was concerned not so much with the problems of an individual as with the much more profound question of mankind in conflict with evil. In *Hamlet* Shakespeare endowed his hero with a universal symbolism, and he shaped all of the elements of his play into a total complex which might provide the emotional equivalent of a Christian view of human life. Hamlet's life-journey may be viewed as the affirmation of a purposive cosmic order. Although *Hamlet* was probably written close upon the completion of *Julius Caesar*,[1] Shakespeare did not continue in it to develop the tragedy of moral choice. He returned instead to the pattern for tragedy he had developed in *Romeo and Juliet*, and some clue to Shakespeare's intentions in *Hamlet* may be found in that earlier work. The crude Senecan revenge formula of the *Ur-Hamlet*, his source,[2] lent itself like the *Romeo and Juliet* story to a kind of tragedy which might explore the growth and maturing of ordinary man in conflict with evil.

Hamlet, like Romeo, comes into a world full of ancient evil not of his own creation. He must oppose this evil, which is more insidious and pervasive than anything in the earlier play. This task is overwhelming in its complexity, and Hamlet can look to no human assistance. His family, his sweetheart, and his school friends all appear to turn against him and to ally themselves with

---

[1] It may be dated in 1600. See Chambers, *William Shakespeare*, I, 423-4; J. Dover Wilson, ed., *Hamlet* (Cambridge, 1936), p. xxii; E. A. J. Honigmann, 'The Date of Hamlet', *Shakespeare Survey* 9 (Cambridge, 1956), pp. 24-34.

[2] For a good treatment of the source problem, see Kenneth Muir, *Shakespeare's Sources I: Comedies and Tragedies* (London, 1957), pp. 110-22. There is a reconstruction of the *Ur-Hamlet* in Whitaker, *Shakespeare's Use of Learning*, pp. 329-46.

the evil force to which he stands opposed. Hamlet makes one
attempt after another to accomplish his goal, but each attempt is
a failure because his plans are marred by those very human shortcomings which reveal him as neither a God-figure nor a pathological study, but as a symbol of ordinary humanity. At the end
of the play Hamlet learns to accept the order of the universe and
to become a passive instrument in the hands of a purposive and
benevolent God. When he has done so, he can accomplish his
mission in spite of his own human failings. Like all men he must
die, but Hamlet's death, like that of Romeo, is also his victory,
for through his encounter with evil he has learned the nature of
evil and the means of opposing it. With this knowledge he is
ready for salvation.[1] The action of Shakespeare's hero is cast in
a pattern which affirms a purposive moral order. The lesser characters serve supporting functions. They stand for moral forces
and moral positions, and taken together, they represent humanity
in the large. The setting is not an isolated castle in a distant
Northern country; the castle of Elsinore is the world.

II

The original Hamlet story had centred about three plots by which
the uncle had tried to entrap and destroy his nephew; each time
Amleth had outwitted his adversary by his greater cunning, and
at last he had destroyed Fengon and attained his victory. This
basic structure Shakespeare retained, but he altered and amplified
it so as to give it a different focus. Again we have a series of con-
tests between Hamlet and Claudius, but now it is not Hamlet's
victory in each encounter that Shakespeare stresses; rather it is
Hamlet's defeat.

The Hamlet Shakespeare shows us in his first act is an ordinary
mortal, bowed down by his human infirmities, by a sense of his
own debasement which reflects the universal burden of original
sin, and by a disgust with the evils of the world which has led him

---

[1] The Christian framework of *Hamlet* has been argued by Roy Walker, *The Time
Is Out of Joint* (London, 1948); G. R. Elliott, *Scourge and Minister*, (Durham, N.C.,
1951); Bertram Joseph, *Conscience and the King* (London, 1953), pp. 130-51; V. K.
Whitaker, *Shakespeare's Use of Learning*, pp. 262-74; Paul N. Siegel, *Shakespearean
Tragedy and the Elizabethan Compromise* (New York, 1957), pp. 99-118; H. S. Wilson,
On the Design of Shakespearian Tragedy, pp. 31-51. A. C. Bradley, *Shakespearean Tragedy*
pp. 171-4, vaguely perceived the religious element in the play, that 'in all that
happens or is done we seem to apprehend some vaster power'.

to the brink of suicide. He is preserved from this final step only by a faith which teaches him that God has 'fix'd / His canon 'gainst self-slaughter' (I.ii.131-2). To him appears his dead father's spirit, and he must not only continue to live in the 'unweeded garden, / That grows to seed' (I.ii.135-6), but he must also take positive action against the evil which blights his world.

The physical obstacles to such action are great, but Shakespeare's emphasis is upon the intellectual obstacles in Hamlet's way, and these are even more imposing. Hamlet must determine whether the ghost speaks truth, and to do so he must cope with theological issues. He must settle the moral issue of private revenge in a benevolent universal order in which God has retained the punishment of the wicked as his own prerogative. He must learn to live with evil in a world in which a man's own mother may be the source of his corruption. He must control the human passions within him which threaten often to destroy the most rational of plans. And he must avoid the damnation of his own soul, for Hamlet has been singled out by God as the castigator of evil, and Elizabethans knew that for such purposes God might employ either a scourge or a minister. A scourge, like Richard III, was an agent of private revenge who in destroying God's enemies damned his own soul; a minister, like Henry of Richmond, was God's instrument who executed public justice and remained untouched by the evil he destroyed. Whether Hamlet act as scourge or minister is a crucial issue in the play.[1]

In the first two acts Shakespeare creates for us the atmosphere of evil which envelops Denmark, and in the appearance of the ghost and the preliminary sparring between Hamlet and Claudius he makes clear the scope of Hamlet's task and the difficulties which beset him. The third act consists of three episodes in each of which Hamlet has an opportunity to entrap the king: the nunnery scene, the mousetrap, and the scene in Gertrude's closet. In each of these situations circumstances place the advantage on Hamlet's side, but in each instance Hamlet spoils his own opportunity, forfeits his apparent advantage by a display of human passion which frustrates his plans. We have what appears to be vacillation and delay, and this theme continues in the fourth act which is taken up largely with Hamlet's departure and the preparations for his return. Ham-

---

[1] See Fredson Bowers, 'Hamlet as Minister and Scourge', *PMLA*, LXX (1955), 740-9, and *Studies in The English Renaissance Drama*, pp. 28-42.

let berates himself in the traditional manner of the avenger, but the delay is not for want of strength or opportunity, as Hamlet tells us:

> I do not know
> Why yet I live to say 'This thing's to do;'
> Sith I have cause and will and strength and means
> To do't.

(IV.iv.43-46)

What Hamlet does not know is that his strength and opportunity are of no avail so long as the moral issues implicit in his task remain unresolved. Hamlet's delay is not the symptom of any peculiar psychological quirk: it is a symbolic statement of the futility of all man's attempts to destroy evil without first learning to know himself and without intellectual faith and certainty. Hamlet has his Christian religion to guide him, but he has not yet learned the answer to his problems which is implicit in that faith. This answer is a simple one, and in the fifth act he finally learns it. When he has done so his mission is accomplished in spite of his own human inadequacies. He dies, but he is victorious. He attains salvation, and there is a new birth of order in Denmark with the agents of evil dead upon the stage and Fortinbras ascending the throne.

Shakespeare keeps the answer to Hamlet's problem before the audience throughout the play. It is mirrored in the Christian stoicism of Horatio. Before the mousetrap scene which is to reveal exactly the contrary qualities in Hamlet, Horatio is fully described:

> for thou hast been
> As one, in suffering all, that suffers nothing,
> A man that fortune's buffets and rewards
> Hast ta'en with equal thanks: and blest are those
> Whose blood and judgement are so well commeddled,
> That they are not a pipe for fortune's finger
> To sound what stop she please. Give me that man
> That is not passion's slave, and I will wear him
> In my heart's core, ay, in my heart of heart,
> As I do thee.

(III.ii.70-79)

Hamlet must become like Horatio. He must learn that evil is a necessary part of God's harmonious order, that man must live with evil while he opposes it as best he can. He must learn that

death is the inevitable end of all, and he must learn that to achieve
justice he must make of himself a passive instrument in the hands
of God, in the faith that God will preserve a just and benevolent
moral order regardless of man's own feeble efforts. When Hamlet
can become impervious to the blows of fortune his mission will
be accomplished. *Hamlet* is controlled by the notion of a divine
providence which guides the affairs of men according to God's
own just and merciful designs. The play asserts the notion which
Shakespeare had more hesitatingly sought to embody in *Romeo
and Juliet*, and to do so Shakespeare shaped his crude Senecan
source into a similar pattern of tragic action.

Hamlet opens, like *Romeo and Juliet*, not with a view of the hero,
but with an impression of the evil into which he is to come.
Shakespeare now uses more subtle devices than the feud scene of
the earlier play; by poetic imagery he creates a mood of evil and
foreboding. It is reflected in the coldness and gloom of the castle
battlements; the rottenness in the state of Denmark is given imaginative expression in Francisco's "tis bitter cold, / And I am sick
at heart" (I.i.8-9). We are made ready for the appearance of the
ghost, an unnatural phenomenon which reflects the perversion of
God's harmonious order which it will be Hamlet's mission to
restore to harmony. The motif of the unnatural is stressed in
Horatio's recollection of the corruptions in nature which Elizabethans believed to accompany corruptions in the world of man
(I.i.112-25). The feeling of ancient evil, insidious and all-corrupt-
ing, is established in the first scene of the play.

From the gloom of the castle walls, we move to the cheerful
splendour of the council chamber, with only Hamlet as a dis-
cordant figure of gloom to remind the audience of the atmosphere
of evil it has just experienced. The second scene of the play prepares us for the task Hamlet is soon to face. We are told of the
political situation in Denmark, and particularly that Hamlet's adversary is a popular king who has come to the throne with the aid
and support of the court:

> nor have we herein barr'd
> Your better wisdoms, which have freely gone
> With this affair along. (I.ii.14-16)

Hamlet's first soliloquy (I.ii.129-59), designed to reveal the cause
of his initial disturbance, contains no mention of the king's usurpation or his own frustrated ambition, but only the shame of

F

Gertrude's marriage. The dispatch of the ambassadors to Norway shows Claudius to be an efficient ruler, and his speech to Laertes is all cordiality and affability. He seems the loving stepfather in his concern for Hamlet, and particularly in his announcement:

> for let the world take note,
> You are the most immediate to our throne;
> And with no less nobility of love
> Than that which dearest father bears his son,
> Do I impart toward you. (I.ii.108-12)

This will further complicate Hamlet's task, for any action against Claudius will appear to the world as that of an unnatural tyrannicide.

An audience watching the play for the first time could not fail to regard Claudius as a kind and gracious king, perhaps overly concerned by the behaviour of his stepson, whose own rude and ungracious replies would not win much sympathy for him. Much of the weakness of *Hamlet* criticism has come from our tendency, so difficult to avoid, to view parts of the play on the basis of a knowledge of the whole which an Elizabethan theatre audience could not have had. We know that Claudius will soon emerge as a ruthless schemer and villain, but the audience viewing the first act has no reason to doubt either his goodness or the accuracy of his description of Hamlet's condition. The soundness of the moral view in which it is couched no contemporary audience could have doubted:

> but to persever
> In obstinate condolement is a course
> Of impious stubborness; 'tis unmanly grief;
> It shows a will most incorrect to heaven,
> A heart unfortified, a mind impatient,
> An understanding simple and unschool'd:
> For what we know must be and is as common
> As any the most vulgar thing to sense,
> Why should we in our peevish opposition
> Take it to heart? Fie! 'tis a fault to heaven,
> A fault against the dead, a fault to nature,
> To reason most absurd; whose common theme
> Is death of fathers, and who still hath cried,
> From the first corse till he that died today,
> 'This must be so.' (I.ii.92-106)

Hamlet suffers from an unnatural grief over the death of his father, 'a will most incorrect to heaven', in that it implicitly denies the justice of God who has decreed his father's death. Like an earlier Romeo, Hamlet too is 'fortune's fool', for he cannot accept the ordinary evil of the world and learn to live with it. Hamlet's excessive grief has the exaggeration of all symbol; it represents the state of man with 'heart unfortified, a mind impatient, / An understanding simple and unschool'd' before he has learned the lesson of faith in the perfection of God's universal order. Hamlet here is not a philosopher. He is the very opposite, man untutored, and therefore unable to bear the burdens of human life. This is the low point which from, like Romeo, he must grow to maturity.

To make this clear is the function of Hamlet's first soliloquy (I.ii.129-59). His body is sallied (assailed),[1] by the evil of the world. He suffers from the weight of original sin as all men do. This is symbolized in part by his mother's incestuous marriage which he sees as the source of his own defilement. The world itself, God's most magnificent creation, to him is merely a place of corruption from which only the fear of death prevents his escape:

> How weary, stale, flat and unprofitable,
> Seem to me all the uses of this world!
> Fie on't! ah fie! 'tis an unweeded garden,
> That grows to seed; things rank and gross in nature
> Possess it merely. (I.ii.133-7)

He knows, however, that God has 'fix'd / His canon gainst self-slaughter' and this knowledge is a sign of the grace of God which he shares as well as original sin. It keeps him from the suicide which is the logical corollary of his view of life, and out of it will come his growth and final salvation.

To such a man the ghost of his father reveals an evil which touches his immediate being and is a reflection in specific terms of the general evil which has already reduced him to despair. The ghost, moreover, imposes upon him the duty of every Christian soul: to combat this evil which distorts God's harmonious order. To do this Hamlet must assert his own natural sense of duty: 'If

[1] Fredson Bowers, 'Hamlet's "sullied" or "solid" flesh: A Bibliographical Case History', *Shakespeare Survey* 9 (Cambridge, 1956), pp. 44-48, has argued well for retention of the Q² 'sallied' as a variant spelling of 'sullied'. Probably Shakespeare intended both meanings at once, 'sullied' and 'assailed'. The Folio 'solid' has little to support it.

thou hast nature in thee, bear it not' (I.v.81), the ghost commands. Hamlet's nature is the bond which unites him to his father and to God, the normal filial feeling which is an emanation on the human plane of the love of God for his creation. The ghost appeals to Hamlet on the basis of those very things which make him the creature of God, separate always from the 'beast who wants discourse of reason'.

But the paradox is that the duty which the ghost commands can be accomplished only by an acceptance of the evil Hamlet must oppose. To have nature in him is for Hamlet to share in the purposes of God, and this involves a submission to God's order in all of its implications. What Hamlet must learn is that man frustrates evil merely by his faith in God and by the cultivation of his own goodness. The ghost indicates the goal which Hamlet must attain, and the play becomes a dramatic symbol of the struggle man must endure in order to learn the answers of faith and submission.

The ghost himself is a symbol of the paradox implicit in the duty he imposes. His nature is uncertain.[1] Shakespeare deliberately may have mingled with his Protestant setting elements of Catholic doctrine – with which all Elizabethans, of course, were familiar – to create this feeling of confusion and uncertainty. The ghost stands for the paradox implicit in an action against evil which is itself a submission to evil. 'But, howsoever thou pursuest this act,' he commands, 'Taint not thy mind, nor let thy soul contrive / Against thy mother aught' (I.v.85-86). The injunctions are antithetical, for how can Hamlet execute a vengeance which God expressly forbids without tainting his mind, damning his soul? And how can he expose his mother's sins and murder her husband without contriving against her? Only by submission to the will

---

[1] There has been much debate over the nature of the ghost. Dover Wilson, *What Happens in Hamlet* (New York, 1933), pp. 52-60, sees the ghost as coming 'not from a mythical Tartarus, but from the place of departed spirits in which post-medieval England, despite a veneer of Protestantism, still believed at the end of the sixteenth century'. R. W. Battenhouse, 'The Ghost in *Hamlet*: A Catholic "Linchpin"?', *SP*, XLVIII (1951), 161-92, sees it rather as 'a spirit from a pagan hell, a region considered purgatorial in classical but not in Catholic doctrine'. Among the many attempts to prove the ghost, Hamlet and Shakespeare all Catholics is that of I. J. Semper, *Hamlet Without Tears* (Dubuque, Iowa, 1946), pp. 14-40. Lily B. Campbell, *Shakespeare's Tragic Heroes* (New York, 1952), pp. 121-8, argues that Shakespeare poses for Hamlet the problem of the ghost's identity and credibility by depicting simultaneously three conflicting current attitudes towards ghosts so that 'if a Papist and King James and Timothy Bright had seen the play, as they all probably did, each would have gone home confirmed in his own opinion about ghosts'.

of God can the seemingly impossible be accomplished. Hamlet's
hysterical confusion when the ghost has departed reflects the confusion which is to mark his action against Claudius. He has already
begun to plan the series of ineffective plots with which the following acts will be concerned. His 'antic disposition' stands for the
folly which is to mark his every scheme.

The interview between Reynaldo and Polonius, with its motif
of petty spying and intrigue, carries the theme of corruption into
the second act, and against this is presented the indirection and
confusion into which Hamlet is led by his attempt to oppose evil
with his 'antic disposition'. Hamlet has been beating about vainly
for a solution to his problem. Ophelia's description of his pathetic
visit to her closet (II.i.77-100) shows that in his helplessness he
has turned to another human being for support. We cannot suppose that Hamlet in the scene Ophelia describes is merely play
acting, posing as a melancholy lover so as to mislead Polonius.
Ophelia's words reveal his tragic and pathetic sincerity. Ophelia
can offer no support to Hamlet when he most needs her – it is her
chief function in the play thus to fail him – and this emphasizes
that man faced with such a task as Hamlet faces can turn to no
other human being for help.

Hamlet has no real plan in the second act, but Shakespeare here
prepares his audience for the first advantage which is by accident
to come to Hamlet at the beginning of the third, in the nunnery
scene with Ophelia. This advantage he forfeits because he has not
yet learned the mastery of passion which must accompany acceptance of God's order. He cannot live in a world in which the
woman he loves may be used as a tool against him. To make sense
of the nunnery scene and of the exchange with Polonius which
precedes it, we must assume that Hamlet appears upon the second
scene of Act II soon enough to overhear the speech in which
Polonius offers to 'loose' his daughter to Hamlet (II.ii.162-7), and
that he knows of Ophelia's part in the plot against him.[1]

The knowledge that Ophelia is to be so used causes Hamlet to
see her as parallel to his mother in her betrayal of his father. Thus
his contemplation of suicide in the 'To be or not to be' soliloquy
(III.i.56-90) recalls for the audience his similar contemplation in
the soliloquy at the end of the second scene of the play, in which
he had dwelt on his mother's perfidy. He is already disillusioned

---

[1] First proposed by J. D. Wilson, *What Happens in Hamlet*, pp. 101-8.

with Ophelia as he approaches her where she awaits him, and the ease with which he finds her now after her previous rejection of him can only confirm his knowledge of her part in the plot against him. In his 'I never gave you aught' (III.i.96) he tells her that she is no longer the woman he had loved. Her puzzling implication that it is he, rather than she, who has changed brings forth the savage 'Ha ha! are you honest?' (102) and then the implicit statement that she has betrayed him, 'That if you be honest and fair, your honesty should admit no discourse to your beauty' (107-8).

But Hamlet cannot accept the fact of Ophelia's apparent betrayal, and coming hard upon the iniquity of his mother, it overwhelms him again with a sense of his own baseness and defilement. He breaks out in a savage imprecation against humanity and himself:

> Get thee to a nunnery: why wouldst thou be a breeder of sinners? I am myself indifferent honest; but yet I could accuse me of such things that it were better my mother had not borne me: I am very proud, revengeful, ambitious, with more offences at my beck than I have thoughts to put them in, imagination to give them shape, or time to act them in. What should such fellows as I do crawling between earth and heaven? We are arrant knaves, all; believe none of us. Go thy ways to a nunnery. Where's your father?
>
> (III.i.122-33)

The final question is the crucial test of Ophelia. Hamlet already knows the answer, but when she lies, 'At home, my lord' (134), his bitterness and fury break forth, and he loses all control. He is savage in his denunciation of womankind. Knowing of the listening eavesdroppers as he does, he might have used this opportunity to mislead them and thus to further his own cause, but instead he is capable only of a wild and futile threat upon the king's life: 'I say, we will have no more marriages: those that are married already, all but one, shall live' (153-5). From this rash and purposeless threat Claudius knows that Hamlet is not a harmless madman suffering from unrequited love. He knows that he is a dangerous adversary who must be watched, and Hamlet's task, by his own passionate outburst, has been rendered more difficult. That we can sympathize with Hamlet's bitterness towards Ophelia, and that few men might have acted otherwise, enforces the universality in Hamlet's characterization, reminds us that the weakness which frustrates his plans is the common weakness of all men.

The play within the play represents Hamlet's first real effort to entrap Claudius. When we relate this 'mousetrap' scene to the total thematic structure of the play, it appears not as a victory for Hamlet, but rather, like the nunnery scene before it, as one of a series of episodes in which Hamlet through his own inadequacy loses an opportunity to accomplish his goal.

Whether we assume that Claudius failed to see the dumb-show, or what is more likely, that he saw it but was able to restrain himself from betraying emotion,[1] we must recognize not only that the dumb-show was necessary for technical reasons, but that it was carefully contrived as part of the duel which goes on throughout the scene between Hamlet and Claudius. By this struggle the dramatic tension is maintained, and the intrusion of the dumb-show – probably against Hamlet's wishes – makes of the *Murder of Gonzago* a two-edged instrument which may be used by Claudius against Hamlet himself. The dumb-show provides the forewarning which Claudius needs so that he can seize the advantage and turn Hamlet's apparent victory into defeat. But Hamlet himself must furnish Claudius with the means to do so, and he does this by his needless insulting of the queen and by the crucial line he utters at the height of his passion: 'This is one Lucianus, nephew to the king' (III.ii.254). Again he loses himself in a wild impulse to threaten Claudius. By making Lucianus nephew instead of brother, Hamlet shapes the play for the watching audience as a threat upon the life of Claudius by his mad nephew, and not as a re-enactment of Claudius' own crime against his father.

Shakespeare carefully contrived the scene so that Hamlet would again destroy his own cause by an unthinking display of passion. His desire to threaten the king and to vent his bitterness against his mother blinds him to the cast his words will give the play he is presenting. Hamlet settles his doubts about the ghost, but he also places himself in a position whereby Claudius can with good reason ship him to England. The 'mousetrap' is Hamlet's first

---

[1] That any valid reading of *Hamlet* must explain the function of the dumb-show and why Claudius shows no reaction to it was pointed out by W. W. Greg, 'Hamlet's Hallucination', *MLR*, xii (1917), 393-421. Dover Wilson, *What Happens in Hamlet*, pp. 138-97, has reconstructed the scene on the supposition that Claudius does not see the dumb-show. That he does see it but is able to control himself has been argued by J. Q. Adams, ed., *Hamlet* (Boston, 1929), p. 265; Harley Granville-Barker, *Prefaces to Shakespeare* (Princeton, 1946), i, 87-88; G. L. Kittredge, ed., *Hamlet* (Boston, 1939), pp. 226-9; W. W. Lawrence, 'Hamlet and the Mouse Trap', *PMLA*, liv (1939), 709-35; G. R. Elliott, *Scourge and Minister*, p. 90; B. Joseph, *Conscience and the King*, pp. 83-84.

important victory, for it convinces him of the king's guilt, but it is also among the worst of his failures, for it leaves him in the king's power, farther than ever from accomplishing his mission.

I would suggest that Claudius saw the dumb-show and was immediately alerted to Hamlet's purpose; the unusual method of murdering a man by poison through the ear – which Shakespeare deliberately chose for this purpose – could refer only to his own crime. For the rest of the play scene Claudius planned carefully, while pretending ignorance of the play's argument, to find some means to turn the tables upon his nephew and then retire from the scene without betraying his guilt to any of the onlookers. There is no reason to suppose that Claudius runs shrieking from the room in terror. The plot depends in large measure upon a Claudius who is a strong, resourceful monarch, not easily panicked. As soon as Hamlet's outburst has made it appear that *The Murder of Gonzago* is a threat upon the king's life, Claudius has every reason to rise and leave the room with a full display of royal dignity and righteous indignation. None of the beholders of the play has reason to believe anything other than that Hamlet has been guilty of a monstrous indiscretion, and that the king is a patient, wronged monarch who is entirely justified in sending his dangerously lunatic nephew to England.[1]

With Hamlet convinced of his uncle's guilt, a major obstacle in his path has been removed, but more basic issues are still unresolved, for Hamlet has not yet learned the acceptance of divine providence, without which no plan can be more effective than his abortive 'mousetrap'. This is made clear by the free opportunity which Shakespeare now gives Hamlet to kill Claudius when he finds him at prayer. Hamlet's failure to do so has been explained usually as either a carry-over from the brutal revenge theme of

---

[1] Dover Wilson has held that this double implication of the 'mousetrap' was part of Hamlet's own careful plan. To Hamlet and Horatio the play was to betray the guilt of Claudius, but at the same time it was to display to the rest of the court an ambitious nephew's plan to kill his uncle out of desire for the throne, and thus furnish a plausible reason for the coming murder of Claudius without reflecting upon the family honour by an exposure of Gertrude. Why Hamlet, so concerned later that Horatio should 'report me and my cause aright' (V.ii.350), should now prefer the stigma of an unnatural tyrannicide to killing Claudius without offering any reason at all, Wilson does not make clear. There is nothing in the text to indicate that family honour is much of an issue in the play. That Hamlet could have planned for the court to view *The Murder of Gonzago* as a mad nephew's brutal announcement that he is about to murder his kindly and benevolent uncle, as Wilson supposes, is impossible to believe.

the source,[1] or as the rationalization of a pathological personality incapable of action.[2]

When we consider the governing theme of the play, however, we see that the scene is symbolic and ritualistic; it is not designed to depict psychological truth, but to underscore dramatically the inability of man to execute the justice of God. Hamlet says that he will not kill Claudius until he can destroy his soul as well as his body. The punishment of Claudius in God's harmonious order must be damnation, but this damnation Hamlet is powerless to decree. To attempt it is to lead only to uncertainty and confusion. The futility of Hamlet's effort is emphasized by the masterful irony of the king's final words:

> My words fly up, my thoughts remain below:
> Words without thoughts never to heaven go.
>
> (III.iii.97-98)

Hamlet is powerless even to know the condition of his adversary's soul, let alone destroy it. This scene which has led to so much critical controversy was not designed primarily to throw light upon the character of Claudius any more than that of Hamlet. It was designed to show the audience that the knowledge which Hamlet has gained from his 'mousetrap' is not enough, to indicate that the deed which Hamlet contemplates is a usurpation of God's prerogative, and to prepare for Hamlet's coming surrender of his vengeance into the hands of God. Until he can do so, further failure awaits him. The death of Polonius will further illustrate the human havoc which is all that Hamlet in his present state can accomplish.

In the closet scene with his mother Hamlet determines finally

[1] See, for instance, Levin Schücking, *The Meaning of Hamlet* (London, 1937), pp. 137-8. That Hamlet's speech is to be taken literally, as in accord with Renaissance notions of proper revenge, has been argued by Hardin Craig, *An Interpretation of Shakespeare*, p. 189; B. Joseph, *Conscience and the King*, pp. 117-19. For G. Wilson Knight, *The Wheel of Fire*, pp. 26, 35-36, the scene provides evidence of Hamlet's deliberate cruelty. Knight sees Hamlet as a 'diseased soul', a figure of death, spreading destruction in a world which otherwise might be healthy and normal. A somewhat similar view is in John Vyvyan, *The Shakespearean Ethic*, 27-61. That Hamlet, as a Renaissance aristocrat, simply cannot bring himself to kill a defenceless man is argued by Peter Alexander, *Hamlet, Father and Son* (Oxford, 1955), pp. 144-7. There is nothing in the scene to support such a contention.

[2] Bradley, *Shakespearean Tragedy*, p. 134; J. Q. Adams, pp. 274-6; E. M. W. Tillyard, *Shakespeare's Problem Plays* (London, 1950), pp. 146-9; Elliott, *Scourge and Minister* pp. 108-11. This view was perhaps most notably expressed by Coleridge.

that she has had no part in the murder of her first husband. The astonishment reflected in her 'As kill a king!' (III.iv.30) corroborates the cumulative evidence of her innocence. Hamlet thus attains a victory similar to that of the play scene, but at the same time his excess of passion leads to the death of Polonius. Although Hamlet succeeds in winning his mother to his side, he also justifies the court's already aroused suspicions that he is a danger to the state. If the king had any fears of removing him to England, he need have them no longer. In spite of his victory, Hamlet is even further from accomplishing his mission.

The reappearance of the ghost has been the subject of much critical controversy. But the ghost himself makes very clear the reason for his coming:

> Do not forget: this visitation
> Is but to whet thy almost blunted purpose.
> But, look, amazement on thy mother sits:
> O, step between her and her fighting soul.
>
> (III.iv.110-13)

The ghost furthers the plot by indicating to the audience that Hamlet now must win his mother to repentance for her sins, and he furnishes, as he had not in his first appearance, a clue to how Hamlet's task may be accomplished. The ghost indicates to Hamlet and the audience the Christian way by which Hamlet must proceed, and of which he thus far has been incapable.

Hamlet's purpose has been blunted by the passion which has thus far marked his every effort to destroy evil as he was commanded. Hamlet himself admits that he is 'lapsed in time and passion' (III.iv.107). His Christian concern for his mother's salvation as opposed to his uncle's damnation is the first move he makes towards his final goal, and this move is heralded by the reappearance of the ghost. It is dramatically effective that the ghost should appear precisely when he does. In an unthinking fit of passion Hamlet has just slain Polonius. He had entered his mother's closet in frenzied excitement, and his passion had been mounting at so furious a pitch that the queen's very life was in danger. In spite of himself, Hamlet has permitted the 'soul of Nero' to enter his bosom. The ghost's sudden appearance sets off this passionate display, for Hamlet's anger subsides as he stares at his father, transfixed in amazement. In his concern for Gertrude the ghost points out for the audience the alternative to the fruit-less passion he has halted. He stands for reason.

The unnecessary murder of Polonius will complicate Hamlet's task even more than his new-found knowledge of his mother's innocence will facilitate it. But the moral implications of his kill-ing Polonius are more important than the physical, for Hamlet has stained his hands with blood, and he fears that in doing so he has forfeited the role of God's minister which he seeks and has become instead a scourge destined to damnation. Hamlet fears that he has compromised one of the objectives implicit in his killing of the king. This is made clear in the brief but important passage in which Hamlet comments upon his deed:

> For this same lord,
> I do repent: but heaven hath pleased it so,
> To punish me with this and this with me,
> That I must be their scourge and minister.
>
> (III.iv.172-5)

God's punishment which Hamlet sees implicit in the dead Polonius is not the revelation of his intentions to Claudius, as most critics have supposed, but rather his coming death, for Elizabethan moral law held that the murder of an innocent man inevitably must be repaid in kind.[1] From this moment the death of Hamlet is a cer-tainty both to the audience and to Hamlet himself. Hamlet must suffer punishment for his attempt to execute the justice of God. In the closet scene he has performed the very deed he had contem-plated while watching Claudius at prayer, and the sinful futility of such action is dramatically underscored in the dead Polonius.

This knowledge of his coming death serves a salutary function, for the first step in Hamlet's regeneration must be an acceptance of the inevitability of death and an awareness of the transitory nature of all earthly things. Thus when we find him with the grave-diggers at the beginning of the fifth act, his talk with them and Horatio stresses this motif: 'Imperious Caesar, dead and turn'd to clay, / Might stop a hole to keep the wind away' (V.i.236-7). That Shakespeare in this scene takes pains to inform the audience that Hamlet is thirty years old, whereas in the early scenes of the play he had appeared much younger, has long been a puzzle. But if we regard the role of Hamlet as a symbolic portrait of the human life-

---

[1] See Fredson Bowers in *PMLA*, LXX (1955), 740-9.

journey, we see that it is necessary for Shakespeare now to tell his audience that Hamlet has grown to maturity. Shakespeare's handling of time is not dictated by a consistent naturalism, but by the requirements of his theme. An audience reared in the symbolic tradition of the morality drama would pay little attention to the logical inconsistency which has so troubled modern commentators.

With the knowledge of death's inevitability must be combined a faith in the providence of God which allows man to face the inevitable unafraid. This faith Hamlet acquires on his sea voyage, and it is the principal mark of his regeneration.[1] He has escaped from the death awaiting him in England not only through his own ingenuity, but also through a series of semi-miraculous accidents without which his most careful plans would have come to nought. It is clear to the new Hamlet whom we meet in the final act that heaven has preserved him, that his own valour could serve him only when supported by divine purpose. This Hamlet affirms for Horatio:

> Rashly,
> And praised be rashness for it, let us know,
> Our indiscretion sometimes serves us well,
> When our deep plots do pall: and that should teach us
> There's a divinity that shapes our ends,
> Rough-hew them how we will.
>
> (V.ii.6-11)

In the fifth act Hamlet has submitted to the will of God, and in this very act of submission he has attained his victory. There is no more confusion about the course to be taken:

---

[1] See S. F. Johnson, 'The Regeneration of Hamlet', *SQ*. III (1952), 187-207. The regeneration of Hamlet in the fifth act has been argued by J. M. Murry, *Shakespeare* (London, 1936), pp. 247-54; C. S. Lewis, 'Hamlet: The Prince and the Poem', *Proc. of the British Academy*, XXVIII (1942), 139-54; Theodore Spencer, *Shakespeare and the Nature of Man* (New York, 1949), pp. 106-9; Hardin Craig, *An Interpretation of Shakespeare*, p. 190; G. R. Elliott, *Scourge and Minister*, pp. 132-206; Francis Fergusson, *The Idea of a Theater* (Princeton, 1949), pp. 130-3; Bertram Joseph, *Conscience and the King*, pp. 130-51; Maynard Mack, 'The World of Hamlet', in *Tragic Themes in Western Literature*, ed. Cleanth Brooks (New Haven, 1955), pp. 30-58; P. N. Siegel, *Shakespearean Tragedy and the Elizabethan Compromise*, pp. 99-118; H. S. Wilson, *On the Design of Shakespearian Tragedy*, pp. 31-48; Fredson Bowers, *PMLA*, LXX (1955), 740-9. Roy Walker, *The Time Is Out of Joint*, p. 143, has written that Hamlet's sea voyage 'is also symbolical of a spiritual journey and the decision to return to Elsinore is for Hamlet in his degree what the decision to go to Jerusalem was to Jesus'. G. Wilson Knight, after reading Walker's work in manuscript, came also to this conclusion in the 1949 edition of *The Wheel of Fire*, pp. 320-3.

> Does it not, thinks't thee, stand me now upon –
> He that hath kill'd my king and whored my mother,
> Popp'd in between the election and my hopes,
> Thrown out his angle for my proper life,
> And with such cozenage – is't not perfect conscience,
> To quit him with this arm? and is't not to be damn'd,
> To let this canker of our nature come
> In further evil?
>
> (V.ii.63-70)

He now can view the death of Claudius not as a sinful act of private vengeance which must be his own damnation, but as a lawful act of public duty, that of a minister of God and not of a scourge.[1]

But Hamlet has no particular plan for killing Claudius, and he seems to feel no need for one. He has only his confidence in the workings of divine providence. When Horatio suggests that the duel may be Hamlet's death and that he postpone it, Hamlet's reply is the Christian stoicism of a man who is ready for death, has learned to live with evil, and will accept whatever providence decrees in the faith that the God who directs it is a just and benevolent one:

> Not a whit, we defy augury: there's a special providence in the fall of a sparrow. If it be now, 'tis not to come; if it be not to come, it will be now; if it be not now, yet it will come: the readiness is all: since no man has aught of what he leaves, what is't to leave betimes? Let be.
>
> (V.ii.230-5)

This is the answer to which Shakespeare finally leads us, the resolution of the paradox in the ghost's command. Such a faith is the only plan that Hamlet needs to combat the evil of the world. The ineffective schemer of the first three acts is no more; Hamlet has become a passive instrument in the hands of divine providence. He will cleanse from Denmark the evil of Claudius just as an earlier Richmond had freed England from the curse of Richard III.

When Hamlet enters the duel with Laertes, the 'antic disposition' which had been the mark of his confused indirection has disappeared, and there can be no doubt of the sincerity with which

---

[1] See John E. Hankins, *The Character of Hamlet* (Chapel Hill, 1941), p. 74; S. F. Johnson, *SQ*, III (1952), 201; Fredson Bowers, *PMLA*, LXX (1955), 740-9.

he addresses Laertes and craves his forgiveness as a fellow human being (V.ii.237-55). Through the workings of divine providence, the plan of Claudius backfires; his guilt is exposed to the entire court; Gertrude is spared by death from the shame of this revelation; and with a stroke of his envenomed sword Hamlet accomplishes his mission. As Hamlet forces the poisoned cup to the king's lips, Shakespeare through Laertes emphasizes that in God's harmonious order evil must destroy itself: 'He is justly served; / It is a poison temper'd by himself' (V.ii.338-9). By submission to the will of God, Hamlet attains his victory. That Hamlet in his death attains salvation is made clear to the audience by Horatio: 'Good night, sweet prince; / And flights of angels sing thee to thy rest' (V.ii.370-1). *Hamlet*, like *Romeo and Juliet* is a play not about defeat, but about victory and salvation.

III

I have suggested that Shakespeare framed the role of Hamlet to represent the life-journey of everyman in an ordered universe ruled by a benevolent God. In this play Shakespeare emerges as a master of dramatic symbolism, able to give to tragedy a universality unknown in the work of his contemporaries. But Shakespeare in his greatest plays combines a symbolic with a realistic technique. The illusion of reality with which Hamlet is informed scarcely needs urging, for there is probably no other figure in the world's literature who has appeared so lifelike. Critics from William Richardson to the present have puzzled over his human peculiarities, endowed him with qualities really their own, loved him and sorrowed over him as though he were a living being and not the creation of an artist to fill one function in a larger dramatic design.

The role of Hamlet in the play we can determine, but really to know Hamlet the man is impossible. We cannot pluck the heart out of his mystery because Shakespeare did not intend that we should. Hamlet cannot be reduced to any simple psychological formula, Elizabethan or modern. I would suggest that the illusion of infinite complexity which Shakespeare created in Hamlet was part of his deliberate purpose, and that it is in accord with the larger intellectual symbolism of the play. In his complexity Hamlet stands for all men.

Hamlet's initial failure to accomplish his mission represents any man's frustration in the face of evil until he has come to terms with cosmic issues, but on the literal level of the action Shakespeare depicts this failure in more specific human terms. It is usually held that Hamlet's outbursts of passion followed by depression are the signs of what Elizabethans called melancholy; but if Hamlet suffers from some mental infirmity, as he himself declares (V.ii.243-50), this is only a symbol of the general infirmity which all men suffer.

Hamlet is describing not only himself, but mankind in general as he looks down from the battlements upon the revelry of the court below:

> So, oft it chances in particular men,
> That for some vicious mole of nature in them,
> As, in their birth – wherein they are not guilty,
> Since nature cannot choose his origin –
> By the o'ergrowth of some complexion,
> Oft breaking down the pales and forts of reason,
> Or by some habit that too much o'er-leavens
> The form of plausive manners, that these men,
> Carrying, I say, the stamp of one defect,
> Being nature's livery, or fortune's star, –
> Their virtues else – be they as pure as grace,
> As infinite as man may undergo –
> Shall in the general censure take corruption
> From that particular fault.
>
> (I.iv.23-38)

What then is this 'vicious mole of nature'? When we consider Hamlet as an individual, it must be his inability to control his passion, those faults which frustrate him at the play scene and in his mother's closet. On the symbolic level, with Hamlet as a symbol of mankind, the 'mole of nature' is original sin which beclouds man's reason and makes it so difficult for him to learn what Hamlet must learn before he can combat evil.

Hamlet's apology to Laertes before the duel has been much debated. Bradley (pp. 220-1) reluctantly concluded that it was mere dissimulation necessary for Hamlet's ends. But we cannot doubt the sincerity of Hamlet's words, if for no other reason than that to have Hamlet here dissimulating would remove sympathy from him when Shakespeare is most careful to build it up before the close of the play. The generous honesty of Hamlet's speech is unmistakable:

> Give me your pardon, sir: I've done you wrong;
> But pardon't, as you are a gentleman.
> This presence knows,
> And you must needs have heard, how I am punish'd
> With sore distraction. What I have done,
> That might your nature, honour and exception
> Roughly awake, I here proclaim was madness.
> Was't Hamlet wrong'd Laertes? Never Hamlet:
> If Hamlet from himself be ta'en away,
> And when he's not himself does wrong Laertes,
> Then Hamlet does it not. Hamlet denies it.
> Who does it, then? His madness: if't be so,
> Hamlet is of the faction that is wrong'd;
> His madness is poor Hamlet's enemy.
> Sir, in this audience,
> Let my disclaiming from a purposed evil
> Free me so far in your most generous thoughts,
> That I have shot mine arrow o'er the house,
> And hurt my brother.

(V.ii.237-55)

The killing of Polonius was one example of the error to which Hamlet's humanly defective nature had brought him. In specific terms, it was the result of that madness, or melancholy by which the universal human weakness is symbolized. This madness, however, has injured Hamlet as much as it has Laertes; it has been the source of all his difficulties from the first appearance of the ghost. That Hamlet now can describe this weakness in retrospect is a sign that he has recovered from it, for at this stage of the play mankind has already learned the lesson necessary for salvation, and Hamlet has overcome his human infirmity. He sees Laertes as his brother, a fellow man sharing the same universal problem: 'For, by the image of my cause, I see / The portraiture of his' (V.ii.77-78). Acknowledgement of the fatherhood and supremacy of God must lead to recognition of the brotherhood of man.

In the general portrait of mankind in conflict with evil, Laertes, Fortinbras and Ophelia represent different moral positions. They are young like Hamlet. Each has had a father killed, and each must struggle against the evil of the world. The defeat of Laertes and Ophelia sets off the victory of Hamlet; the victory of Fortinbras parallels that of Hamlet and gives it a more universal significance.

Laertes returns to the dark world of Denmark, full of the same ancient evil which oppresses Hamlet, to find that his father has been murdered. He too seeks redress, but unlike Hamlet he is ready to damn his own soul in the pursuit of it. There are no moral issues for Laertes:

> To hell, allegiance! vows, to the blackest devil!
> Conscience and grace, to the profoundest pit!
> I dare damnation. To this point I stand,
> That both the worlds I give to negligence,
> Let come what comes; only I'll be revenged
> Most throughly for my father.
>
> (IV.v.131-6)

He scorns both the 'conscience' which causes Hamlet to examine the moral and religious implications of his duty, and the 'grace' which Hamlet allows to guide him and to which he owes his victory. The one is dependent upon the other.

Claudius here stands in a relation to Laertes parallel to that of the ghost to Hamlet. The ghost had demanded that Hamlet oppose evil in accord with a Christian moral order, and in Gertrude's closet he had upheld the ideal of mercy. Claudius, on the other hand, is the spirit of evil itself, and he seconds Laertes in a revenge which will defy God's moral law. 'What would you undertake,' he asks, 'To show yourself your father's son in deed / More than in words?' and Laertes replies, 'To cut his throat i' church' (IV. vii.125-7). How markedly this contrasts with the refusal of Hamlet to kill Claudius at prayer. Laertes in his delusion will assume the justice of God in open defiance of God, and this Claudius, the force of evil, encourages: 'No place, indeed, should murder sanctuarize; / Revenge should have no bounds' (128-9).

Laertes is led by evil into the very action which Hamlet had been able to avoid. His instigator to revenge is indeed the 'goblin damned' which Hamlet feared his father's ghost might be. Laertes lives and dies as 'fortune's fool', unable to control his passion, a rebel against order, and, in contrast to Hamlet, a failure in his cause. The excessive passion of Laertes is made particularly clear in the graveyard scene. His leaping into Ophelia's grave represents the same kind of passionate excess of grief we have noted in Hamlet's initial defiance of reason by excessive mourning for his father.

That Hamlet can rebuke Laertes for such display is a sign of his

G

own growth. Shakespeare in this scene makes clear the relation of
Hamlet to Ophelia:

> I loved Ophelia: forty thousand brothers
> Could not, with all their quantity of love,
> Make up my sum.   (V.i.292-4)

At the same time Shakespeare uses Laertes to show the mastery
over passion which Hamlet has attained, for he can now control
his grief as Laertes cannot. There is a popular stage tradition
which would have Hamlet leap into the grave with Laertes at this
point, but there is no warrant for this either in the good quarto or
the Folio texts, the notion being based upon a stage direction in
the corrupt first quarto which Nicholas Rowe took over and which
most subsequent editors have followed.[1] Hamlet does not abandon
himself to the 'towering passion' which Laertes' words provoke.[2]
Hamlet's speech (V.i.297-307) is one of scornful derision for Laertes, showing to him the unreason of his own behaviour: 'Nay, an
thou'lt mouth, / I'll rant as well as thou' (V.i.306-7). Hamlet has
learned to see such passion as he himself had once exhibited merely
as meaningless and futile rant.[3] It is Laertes who leaps out of the
grave to attack Hamlet, as the restraint of Hamlet's reaction makes
clear:

> Thou pray'st not well.
> I prithee, take thy fingers from my throat;
> For, though I am not splenitive and rash,
> Yet have I in me something dangerous,
> Which let thy wiseness fear: hold off thy hand.
>
>   (V.i.282-6)

[1] See Granville-Barker, *Prefaces to Shakespeare*, I, 39n.

[2] For instance, Bradley, *Shakespearean Tragedy*, p. 124; Schücking, *The Meaning of Hamlet*, pp. 163-4; Dover Wilson, *What Happens in Hamlet*, p. 270; Wilson Knight, *The Wheel of Fire*, p. 22; Tillyard, *Shakespeare's Problem Plays*, pp. 17-18; Stirling, *Unity in Shakespearian Tragedy*, pp. 70-72. E. E. Stoll sees Hamlet's behaviour here as 'so outrageous and bombastic, so incongruous with the character which Shakespeare has given the hero, that it merits no serious consideration'. See *Hamlet the Man*, English Assoc. Pamphlet No. 91 (1935), p. 11. For Stoll the scene is mere stage spectacle. This view is the logical consequence of a conception of Hamlet as here unable to control his passion. So viewed, the scene would have no meaning in the total structure of the play.

[3] The quiet dignity of Hamlet in contrast to the fury of Laertes has been noted by Granville-Barker, *Prefaces to Shakespeare*, I, 138; Walker, *The Time is Out of Joint*, p. 137; Joseph, *Conscience and the King*, p. 162. Of this episode G. R. Elliott writes, 'All the more significant, then, is Hamlet's control, not perfect but extraordinary, of his present "towering passion" (V.ii.80). He will not let it put him beside himself as it did on earlier occasions.' See *Scourge and Minister*, pp. 170-1.

Hamlet by the fifth act has learned to master his own passion in the face of evil. The chief function of Laertes is, by contrast, to make this clear.

Fortinbras speaks scarcely two dozen lines in the play, and yet his shadow lies across it from the first scene to the last. His situation too is closely parallel to that of Hamlet. His uncle rules Norway, although he is the dead king's son and heir, and he feels the burden of restoring to Norway the lands she has lost, just as Hamlet feels that of avenging his father. This purpose Fortinbras undertakes at the same time that Hamlet undertakes his, but Fortinbras is deflected from his purpose by the embassy of Cornelius and Voltimand, designed possibly to parallel Rosencrantz and Guildenstern, who similarly attempt to frustrate the purposes of Hamlet. Hamlet and Fortinbras both accomplish their missions, for whereas Hamlet destroys evil, Fortinbras recovers not only his lands, but all of Denmark as her new king. The method he initially contemplates is as contrary to God's moral order as the futile plans of Hamlet, for Fortinbras' father has been fairly and honourably killed in battle, and the lands in question lawfully forfeited.

Fortinbras will expose his mortal life 'to all that fortune, death and danger dare, / Even for an egg-shell' (IV.iv.52-53), but he knows also how to accept his fate and the moral law of the universe in the manner of the mature stoical man. His uncle's command that he abandon his Danish expedition is an assertion of moral law, and this Fortinbras accepts, although it blunts his original purpose. This act of submission is parallel to the final submission of Hamlet. Its result also is victory. His original unlawful adventure might have won him some land in the hazard of uncertain battle; his submission makes him the new king of Denmark, for providence guides him to Elsinore at the proper moment. He attains the kind of victory over natural impulse which makes him the perfect ruler for the new Denmark which will follow the destruction of the ancient evil of which Claudius has been symbol. Fortinbras stands for the rebirth of order.

Shakespeare's realism has made of Ophelia a pathetic and poignant figure, but her role in the total design is nevertheless a subsidiary one. She is used, like Laertes and Fortinbras, primarily to focus attention upon another approach to the general human problem with which the play is concerned. In the original legend her archtype was a whore used to trap Hamlet. Shakespeare retains her role as the decoy – and there is no evidence that she is an unwilling one – but he transforms her into a simple, virtuous young girl who we are given every reason to believe has loved Hamlet and been loved in return. She becomes a symbol of the human love to which Hamlet turns for support, and her rejection of him emphasizes symbolically that man faced with Hamlet's task must rely upon himself alone.

Ophelia's madness is related to the central theme of the play, for Ophelia parallels Hamlet in that she must learn to live with evil in a world in which her lover may go mad and murder her father, and in which there is not a single soul to whom she can turn for aid in her abandonment. Like Laertes, but unlike Hamlet and Fortinbras, she is incapable of growth, and thus her end is madness and suicide. Hamlet suffers because he questions moral law and seeks for answers; Ophelia suffers by contrast because she is incapable of such questioning. Her moral law is her father's word, and she is incapable of discovering that her father is an instrument of evil. 'I shall obey, my lord' (I.iii.136) is her only reply to the great moral issues which every human being confronts. Her obedience to her father causes her to see love as madness and lust, to reject her fellow man in Hamlet, and in the nunnery scene to become, like her brother Laertes, an instrument of evil in spite of her own natural inclinations towards the good. Ophelia is the dramatic symbol of moral blindness; her virtue is the 'cloistered virtue' which Milton scorned. Hamlet's acceptance of the will of God comes only after prolonged struggle; without this struggle there can be no knowledge and no salvation. This truth the 'maimed rites' of Ophelia illustrate with a tragic poignancy. In her pain and death there is no victory.

The remaining characters serve similar thematic functions. Some are more fully developed than others, but none is designed primarily as a portrait from life. Dramatic functions often create inconsistencies which are difficult to reconcile. This is true of Polonius whose role as the principal agent of an evil force is difficult to reconcile with that of the loving father in whom Ophelia places her trust and who is certainly devoted to her. This view of him is in the play, but it is inconsistent with the brutality of his treatment of Ophelia before and after the nunnery scene, with the coarse animal imagery of his 'At such a time I'll loose my daughter to him' (II.ii.162).

Particularly troublesome have been the two speeches in which Claudius acknowledges his murder of his brother and seems to show remorse for his crime. To modern audiences these add to the realism of his portrait, revealing a peculiar mixture of good and evil which may be part of the most hardened criminal. To a Renaissance audience these speeches would win no sympathy for Claudius.[1] They would exhibit in him only what all sinners feel, horror of the crime and dread of its consequences. They would not show remorse, for Claudius expresses no contrition; he will not surrender the effects of his crime or do penance for it. He is, in fact, a conventional portrait of a sinner unrepentant and destined for damnation. The imagery of Claudius' speeches recalls the futile sacrifices of the Biblical Cain, which God rejected.

These speeches serve also important mechanical functions. As Ophelia goes to her encounter with Hamlet in the lobby, Claudius speaks an aside:

> How smart a lash that speech doth give my conscience!
> The harlot's cheek, beautied with plastering art,
> Is not more ugly to the thing that helps it
> Than is my deed to my most painted word:
> O heavy burthen! (III.i.50-54)

Thus Shakespeare brands him as a hypocrite, one whose deed contradicts his word, whose seeming virtue is the plaster over the ugly reality of the whore. But at the same time Shakespeare uses this speech to resolve the doubts of the audience about the ghost. To appreciate fully the ensuing action, the audience must be certain of Claudius' guilt, and after this speech it can have no further doubt.

The symbolic function of Claudius' prayer scene we already have noted. We cannot allow these seeming signs of remorse or the attractive features of Claudius, his love for Gertrude and his courage in confronting Laertes, to obscure the fact that his function in the play is to stand for evil. One of the traditional aspects of evil – mirrored in the Vice of the medieval morality plays – was false appearance. Evil, like Claudius, may look attractive, but inwardly it is foul and rotten. In learning the nature of evil Hamlet must learn to distinguish appearance from reality. The semblance

---

[1] See Joseph, pp. 80-82; M. D. H. Parker, *The Slave of Life* (London, 1955), pp. 150-3.

of good with which the villainy of Claudius is cloaked supports the intellectual content of the play. It is a motif which Shakespeare is further to develop in *Othello*.

IV

In the plays from *King John* through *Julius Caesar* Shakespeare had learned to reflect political issues in specific human terms. These plays have a limited range, for the problems themselves concentrate upon only one area of human experience, although as always in Shakespeare the political issues cannot be divorced from the ethical. In *Hamlet* Shakespeare went beyond these plays. He tried to give dramatic form to the problem of man's life on earth, its meaning and its direction in the face of an ever-present evil and an inevitable death. We have seen how he had conceived of these issues as the proper sphere of tragedy in such early plays as *Titus Andronicus* and *Romeo and Juliet*, where his artistry was not yet equal to the magnitude of the task. In *Hamlet* he mirrored in the struggle and death of one man a higher degree of life's complexity than had ever before been reflected in drama, and he ordered all the elements of his play so as to lead his audience to a positive affirmation of a Christian moral order. To view *Hamlet* as merely the case study of an individual is to belittle the genius of Shakespeare and to slight his artistry.

In *Hamlet* Shakespeare refined and developed the pattern of tragic action which he had first developed out of Senecan antecedents in *Romeo and Juliet*. This type of tragedy he never again attempted. In his next play, *Othello*, he returned to the pattern of moral choice with which he had experimented in *Julius Caesar*, and now he developed it so that it could encompass not a specific political issue, but like *Hamlet* all of human experience. With this pattern of moral choice he continued to experiment for the remainder of his career as a writer of tragedy.

CHAPTER FIVE

The Pattern of Moral Choice:
Othello

I n *Othello* Shakespeare again gave dramatic form to a Christian
view of mankind's encounter with evil, the destructive power
of that evil, and man's ability to attain salvation in spite of it.[1]
He did so with a neatness and precision which reveal that he had
matured as an artist in the brief years since the completion of
Hamlet. Now he evolved a more perfect dramatic form which
might in the domestic setting of one man's fall – closer to the
immediate world of his audience than that of any other of his
tragedies – mirror the fall of all men, just as Judeo-Christian tradition had reflected it in the fall of Adam; and as the paradox of
the fortunate fall assured to man the hope of redemption, Shakespeare reflected also this universal hope in *Othello.*[2]

Critics since the time of Thomas Rymer and his *Short View of
Tragedy* (1693) have debated the credibility of the action and the
motivation of character in *Othello.* Rymer dismissed the play as

---

[1] It was completed probably in 1602 or 1603. See J. Dover Wilson, ed., *Othello*
(Cambridge, 1957), pp. xiii-xv, for the best evidence as to the date.

[2] The Christian framework of *Othello* has been recognized by G. Wilson Knight,
The Wheel of Fire, pp. 97-119; S. L. Bethell, 'Shakespeare's Imagery: The Diabolic
Images in *Othello*', *Shakespeare Survey 5* (Cambridge, 1952), pp. 62-80; G. R. Elliott,
Flaming Minister: A Study of Othello as Tragedy of Love and Hate (Durham, N.C.,
1953); M. D. H. Parker, *The Slave of Life,* pp. 125-9; R. B. Heilman, *Magic in the
Web* (Lexington, Ky., 1956); Paul N. Siegel, *Shakespearean Tragedy and the Eliza-
bethan Compromise,* pp. 119-41; H. S. Wilson, *On the Design of Shakespearian Tragedy,*
pp. 52-67.

This has not been a dominant point of view. For A. C. Bradley, *Othello* conveyed
the 'impression of darkness and fatefulness, . . . the absence of direct indications of
any guiding power', *Shakespearean Tragedy* (London, 1949), p. 181. In more recent
times this view has persisted in such works as Clifford Leech, *Shakespeare's Tragedies
and Other Studies in Seventeenth Century Drama* (London, 1950), pp. 8-9; Geoffrey Bush,
Shakespeare and the Natural Condition (Cambridge, Mass., 1956), pp. 53-61.

'a Bloody Farce, without salt or savour' (p. 146), and in spite of many attempts to justify the play in terms of ordinary human behaviour, so acute a critic as T. S. Eliot can still remark that 'Rymer makes out a very good case' of which he has 'never seen a cogent refutation'.[1] It has been argued even that Shakespeare deliberately created impossible characters and an inconceivable situation so as to shock his audience.[2] To argue the credibility of the characters in *Othello* is a fruitless enterprise; that Shakespeare endowed them with as much of the illusion of reality as his art allowed we cannot doubt, but we must also admit that the events of the play are not such as would likely occur in ordinary life. Seen as a case study of individuals or as the account of a particularly exciting murder, the play emerges as faulty and deficient. When we consider *Othello*, however, in the non-naturalistic, symbolic tradition of Shakespeare's theatre, as the emotional equivalent of universal human experience, it emerges among the masterpieces of all time.

From the seventh novel of the third day of Giraldi Cinthio's *Hecatommithi* Shakespeare took the bare outline of his story.[3] All of Cinthio's tales were designed to illustrate moral lessons relating to marriage, and this one held up the fate of the heroine as an example of what happens to a girl who marries a man of different race, religion and social customs (*la natura, il Cielo, il modo della vita*). The story is crude and sordid, and the principal characters are little more than two rather brutal criminals who murder for the most ignominious reasons and who attempt to evade the consequences of their crime. Shakespeare, however, was not interested in presenting a factual report of a sordid crime. He reduced the immediate details of the intrigue to an insignificant level, so altering the time sequence of his source, for instance, as to give Desdemona and Cassio no opportunity to commit the offence of which Iago accuses them.[4] What emerges is not a logical and coherent

---

[1] *Selected Essays: 1917-1932* (New York, 1932), pp. 97n, 121n. The refutation is attempted by Leech, *Shakespeare's Tragedies*, pp. 87-110.

[2] See Robert Bridges, *Collected Essays etc.* (London, 1927), I, 23-25; E. E. Stoll, *Othello: An Historical and Comparative Study* (Minneapolis, 1915), *Art and Artifice in Shakespeare*, pp. 6-55, 'Source and Motive in *Macbeth* and *Othello*', *RES*, XIX (1943), 25-32.

[3] On the source see Kenneth Muir, *Shakespeare's Sources*, I, 122-40; H. B. Charlton, *Shakespearian Tragedy*, pp. 113-40; Dover Wilson, pp. xiii-xxiv.

[4] On Shakespeare's manipulation of time in *Othello*, see in particular Granville-Barker, *Prefaces to Shakespeare*, II, 24-30; Charlton, *Shakespearian Tragedy*, pp. 130-2; Dover Wilson, pp. xxx-xxxvi; M. R. Ridley, ed., *Othello* (London, 1958), pp. lxvii-lxx.

account of a specific event, but an imaginative impression of evil's operation which must be grasped in its totality with slight regard to the logic of its particular parts. By scanting the particular detail Shakespeare is able to focus upon the total poetic impression. So compelling is his artistry that few beholders of the tragedy in the theatre ask the questions which have so bothered generations of critics.

Cinthio's account, however, provided the basic ingredients for the kind of drama Shakespeare now envisaged. There was the central situation of a man choosing evil through deception and then suffering remorse for his error. There was the suggestion that the girl had loved the Moor because of his great virtues, and there was Cinthio's emphasis upon the unnaturalness of the marriage. The delusion and remorse of Othello offered the same scope for a tragedy of moral choice as had the delusion and remorse of Brutus in *Julius Caesar*. The motif of the unnatural could be altered in focus so that one of the marks of Othello's delusion might be his conception as unnatural of what was really a reflection of God's harmonious order, and his corollary acceptance as natural and 'honest' of what was really Satanic. Thus Shakespeare could pose for Othello the problem he had posed for Hamlet, that of distinguishing the mask of goodness from actual goodness, and in the inability of Othello to do so until too late, he might again express what he had mirrored in Claudius, that evil operates through deception.

Othello is of great potential virtue, but when he comes upon the scene he is, like the early Hamlet, as yet untried. In spite of his age he has not yet encountered the evil of the world. The play will be his baptism; he will encounter evil as Adam had encountered it, and like Adam he will fall, but in his own destruction he will learn the nature of evil. He will learn to distinguish true virtue from seeming virtue, and from his tragedy he will emerge the kind of man who is capable of salvation. Shakespeare says in the destruction of Othello, as in that of Hamlet, that true virtue and wisdom may come to man only through suffering, struggle and self-mastery. It is the tragedy of human life that this must be so.

In *Hamlet* evil had been passive. Claudius might never have acted against Hamlet, for he was content to let his crime lie buried in the past, but Hamlet had been faced with the task of active struggle against evil. In *Othello* evil is an active force embodied in

Iago. He is a dramatic symbol of evil whose function is to cause the downfall of Othello, and although Shakespeare endows him with an illusion of reality so supreme in its artistry that it has escaped analysis as thoroughly as that of Hamlet, in the larger symbolic design of the play he needs no specific motivation. Othello is posing the chief question in the minds of his audience when he asks, 'Will you, I pray, demand that demi-devil / Why he hath thus ensnared my soul and body?' (V.ii.301-2); Shakespeare's only answer is to affirm the inscrutability of evil, its self-sufficiency which needs no motive beyond the fact of its existence: 'From this time forth I never will speak word. / Demand me nothing: what you know you know' (V.ii.303-4).

To emphasize that evil needs no specific reason to seduce man, that its very nature is to do so, Shakespeare availed himself of the long dramatic tradition of the morality Vice which was so much a part of the age in which he worked, and whose features his audience immediately could recognize.[1] Iago has all of the characteristics of the traditional Vice, the bluff good nature, the sense of humour, and there is even the gull, Roderigo, whom he dupes. Iago is the masquer, or dissimulator, the conventional figure of evil disguised as good.

Shakespeare achieves directness and precision in this play by symbolizing his force of evil in terms of one specific sin. This is jealousy, in Renaissance terms an aspect of the deadly sin of envy, the antithesis of love which springs from the perversion of love by fear.[2] Iago is the dramatic symbol of jealousy itself, and he mirrors jealousy in all of its possible forms. He is jealous of Cassio's position (I.i.8-33). His suspicions of Emilia, of which Shakespeare reminds the audience throughout the play (I.iii.392-6, II.i.304-8, IV.ii.145-7) show the same kind of sexual jealousy he is to arouse in Othello. His lust for Desdemona (II.i.300-2) springs from envy of the happiness of Othello. Iago in his soliloquies reveals himself to the audience as a personification of jealousy; he does so as thoroughly as any personification of a deadly sin had ever exposed himself in the medieval morality drama. It is unlikely that a Jacobean audience could have failed to grasp the symbolism with which Iago is endowed.

Just as Iago stands for jealousy, Desdemona stands for its very

---

[1] See Bernard Spivack, *Shakespeare and the Allegory of Evil* (New York, 1958).
[2] See Lily B. Campbell, *Shakespeare's Tragic Heroes*, pp. 148-74.

opposite, the cardinal virtue of love. It is love in the highest scale
of Christian neo-Platonism, love of the mind and understanding:

> I saw Othello's visage in his mind,
> And to his honours and his valiant parts
> Did I my soul and fortunes consecrate.
>
> (I.iii.253-5)

It is all bounty, all trust and all forgiveness. In the perfection of
her love Desdemona reflects the love of Christ for man; she stands
both for self-sacrifice and for redemption. Othello is like the conventional morality play hero between the Satanic Iago and the
angelic Desdemona. Both vie for his soul, and in his human imperfection he chooses wrongly.

Shakespeare constructed *Othello* so that dramatic emphasis would
be placed upon the process of this wrong moral choice. In the first
two acts he makes clear the symbolism of the various characters,
and he provides a setting for the temptation of Othello which
occupies the long third scene of the third act. This is the crucial
scene of the play, and it ends with a symbolic union of Othello
and Iago. The fourth act is devoted to evil's operation, the rapid
degeneration of Othello from man of reason to its bestial opposite.
That Othello should succumb to the shallow plot of the handkerchief has puzzled many critics, but when he does so he has already
forfeited the powers of reason, and all of his behaviour is a negation of reason; this the very speciousness of Iago's plot serves to
emphasize. In the fourth act also we see the perversion of values
which Othello's delusion entails as he comes to see the world
through the eyes of Iago, with the culminating instance of Desdemona, symbol of divine love, treated as though she were a
whore.

Shakespeare never slackens his pace. Othello's madness mounts
in an ever-increasing fury until he commits the culminating sin.
He takes upon himself the justice of God and murders Desdemona
in what his delusion tells him is justice, but what is really a devilish
and bestial revenge. The murder occurs in the second scene of the
final act. It is followed by an immediate revelation to Othello of
his error. He recognizes his wrong moral choice, casts off Iago,
and before his death he undergoes remorse and penance. Finally
by an act of will he executes true justice upon himself. He dies in
reunion with Desdemona, and in his expiation for his sin he merits

divine mercy. In spite of the tortures of hell which Othello en-
visions for himself, the audience is assured of his eventual salvation. *Othello* reflects the traditional pattern of the Christian soul
ensnared by sin, but who through suffering and self-knowledge
learns to overcome it. The audience participates emotionally in
Othello's anguish, and it recognizes at the end the promise of
salvation which affirms order, justice and mercy in the universe.
It experiences a sense of tragic reconciliation.

II

Like *Hamlet*, *Othello* begins with evil; it is not the pervasive darkness and gloom which hangs over Elsinore, but a specific agent of
evil who wears the outward signs of virtue, life and conviviality.
In Iago we see evil as deception and as a direct challenge to the
order and harmony of the universe. Iago's superficial brilliance
and self-control is the 'reason' of Renaissance scepticism which in
Shakespeare's day was challenging the great vision of harmony,
order and degree which Christian humanism carried over from
the Middle Ages and which was most notably embodied in the
writings of Richard Hooker.

Iago reveals himself as an active force of evil in the opening
scene of the play. To Roderigo alone is granted insight from the
beginning into the true Iago, but Roderigo is a fool who cannot
perceive the implications of what he sees until it is too late. Iago's
single word of admiration in the play is for evil servants who
secretly betray their masters:

> Others there are
> Who, trimm'd in forms and visages of duty,
> Keep yet their hearts attending on themselves,
> And, throwing but shows of service on their lords,
> Do well thrive by them and when they have lined
>   their coats
> Do themselves homage: these fellows have some soul;
> And such a one do I profess myself.

(I.i.49-55)

Iago stands for social disintegration. In the harmonious world
order of which Shakespeare's contemporaries liked to conceive,
servants had their just place, their rights and their obligations.
They were loyal to their masters out of love, and their masters
repaid them with care and protection, all as a part of a social order

whose perfection reflected the love of God for man. The true
servant of such a system, Iago sees as:

> a duteous and knee-crooking knave
> That, doting on his own obsequious bondage,
> Wears out his time, much like his master's ass,
> For naught but provender, and when he's old, cashier'd:
> Whip me such honest knaves.
>
> (I.i.45-49)

[margin note: Iago appears to be good]

Such a servant Iago appears to be, but his semblance of loyalty is
but a mask. He is always the self-seeker. He shares none of the
'love and duty' which hold together the social order and link it to
God Himself. Iago is all seeming, false appearance:

[margin note: But but he is realy self centered]

> In following him, I follow but myself;
> Heaven is my judge, not I for love and duty,
> But seeming so, for my peculiar end:
> For when my outward action doth demonstrate
> The native act and figure of my heart
> In compliment extern, 'tis not long after
> But I will wear my heart upon my sleeve
> For daws to peck at: I am not what I am. (I.i.58-65)

The supreme egotism of Iago is a manifestation of the code of
'reason' by which he lives. True human reason in terms of Renaissance Christian humanism was a reflection of the supreme wisdom
of God, and it consisted of attuning one's own will to the purposes of God, a recognition that human events are reflections of
divine purpose. Iago's 'reason' is the sin of pride, for it denies the
supremacy of God and sees man as the sole author of his destiny,
able to control himself and others by the power of his mind. This
is expressed in his speech to Roderigo:

[margin note: instead he acts out of he is the auther]

> Virtue! a fig! 'tis in ourselves that we are thus or thus. Our
> bodies are our gardens, to the which our wills are gardeners; so
> that if we will plant nettles, or sow lettuce, set hyssop and weed up
> thyme, supply it with one gender of herbs, or distract it with many,
> either to have it sterile with idleness, or manured with industry, why,
> the power and corrigible authority of this lies in our wills. If the
> balance of our lives had not one scale of reason to poise another of
> sensuality, the blood and baseness of our natures would conduct us
> to most preposterous conclusions: but we have reason to cool our
> raging motions, our carnal stings, our unbitted lusts, whereof I take
> this that you call love to be a sect or scion.
>
> (I.iii.322-37)

Iago would control human passion by an act of will unrelated to the will of God; his action reveals an unbridled passion which gives the lie to his own protestation. In denying the purposes and the power of God, Iago strikes at the root of Christian humanism, for the 'natural law' which it saw as the guiding principle in human affairs was a reflection of the divine law of God, an emanation of God's love for his creation and of the harmonious order by which he ruled the universe. Iago, like the later Edmund, stands outside morality. He can see man only as a creature of animal passion, cut off from the grace of God. Love, the guiding principle in God's plan, is only 'a lust of the blood and a permission of the will' (I.iii.339-40).

Bradley (pp. 236-7) marvelled that the supreme intellect of Iago should finally betray him into such colossal errors as his misjudging both the relationship between Othello and Desdemona and the character of his own wife, Emilia. But it is in the very nature of Iago's intellect that this should be so; for such 'reason', standing outside of moral law, can never recognize the truth of moral law; it can perceive the signs of God's benevolence only as their very opposites. The love of Othello and Desdemona, a love of mind divorced from physical passion, can appear to Iago only as 'a frail vow betwixt an erring barbarian and a super-subtle Venetian' (I.iii.362-4). Viewing love as animal lust he can only conclude that Desdemona will be governed by lust:

> Her eye must be fed; and what delight shall she have to look on the devil? When the blood is made dull with the act of sport, there should be, again to inflame it and to give satiety a fresh appetite, loveliness in favour, sympathy in years, manners and beauties; all which the Moor is defective in: now, for want of these required conveniences, her delicate tenderness will find itself abused, begin to heave the gorge, disrelish and abhor the Moor; very nature will instruct her in it and compel her to some second choice.
>
> (II.i.227-37)

He can perceive only the outward appearance of Othello; he cannot see the qualities for which Desdemona married him, and thus their relationship seems only a product of lust which lust must destroy. Out of Iago's failure of perception will come his own destruction, but this failure is inherent in the very 'reason' by which he lives.

Iago is revealed to the audience as a demi-devil, the incarnation of evil itself, the negation of moral law. This is not, however, how he appears to the other characters in the play: 'Divinity of hell! / When devils will the blackest sins put on, / They do suggest at first with heavenly shows, / As I do now' (II.iii.356-9). To the rest of the world, and particularly to Othello, he is always 'honest' Iago, and we must remember that 'honest' has also the implications of chaste. Like the Claudius of *Hamlet*, Iago is evil in its traditional role, disguised as good. He stands for false appearance, and it is fitting that Shakespeare should give to him the celebrated lines on reputation:

> Good name in man and woman, dear my lord,
> Is the immediate jewel of their souls:
> Who steals my purse steals trash; 'tis something,
>   nothing;
> 'Twas mine, 'tis his, and has been slave to thousands;
> But he that filches from me my good name
> Robs me of that which not enriches him
> And makes me poor indeed.   (III.iii.155-61)

Only the name, the outward appearance, is the immediate jewel of his soul. This reputation theme runs through the entire play,[1] but Shakespeare makes a careful distinction between a just self-esteem which a man in his honour must defend and a worship of false appearance without regard to the inner reality. Such a concern for reputation is a manifestation of pride, for it is the sin of cherishing only appearance as that part of man which distinguishes him from the beast, and thus it is a denial of God. This false concern for reputation Iago arouses in Othello, leading him to the murder of Desdemona in the delusion that only thus can he preserve his good name.

Cassio serves various dramatic functions in the play, and one of them is to emphasize this theme of reputation. When Othello dismisses him from his post it is the loss of this kind of worldly appearance that Cassio laments:

> Reputation, reputation, reputation! O, I have lost my reputation!
> I have lost the immortal part of myself, and what remains is bestial.
> My reputation, Iago, my reputation!
>
>   (II.iii.262-5)

---

[1] See Brents Stirling, *Unity in Shakespearian Tragedy*, pp. 111-38; G. R. Elliott, *Flaming Minister*, p. 94ff.

Iago is wearing the mask of seeming virtue when he replies:

> As I am an honest man, I thought you had received some bodily
> wound; there is more sense in that than in reputation. Reputation is
> an idle and most false imposition: oft got without merit, and lost
> without deserving: you have lost no reputation at all, unless you
> repute yourself such a loser.
>
> (II.iii.266-71)

We cannot doubt that this is Shakespeare's comment; Iago states
it as 'an honest man', and that he should be the one to voice this
view need not surprise us when we remember the wisdom of the
advice which Claudius had offered to Hamlet while wearing a
similar mask of seeming virtue.

Cassio is deluded like Othello by the seeming virtue of Iago:
'I never knew / A Florentine more kind and honest' (III.i.42-43).
This parallel is not his only function in the play. He is used also as
a symbol of the true friendship which Othello rejects. His is a
genuine honesty contrasted to the seeming honesty of Iago; his
conviviality and good fellowship stem, as opposed to Iago's, from
a real trust and love of his fellow men. In spite of his deception by
Iago, Cassio does not allow himself to be deeply tainted by evil as
Othello does. He maintains to the end his faith in Desdemona,
symbolically a hope that true love and virtue will restore him to
the felicity which his weakness has lost him. Like Banquo in
Macbeth, Cassio stands for ordinary man, with his mixture of good
and evil. He never surrenders his soul to evil, and he emerges
triumphant in spite of his encounter with Iago. Thus he can rule
in Cyprus at the end of the play, a symbol of rebirth.

Just as in Iago Shakespeare pictures evil in the guise of good,
in Othello he pictures true virtue wearing all the outward signs of
evil. To do so he developed the suggestion in Cinthio that the
marriage was unnatural. Cinthio had not dwelt on the blackness
of the Moor, mentioning it only once in his story; but Shakespeare seized upon it as a poetic symbol by which he could emphasize the theme of the unnatural. That Shakespeare intended his
audience to think of Othello as a Negro of very dark complexion
is clear.[1] We must recognize that a Jacobean audience could not

---

[1] See Bradley, *Shakespearean Tragedy*, pp. 198-202; Granville-Barker, *Prefaces to
Shakespeare*, II, 116-17; Charlton, *Shakespearian Tragedy*, pp. 117-18; Dover Wilson,
pp. ix-xii; M. R. Ridley, pp. l-liv.

have failed to view the marriage of a white Italian girl to a black African with some horror. Cinthio himself had told the story as an example of a marriage contrary to nature. This is not to attribute racial prejudice to Shakespeare. It is, on the contrary, the most astounding evidence of his freedom from such feeling, for the marriage to which he gives the outward appearance of an evil act contrary to nature, he shows in reality to be the noblest type of spiritual union.

In the Renaissance the colour black was a symbol of lechery – it is commonly so used in the emblem books of the period – and it was also the colour of the devil, whose redness is a fairly recent innovation. We have seen the use which Shakespeare made of this belief in the Aaron of *Titus Andronicus*. To Shakespeare's audience Othello, like Aaron, would have all the outward appearance of the 'blacker devil' (V.ii.131) which Emilia calls him. His marriage to Desdemona would appear as an aberration in nature. Iago awakens Brabantio with a description of the marriage in these terms, punctuated by images of brute sexuality:

> 'Zounds, sir, you're robb'd; for shame, put on your gown;
> Your heart is burst, you have lost half your soul;
> Even now, now, very now, an old black ram
> Is tupping your white ewe. Arise, arise;
> Awake the snorting citizens with the bell,
> Or else the devil will make a grandsire of you.   (I.i.86-91)

Brabantio voices the normal feelings of the audience in his incredulity at an event seemingly past reason:

> Damn'd as thou art, thou hast enchanted her;
> For I'll refer me to all things of sense,
> If she in chains of magic were not bound,
> Whether a maid so tender, fair and happy,
> So opposite to marriage that she shunn'd
> The wealthy curled darlings of our nation,
> Would ever have, to incur a general mock,
> Run from her guardage to the sooty bosom
> Of such a thing as thou, to fear, not to delight.
> Judge me the world, if 'tis not gross in sense
> That thou hast practised on her with foul charms,
> Abused her delicate youth with drugs or minerals
> That weaken motion.
>
> (I.ii.62-75)

H

He can only account for his daughter's apparent defiance of nature and reason by the unnatural powers of a devil who can command the use of exotic drugs.

This motif of unnatural union runs through the first two acts of the play, juxtaposed in thematic counterpoint against the twin motif of Iago's honesty. Othello has the blackness of Satan, Iago the whiteness of truth and virtue. True virtue bears the mark of evil, and evil is marked with the semblance of honesty. Shakespeare assures the audience of the falsity of these outward signs, that Iago is only seeming honest, and that Othello, in spite of his appearance, is a man of true nobility whom Desdemona can love for 'his honours and his valiant parts' (I.iii.254). We see his calm bearing and his dignity before the council, and he himself is made to deny the very lechery of which his colour is the outward sign:

> Vouch with me, heaven, I therefore beg it not,
> To please the palate of my appetite,
> Nor to comply with heat – the young affects
> In me defunct – and proper satisfaction,
> But to be free and bounteous to her mind.
>
> (I.iii.262-6)

Yet so shocking is Shakespeare's deliberate reversal of normal appearances that the audience must be left still incredulous, with an uncertain fear that appearance may still be truth. This fear is supported by Brabantio's warning: 'Look to her, Moor, if thou hast eyes to see: / She has deceived her father, and may thee' (I.iii.293-4). Upon this seeming violation of nature, Iago will work in his temptation of Othello. He will cause Othello to see Desdemona as Brabantio has seen her, and thus to cast off as foul and unnatural what appears to be so, but which in reality is the very opposite.

III

The temptation scene of the third act is cast in the conventional pattern of the morality drama. Othello undergoes a struggle during which he must choose between the two forces which vie for his soul, Iago on the one hand and Desdemona on the other. At the end of the scene Othello rejects Desdemona and embraces Iago in a symbolic ritual union, and from thenceforth he sees the world with the eyes of Iago. The tools with which Iago will work already have been prepared for in the first two acts. He will rely upon his own appearance as honest, which Othello has not yet learned to question, and he will work upon the seeming perversion of nature in Othello's own marriage, appealing to Othello's ignorance of life and to the fears and uncertainties which accompany his human inability to distinguish between appearance and reality. Iago will arouse in Othello a false sense of the demands of honour and reputation, which will reflect the love of mere appearance for which Iago from the first has stood. Othello, in the delusion of his wrong moral choice, will live by the code of Iago.

The temptation scene has been widely criticized as incredible. Considered coldly and objectively, Othello's fall does seem difficult to accept, but the audience does not coldly evaluate; it is caught up in the emotional intensity of the scene whose total poetic impact conveys an imaginative impression of man's fall. Shakespeare's artistry infuses the scene with an illusion of reality which is remarkably effective in the theatre. The very speed of the action carries the audience along in Iago's spell and gives it no opportunity to consider questions of logical probability. Shakespeare has carefully provided in the first two acts certain elements which will make the seduction of Othello plausible. He has stressed his simple trust in Iago, his unfamiliarity with civilized life and particularly with Venetian women, his role as an alien in an ever potentially hostile society. Perhaps most significantly, by a series of events Shakespeare has caused Othello to doubt his own powers of judgement and perception.[1] His marriage to Desdemona has resulted in an accusation of witchcraft from one who has always been his friend. Cassio, the officer he had so carefully chosen, in his drunkenness has caused Othello to question the wisdom of that choice. Othello is now ready to question the goodness of Desdemona in which he had believed as firmly as in the friendship of Brabantio and the soldiership of Cassio.

Iago's offensive begins with his 'Ha! I like not that' (III.iii.35) as Cassio departs, but this initial suggestion has no effect upon Othello. He is, as Shakespeare later tells us 'not easily jealous' (V.ii.345), and he does not begin to succumb until much later in the scene. The presence of Desdemona counteracts the force of Iago's insinuations, just as the good angel of the morality drama checks the power of the evil one. It is only after Desdemona has left the scene some eighty-five lines after Iago's initial onslaught

[1] Bradley, *Shakespearean Tragedy*, p. 193.

that Othello begins to rise to Iago's bait. As Desdemona leaves, Othello affirms for the audience the strength of his union with her:

> Excellent wretch! Perdition catch my soul,
> But I do love thee! and when I love thee not,
> Chaos is come again.
>
> (III.iii.90-92)

Iago excites Othello's natural curiosity by his veiled remarks touching the honesty of Cassio, and by the implication that he has secret knowledge which he will not reveal. There is no evidence of jealousy on Othello's part, however, until Iago himself raises the issue:

> O, beware, my lord, of jealousy;
> It is the green-eyed monster which doth mock
> The meat it feeds on: that cuckold lives in bliss
> Who, certain of his fate, loves not his wronger;
> But, O, what damned minutes tells he o'er
> Who dotes, yet doubts, suspects, yet strongly loves!
>
> (III.iii.165-70)

This suggestion Othello at first resists with the memory of Desdemona's virtue and with a true awareness of his own excellence for which Desdemona married him:

> Why, why is this?
> Think'st thou I'ld make a life of jealousy,
> To follow still the changes of the moon
> With fresh suspicions? No; to be once in doubt
> Is once to be resolved: exchange me for a goat,
> When I shall turn the business of my soul
> To such exsufflicate and blown surmises,
> Matching thy inference. 'Tis not to make me jealous
> To say my wife is fair, feeds well, loves company,
> Is free of speech, sings, plays and dances well;
> Where virtue is, these are more virtuous:
> Nor from mine own weak merits will I draw
> The smallest fear or doubt of her revolt;
> For she had eyes, and chose me.
>
> (III.iii.176-89)

Othello's awareness of how jealousy operates, evident in these lines, is in effect a rejection of jealousy, just as the speech is a reaffirmation of those convictions which Iago seeks to undermine.

To this point of the scene, Iago has still been unsuccessful. He cannot shake Othello's faith in himself and in Desdemona. Now he turns to Othello's ignorance of Venice:

> I know our country disposition well;
> In Venice they do let heaven see the pranks
> They dare not show their husbands; their best conscience
> Is not to leav't undone, but keep't unknown.
>
> (III.iii.201-4)

Here Othello is vulnerable, and for the first time there is the beginning of belief in Othello's half-credulous reply: 'Dost thou say so?' (205). Once Othello has been prepared to believe that the virtue of Venetian women may be a seeming virtue, Iago can remind him of the seeming treachery of Desdemona to her father:

> She did deceive her father, marrying you;
> And when she seem'd to shake and fear your looks,
> She loved them most.
>
> (III.iii.206-8)

With the motifs of evil wearing the guise of good and of Desdemona's apparent defiance of nature, Iago gains his first victory, for Othello is forced to reply, 'And so she did' (209).

Othello himself now raises the issue of 'nature erring from itself' (227), and this gives Iago his opportunity to evoke the motif of the unnatural in words which echo those of Brabantio before the Venetian council:

> Not to affect many proposed matches
> Of her own clime, complexion, and degree,
> Whereto we see in all things nature tends –
> Foh! one may smell in such a will most rank,
> Foul disproportion, thoughts unnatural.
>
> (III.iii.229-33)

Othello is now drawn to the side of Iago. He is ready to entertain the idea that Desdemona may not be what she has appeared to be. He can now accept the vision of Iago as the measure of human affairs:

> This fellow's of exceeding honesty,
> And knows all qualities, with a learned spirit,
> Of human dealings.
>
> (III.iii.258-60)

He dwells himself on his blackness and his years which, if love were the mere animal lust which it is to Iago, might furnish reasons for the supposed infidelity of his wife:

> Haply, for I am black
> And have not those soft parts of conversation
> That chamberers have, or for I am declined
> Into the vale of years, – yet that's not much –
> She's gone. I am abused; and my relief
> Must be to loathe her. O curse of marriage,
> That we can call these delicate creatures ours,
> And not their appetites!
>
> (III.iii.263-70)

The symbol of spiritual union has become to him a creature of sensual appetite.

At this moment Desdemona again appears and the struggle for Othello's soul is renewed; he rejects the doubts he has entertained:

> If she be false, O, then heaven mocks itself!
> I'll not believe't.
>
> (III.iii.278-9)

But as she tries to bind his temples, he feels the horns of the cuckold. The poison of Iago has done its work, and when we see Othello again, he is possessed with Iago's own perversion of reputation. His honour is at stake, and he bids farewell to the soldier's life which he cannot enjoy while his name is soiled:

> I had been happy, if the general camp,
> Pioners and all, had tasted her sweet body,
> So I had nothing known. O, now, for ever
> Farewell the tranquil mind! farewell content!
> Farewell the plum'd troop, and the big wars,
> That make ambition virtue! O, farewell!
> Farewell the neighing steed, and the shrill trump,
> The spirit-stirring drum, the ear-piercing fife,
> The royal banner, and all quality,
> Pride, pomp and circumstance of glorious war!
> And, O you mortal engines, whose rude throats
> The immortal Jove's dread clamours counterfeit,
> Farewell! Othello's occupation's gone!
>
> (III.iii.345-57)

The final line echoes the earlier lament of Cassio (II.iii.262-5). It is no longer the reality of Desdemona's virtue that he wishes; he would be happy embracing an evil hidden from him. Othello has set his value upon the false appearance which is the mark of Iago. This concern for reputation is in marked contrast to Othello's modesty in the first act:

> 'Tis yet to know, –
> Which, when I know that boasting is an honour,
> I shall promulgate – I fetch my life and being
> From men of royal siege, and my demerits
> May speak unbonneted to as proud a fortune
> As this that I have reached.

> (I.ii.19-24)

His awareness of his own worth here is a source of self-confidence and assurance. He keeps his noble lineage hidden from the world, and he will not promulgate it until boasting becomes the honour which he knows that it never can be.

Jealousy now has worked deeply into the mind of Othello, but Iago's victory is still not complete. Othello is wavering between the two forces which vie for his soul, and in his bewilderment he demands proof:

> By the world,
> I think my wife be honest and think she is not;
> I think that thou art just and think thou art not.
> I'll have some proof. Her name, that was as fresh
> As Dian's visage, is now begrimed and black
> As mine own face. If there be cords, or knives,
> Poison, or fire, or suffocating streams,
> I'll not endure it. Would I were satisfied!

> (III.iii.383-90)

But jealousy has benumbed his reason, and whatever proof Iago has to offer, Othello is now ready to accept as truth. He accepts without question the shallow lie about Cassio's dream. Upon this falsehood he renounces love and in its place accepts hatred and revenge:

> O, that the slave had forty thousand lives!
> One is too poor, too weak for my revenge.
> Now do I see 'tis true. Look here, Iago;
> All my fond love thus do I blow to heaven.

> 'Tis gone.
> Arise, black vengeance, from thy hollow cell!
> Yield up, O love, thy crown and hearted throne
> To tyrannous hate! Swell, bosom, with thy fraught,
> For 'tis of aspics' tongues!
>
> (III.iii.441-9)

We are ready for the ritual union of Othello with Iago. The language of Othello assumes a highly formal tone as he calls upon 'yond marble heaven' and he kneels: 'In the due reverence of a sacred vow / I here engage my words' (460-2). Iago kneels beside him, revealing again his Satanic origins as he swears not by God, but by the stars and elements:

> Witness, you ever-burning lights above,
> You elements that clip us round about,
> Witness that here Iago doth give up
> The execution of his wit, hands, heart,
> To wrong'd Othello's service!   (III.iii.463-7)

The natural order is reversed as Othello completes his link with evil:

> Damn her, lewd minx! O, damn her!
> Come, go with me apart; I will withdraw,
> To furnish me with some swift means of death
> For the fair devil. Now art thou my lieutenant.
>
> (III.iii.476-9)

To Othello in his tragic delusion Desdemona is the devil and Iago his lieutenant. He is united to a destructive force who now confirms the league between them: 'I am your own forever' (480).

There is an awful solemnity in this scene. Othello in his delusion would convert his sinful vengeance into the guise of a lawful justice, his hatred into duty, and he does so by cloaking his action in the appearance of formal ritual. His delusion parallels that of the earlier Brutus in his desire to carve Caesar as a dish fit for the gods, to make a solemn sacrifice out of a brutal murder. From this point onward Othello will see with the vision of Iago, to whom he is united. Truth will appear as falsehood, love and loyalty as lust and betrayal. Always in his delusion Othello will see himself as the instrument of justice executing his duty in a solemn ritual, although his court-room will be a brothel and his act of justice the destruction of love and truth.

IV

The fourth act is designed to display the degeneration of Othello
from the natural man of the first two acts, endowed with grace and
reason, to the bestial antithesis of which Iago has been symbol.[1]
Before the visiting Venetian lords Othello strikes Desdemona, and
Lodovico underscores for the audience the new Othello which this
represents by recapitulating for us an image of the man Othello
was:

> Is this the noble Moor whom our full senate
> Call all in all sufficient? Is this the nature
> Whom passion could not shake? Whose solid virtue
> The shot of accident, nor dart of chance,
> Could neither graze nor pierce?
>
> (IV.i.275-9)

It is fitting that Iago should be the one to reply with ironic under-
statement: 'He is much changed' (279).

In the first act there had been a stately grandeur in Othello's
speech as he affirmed to the Venetian council his love for Desdemona as a thing of mind and spirit, divorced from all sensual
passion (I.iii.262-6). Now he speaks in a chaotic, disjointed prose
as he shows his mind full of the perverted sexuality which has
been Iago's mark. He tortures himself with sensual imaginings as
he accepts Iago's false description of Desdemona:

> Lie with her! lie on her! We say lie on her, when they belie her.
> Lie with her! That's fulsome. – Handkerchief – confessions – hand-
> kerchief! To confess, and be hanged for his labour; – first, to be
> hanged, and then to confess. – I tremble at it. Nature would not
> invest herself in such shadowing passion without some instruction.
> It is not words that shake me thus. Pish! Noses, ears, and lips. – Is't
> possible! – Confess – handkerchief! – O devil!
>
> (IV.i.35-43)

And he falls into a trance which signifies the total collapse of
reason. There is no lie which Othello will not now accept. This
the episode of the handkerchief is used to illustrate. Shakespeare

---

[1] That this change is supported by the shifting imagery of the play has been
shown by W. H. Clemen, *The Development of Shakespeare's Imagery*, p. 127. See also
Wilson Knight, *The Wheel of Fire*, pp. 97-119; M. M. Morozov, 'The Individual-
ization of Shakespeare's Characters Through Imagery', *Shakespeare Survey 2* (Cambridge, 1949), pp. 83-106; Caroline F. E. Spurgeon, *Shakespeare's Imagery and What
it Tells Us* (New York, 1935), pp. 335-8; S. L. Bethell in *Shakespeare Survey 5*, pp. 62-
80; Dover Wilson, pp. xiv-xlvi; Heilman, *Magic in the Web*, particularly pp. 99-136.

makes it a trick far less likely of success than it is in Cinthio, and by the ease of Othello's deception he shows the collapse of his reason.

As the madness of Othello grows in intensity, alongside of it emerges a grotesque solemnity: the murder to which his delusion leads him is converted into a ceremonial act of sacrificial justice. Othello sees himself as the administrator of the justice of God. When Iago suggests that Othello 'do it not with poison, strangle her in her bed, even the bed she hath contaminated', the reply is an assertion not of revenge but of justice: 'Good, good: the justice of it pleases: very good' (IV.i.220-2). Othello's grotesque parody of justice is expressed in the terrible second scene of the fourth act where he arraigns Desdemona and Emilia as in a court of law, cross-examining each in a tone of official inquiry. But the court-room is a brothel, and Desdemona is 'the cunning whore of Venice / That married with Othello' (IV.ii.89-90). Othello's very questions are a perversion of justice, for his mind can now admit no true verdict. The grotesque perversion of this mock judicial inquiry recalls the simple grandeur of Othello's answering to justice before the Venetian council in the first act. These two judicial scenes reflect the two poles of Othello's development, the madness of the later scene recalling the reason of the earlier. They focus also upon the theme of justice; reason causes it to reflect the law of God, but madness perverts it to the very opposite.

It is in this mock judicial mood that Othello approaches the bed where Desdemona is to be murdered:

> It is the cause, it is the cause, my soul, –
> Let me not name it to you, you chaste stars! –
> It is the cause. Yet I'll not shed her blood;
> Nor scar that whiter skin of hers than snow,
> And smooth as monumental alabaster.
> Yet she must die, else she'll betray more men.
>
> (V.ii.1-6)

We remember the futile wish of Brutus to destroy Caesar's spirit as it seems to him that justice demands, and at the same time not to shed his blood. The presence of Desdemona is almost enough to shatter Othello's delusion; it is his perverted sense of justice which sustains him in his purpose:

> Ah, balmy breath, that dost almost persuade
> Justice to break her sword!   (V.ii.16-17)

He destroys love in a pose of self-sacrificing duty which is a mockery of the justice which in his delusion he sees himself upholding. Othello blinds himself to reality by the very calmness of the ritual execution.

No sooner is the deed completed than the world of reality intrudes with the sound of Emilia's voice. Othello now comes to recognize the delusion under which he has laboured; he sees the true Iago for the first time, and he rushes at him in fury:

> Are there no stones in heaven
> But what serve for the thunder? – Precious villian!
> (V.ii.234-5)

With this the union between them is broken, and cut off from evil Othello now shows a true sense of justice. He sees that the punishment for his sin is damnation. This change in him is signalized by a loss of concern for the outward signs of reputation:

> I am not valiant neither,
> But every puny whipster gets my sword:
> But why should honour outlive honesty?
> Let it go all.
> (V.ii.243-6)

Reputation not based upon true substance has no meaning for him; he has sacrificed his honour, let the world repute him a weakling. He looks at Iago and sees the devil in him:

> I look down towards his feet; but that's a fable.
> If that thou be'st a devil, I cannot kill thee.
> (V.ii.286-7)

He can only wound Iago, and Shakespeare may be suggesting that the force of evil in the world never can be finally destroyed, for Iago alone among Shakespeare's villains still lives at the end of the play, although we know that he will be tortured.

When Emilia had begun to shatter Othello's delusion, he had seen damnation as the consequence of his error:

> O, I were damn'd beneath all depth in hell,
> But that I did proceed upon just grounds
> To this extremity.
> (V.ii.137-9)

Now he sees Desdemona not as an angel of divine mercy, but as a spirit of heavenly justice who will demand his damnation, and he conjures up the tortures of hell:

> O ill-starr'd wench!
> Pale as thy smock! when we shall meet at compt,
> This look of thine will hurl my soul from heaven,
> And fiends will snatch at it. Cold, cold, my girl!
> Even like thy chastity. O cursed slave!
> Whip me, ye devils,
> From the possession of this heavenly sight!
> Blow me about in winds! roast me in sulphur!
> Wash me in steep-down gulfs of liquid fire!
> O Desdemona! Desdemona! dead!
> Oh! Oh! Oh!
>
> (V.ii.272-81)

It is essential to the dramatic design that Othello think of himself as destined for hell, for with this belief his killing of himself becomes an act of true justice, and not just a means of escape from a painful world. But there is a tragic irony in Othello's belief, for Desdemona, the audience knows, stands for mercy and forgiveness. Othello, like Angelo in *Measure for Measure*, is 'most ignorant of what he's most assured', for by his penance and expiation he may win salvation after all. The fire of hell which he now suffers in his mind is a kind of purgatory. The final words of Desdemona had been an assumption of Othello's guilt parallel to that of Christ for the sins of mankind. To Emilia's 'O, who hath done this deed?' she had replied, 'Nobody; I myself. Farewell: / Commend me to my kind lord' (V.ii.123-5).

Desdemona is endowed, like Othello and Iago, with the illusion of reality, but in the total scheme of the play she stands from first to last as an incarnation of self-sacrificing love. She is a reflection of Christ, who must die at the hands of man, but out of whose death may spring man's redemption. We must note that Desdemona undergoes a temptation which parallels that of Othello and which is much like the temptation of Christ in the wilderness. She is offered the bait of evil by Emilia in a scene which parallels that of Othello's seduction by Iago.[1] Emilia justifies sin by the logic of Iago which postulates a world without heavenly control. To sin

---

[1] See P. N. Siegel, *Shakespearean Tragedy and the Elizabethan Compromise*, p. 132; G. R. Elliott, *Flaming Minister*, p. 205.

for the price of the whole world, Emilia argues, would be no sin, for 'Why, the wrong is but a wrong i' the world; and having the world for your labour, 'tis a wrong in your own world, and you might quickly make it right' (IV.iii.80-83). This logic Desdemona rejects, and then Emilia suggests that men themselves are to blame for the sins of their wives, and she argues a principle of vengeance:

> But I do think it is their husbands' faults
> If wives do fall: say that they slack their duties,
> And pour our treasures into foreign laps,
> Or else break out in peevish jealousies,
> Throwing restraint upon us; or say they strike us,
> Or scant our former having in despite;
> Why, we have galls, and though we have some grace,
> Yet have we some revenge.
>
> (IV.iii.87-95)

Emilia lists the very sins against Desdemona of which Othello has been guilty. Desdemona's reply foreshadows her role in the final act, for she is all mercy and all forgiveness, no matter what crimes are done against her:

> Good night, good night: heaven me such uses send,
> Not to pick bad from bad, but by bad mend!
>
> (IV.iii.105-6)

The evil of her murder she will repay with forgiveness and mercy, out of evil creating good. Her unconquerable love for Othello will be his redemption.

Thus, although Othello dies accepting damnation as his just desert, Shakespeare by his careful delineation of Desdemona as a symbol of mercy has prepared the audience for the salvation of Othello in spite of all. Othello dies truly penitent. He takes the step which Claudius, in spite of his fears of damnation, cannot take. Othello destroys himself in an act of expiation, and his final words are a reminder to the audience of his union in death with the goodness he had tried to destroy:

> I kiss'd thee ere I killed thee: no way but this;
> Killing myself, to die upon a kiss.
>
> (V.ii.358-9)

The audience knows that in his renunciation of evil, his penance and expiation, Othello has merited salvation.[1]

---

[1] The salvation of Othello has been most convincingly argued by Parker, *The*

The calm measured cadence of Othello's death speech recalls his earlier speeches before the Venetian council. It is a renunciation of the values of Iago. Othello denies the dues of reputation, of just reward for his services to Venice. He asks that his deed be considered without bias and in terms of the very justice he had violated in the murder of his wife:

> Soft you; a word or two before you go.
> I have done the state some service, and they know't.
> No more of that. I pray you, in your letters,
> When you shall these unlucky deeds relate,
> Speak of me as I am; nothing extenuate,
> Nor set down aught in malice.   (V.ii.338-43)

He appeals to the mercy of the onlookers, naming himself an ordinary man, no more vicious than others, but with the very human weaknesses which can lead to error and corruption. He confesses that he has destroyed his greatest good, not willingly, but in the ignorance of delusion, and in his tears he expresses his sincere contrition:

>   then must you speak
> Of one that loved not wisely but too well;
> Of one not easily jealous, but being wrought,
> Perplexed in the extreme; of one whose hand,
> Like the base Indian, threw a pearl away
> Richer than all his tribe; of one whose subdued eyes,
> Albeit unused to the melting mood,
> Drop tears as fast as the Arabian trees
> Their medicinal gum.   (V.ii.343-51)

And with this, as he had once executed justice upon the infidel Turk, he executes it upon himself:

> And say besides, that in Aleppo once,
> Where a malignant and a turban'd Turk
> Beat a Venetian and traduced the state,
> I took by the throat the circumcised dog,
> And smote him, thus.   (V.ii.351-5)

Slave of Life, pp. 126-9; and Elliott, *Flaming Minister*, pp. 230-42. That Othello is damned has, on the contrary, been argued by Siegel, pp. 131-41; Bethell, *Shakespeare Survey 5*, pp. 62-80; Granville-Barker, *Prefaces to Shakespeare*, II, 83; Arthur Sewell, *Character and Society in Shakespeare*, pp. 94-97. H. S. Wilson, *On the Design of Shakespearian Tragedy*, pp. 66-67, holds that Shakespeare is ambivalent, leaving the audience to draw its own conclusions.

He destroys the evil within himself, asserting true justice as opposed to the perversion of justice which had led him to kill Desdemona. The speech reveals a new self-knowledge and self-understanding. It is a calm summation of Othello's life-journey.

Othello is a tragedy of human weakness and imperfection leading to a wrong moral choice. There is consequent degeneration and a destruction of human value, but at the end, through the operation of divine grace, there is a recognition of error, with consequent remorse, expiation, and the promise of salvation. *Othello* asserts the mercy of God as surely as Shakespeare proclaimed it in *Measure for Measure*, written probably in the same year. The regeneration of Othello is confined to the last scene of the play, but in *King Lear* Shakespeare is to make this process of human regeneration his major focus of dramatic interest. In *Othello* it is the process of seduction with which Shakespeare is most concerned, and this emphasis gives its form to the total play. In the mercy and forgiveness of Desdemona, which triumphs after all, and in the destruction of Iago, who is crushed by the evil he himself sets loose, we have as in *Hamlet* an affirmation of a just and benevolent moral order. The succession of Cassio to Othello's place will herald a rebirth like that of the accession of Fortinbras to the throne of Denmark.

The tragedy of *Othello*, in its neatness and precision of construction, parallels more closely than any of Shakespeare's other plays what may be called the prototype of tragedy in Christian Europe, that of Adam in the garden of Eden. *Othello* expresses more perfectly than any of the other plays the paradox of the fortunate fall through which the Christian world could postulate a merciful and purposive God in spite of Adam's tragedy. The play is Christian in its symbolism and in the central intellectual proposition which shapes and controls the action, character and poetry of which it is comprised. *Othello* couches its universal propositions in terms of specific action and specific character, which in the speedy movement of the scenes retain an illusion of reality in spite of the logical inconsistencies which the scholar's study may reveal. It creates an emotional equivalent for its central idea and a tension between emotion and intellect which is the essence of tragedy. We participate fully in the horror which falls upon Othello, while rationally we are assured and seconded in our faith in divine order.

CHAPTER SIX

The Pattern of Regeneration:
King Lear

I n *King Lear* Shakespeare's emphasis is upon the process of human regeneration, the self-knowledge, penance, and expiation for sin upon which he had touched only lightly in the final scene of *Othello*. That Shakespeare now chose for his hero an old man was thematically appropriate, for his concern is with a spiritual rebirth for which man never can grow too old. Shakespeare juxtaposes dramatically the physical age of his hero against the new manhood he attains through suffering; he affirms that Lear's four score years of pride and self-deception were merely the prelude to life, and not true life at all.[1]

The cruelty and the suffering in *King Lear* have led many critics to call the play a secular tragedy in which Shakespeare offers neither insight into the cause of human suffering nor hope for man other than in stoical submission.[2] Such a view tends to take the play's savagery out of its context in the larger design, to see *Lear* as a disordered mass of impressions, rather than as a neatly unified whole, every element of which is designed to give dramatic form to a thematic statement. The suffering of Lear and Gloucester is presented with all the immediate intensity of which Shakespeare is capable in order to emphasize that the process of regeneration is a purgatorial one. If Shakespeare is to assert the power of man to overcome evil, the forces of evil must be shown in their most

---

[1] It was written, probably, sometime in 1605. See Kenneth Muir, ed., *King Lear* (London, 1952), pp. xxiii-xxiv; Chambers, *William Shakespeare*, I, 467-9.

[2] *Lear* was called a non-Christian play in the nineteenth century by Edward Dowden, *Shakespeare, His Mind and Art* (New York, 1903), p. 240; and more recently by Theodore Spencer, *Shakespeare and the Nature of Man*, pp. 135-52; D. G. James, *The Dream of Learning*, pp. 69-121; Arthur Sewell, *Character and Society in Shakespeare*, pp. 120-1; Geoffrey Bush, *Shakespeare and the Natural Condition*, pp. 87-104.

uncompromising terms. *King Lear* is a triumph of dramatic construction which in its total effect, like *Hamlet* and *Othello* affirms justice in the world, which it sees as a harmonious system ruled by a benevolent God.[1]

All the elements of *King Lear* are shaped by the theme of regeneration which dominates the whole. To find a fitting dramatic form for this new theme, Shakespeare had to extend and develop the pattern for tragedy he had evolved in *Othello*. Again he availed himself of the morality play formula which was so much a part of the dramatic tradition of his age.[2] The didactic and homiletic tradition of medieval drama afforded tools by which Shakespeare might shape a complex of action to reflect the universal role of man in conflict with evil. To reinforce his theme Shakespeare now employed a new device, the parallel tragedy of Gloucester. The double action offers us another hero who is Lear on a slightly lower social plane, and his career by paralleling closely that of Lear reinforces the universal validity of the play's theme.

All the characters perform symbolic functions. The primary focus is upon Lear, and to a lesser extent upon Gloucester; they stand together for humanity at large. The other characters serve secondary supporting functions, each symbolic of some force of good or evil acting upon humanity. The theatre of the action is not only the single world of man, but also its corresponding planes in the scheme of creation: the family, the state, and the physical universe. The universality of theme is reinforced by the vagueness of the place setting; the audience watches not only Lear's little kingdom, but the great world itself.

[1] This has been argued most convincingly by J. F. Danby, *Shakespeare's Doctrine of Nature*. See also V. K. Whitaker, *Shakespeare's Use of Learning*, pp. 300-13; Robert Speaight, *Nature in Shakespearian Tragedy*, pp. 89-121; P. N. Siegel, *Shakespearean Tragedy and the Elizabethan Compromise*, pp. 161-88; M. D. H. Parker, *The Slave of Life*, pp. 130-43; R. B. Heilman, *This Great Stage: Image and Structure in King Lear* (Baton Rouge, 1948); G. L. Bickersteth, 'The Golden World of *King Lear*', *Proc. of the British Academy*, xxxii (1946), 147-71. H. S. Wilson, *On the Design of Shakespearian Tragedy*, pp. 182-9, and G. Wilson Knight, *The Wheel of Fire*, pp. 177-206, although they deny the specifically Christian framework of the play, point nevertheless to the Christian ethics implicit in it, that *Lear* is 'equivalent to the statement that goodness is the natural goal of man, and the aim of evolution. Therefore at the end the danger of the evil-doers is crushed. The good forces, not the evil win: since good is natural, evil unnatural to human nature' (Knight, p. 202).

[2] See O. J. Campbell, 'The Salvation of Lear', *ELH*, xv (1948), 93-109; Danby, p. 40; J. L. Rosier, 'The *Lex Aeterna* in *King Lear*', *JEGP*, liii (1954), 574-80; Watkins, *Shakespeare and Spenser*, pp. 106, 110.

II

As he faces the purifying forces of the storm upon the heath, King
Lear who 'hath ever but slenderly known himself' (I.i.297) speaks
of himself as 'a man / More sinn'd against than sinning' (III.ii.
58-59). To take the old man at his word is to ignore the context
in which the line occurs. If *King Lear* is viewed as the story of a
foolish old man tortured by those he loves, the play loses its
cosmic scope and becomes little more than a pathetic melodrama.
In the scheme of regeneration Lear must come to know himself;
this he does in the purifying agony of the storm. The first two
acts emphasize Lear's initial lack of self-knowledge, and they deliberately exhibit him not so much as the victim of evil forces, but
as the instigator of the evil forces in the play. Our knowledge of
the total play sometimes causes us to forget that an audience viewing it for the first time would not at the end of the first two acts
regard Lear as more sinned against than sinning.[1] Dramatically
the speech serves to underscore the self-ignorance of Lear at the
beginning of the heath scenes which are to bring him a self-
knowledge through suffering.

Lear himself has unleashed the forces of evil which cause his
suffering, and only when he himself has come to realize this and
he no longer sees himself as more sinned against than sinning is
his regeneration possible. If evil is symbolized in Goneril and
Regan, we must remember that it was Lear who brought them
into being: 'But yet thou art my flesh, my blood, my daughter; /
Or rather a disease that's in my flesh, / Which I must needs call
mine' (II.iv.224-6). Lear comes in his madness to acknowledge his
own responsbiility for the evil of his daughters: 'Judicious punishment! 'twas this flesh begot / Those pelican daughters' (III.iv.
76-77). To understand the enormity of Lear's sin, we must recognize the peculiar position of the king in the highly ordered world
which Renaissance Christian humanism carried over from the
Middle Ages.

Lear's resignation of his throne and division of his kingdom
would have been regarded by a Jacobean audience with a horror
difficult for a modern audience to appreciate, for these acts were
a violation of the king's responsibility to God, and they could

---

[1] This statement, as Danby has indicated (pp. 183-4), is 'a reversal of the judgement we have been making on Lear in the first two acts'.

result only in the chaos on every level of creation which is the subject of the play.[1] By his resignation of rule Lear disrupts the harmonious order of nature. He chooses the lesser finite good of power without responsibility, rather than the greater infinite good of God's order which decrees that the king rule for the good of his people until God relieves him of his responsibility by death.

These political implications I have already treated.[2] Although *King Lear* is more than a history play and the tragedy is more than a political one, the political aspects of Lear's initial act are of crucial importance, for they contribute to the cosmic breadth of the whole. The state is only one of the planes on which the action occurs, but we must remember that in the Renaissance world view the state was a middle link between the physical universe and individual man, and that all three planes of creation were in close harmony with one another. Lear's initial crime makes its reverberations felt both above and below, corrupting the entire scale of creation.

In this political dimension of Lear we may perceive some of the growth in Shakespeare's tragic vision beyond *Othello*. In that play evil's operation had been restricted to the soul of a single man. In *Lear* Shakespeare learned to extend the arena of his tragedy to all the planes of creation, to mirror the wrenching of Lear's soul in the upheaval of the storm and in the political disorder descending upon all Britain. Evil, further, is stripped now of the surface charm worn by Iago; it is exposed in all its naked, coarse brutality. It is more pervasive in that it is no longer concentrated in one demonic figure; we see it equally in Goneril, Regan, Edmund and Cornwall, and it infuses itself down the social scale to the lowly Oswald.

But if evil is more insidious and pervasive in *Lear* than Shakespeare ever before had portrayed it, man's triumph is also more clearly delineated. The audience is left with little doubt of the final salvation of Lear and Gloucester, for the major emphasis of the play is upon their regeneration. In *King Lear* Shakespeare drew the conflict between good and evil more profoundly and on a

---

[1] See Hardin Craig, *An Interpretation of Shakespeare* (New York, 1948), pp. 206-19. Theodore Spencer, *Shakespeare and the Nature of Man*, p. 142, calls it a violation both of Natural Law and the Law of Nations.

[2] *The English History Play in the Age of Shakespeare*, pp. 248-53. On the evolution of the Lear story, see Wilfred Perett, *The Story of King Lear from Geoffrey of Monmouth to Shakespeare* (Berlin, 1904),

wider canvas than he had drawn it in *Othello*. Man, society and
physical nature are all engulfed by evil, but all are able to emerge
and triumph in spite of it. To this conception of evil's operation
he was to return in *Macbeth*.

From Lear's question to Cordelia, 'What can you say to draw /
A third more opulent than your sisters?' (I.i.87-88), we know that
Lear already has decided before the 'love contest' upon the precise
terms of the division of his kingdom. In his 'I loved her most, and
thought to set my rest / On her kind nursery' (I.i.125-6), we see
that his plan to divide his residence between Goneril and Regan
was merely a hasty afterthought. Lear's sin was a deliberate moral
choice made before the 'love contest', and not the hasty result of
his frustration. The foolish 'love contest', with all the irrational
behaviour to which it gives rise, is merely part of the general chaos
provoked by that initial decision. The illogic in the opening scenes
of the play is deliberate; Lear's foolish spur-of-the-moment alter-
ation of his careful plans and Gloucester's incredible gulling by
Edmund are reflections of the general chaos and irrationality into
which society has been plunged by Lear's initial decision to divide
his kingdom and abandon his responsibility to God.

This deliberate illogic pervades the first act, designed to make
clear to the audience the magnitude of Lear's initial sin and its
effect upon the total cosmos, perverting both the laws of society
and the reason of individual man. It is evident in Lear's confusion
of appearance with reality which causes him to accept the false
protestations of love by Goneril and Regan and to reject the true
love of Cordelia. She loves her father 'According to my bond; nor
more nor less' (I.i.95). This is the bond of nature – the same bond
which links Hamlet to his father and enjoins him to combat evil
– which ties the child to its parent in God's harmonious world
order.[1] It is proper that Cordelia's statement of filial love should
be straightforward and free from the extravagant sentimentality
which marks the flattery of her sisters:

> Good my lord,
> You have begot me, bred me, loved me: I
> Return those duties back as are right fit,
> Obey you, love you, and most honour you.
> Why have my sisters husbands, if they say
> They love you all? Haply, when I shall wed,

[1] See Danby, *Shakespeare's Doctrine of Nature*, pp. 125-9.

That lord whose hand must take my plight shall carry
Half my love with him, half my care and duty:
Sure, I shall never marry like my sisters,
To love my father all.

(I.i.97-106)

This expression of love is rational: it recognizes the laws of God
and society, duty to father and to husband. This in his delusion
Lear cannot see, and he rejects the bond of nature upon which
Cordelia's argument is based.

This same perversion is in Lear's banishment of Kent, a symbol
of loyalty and respect for authority. It is implicit also in Lear's
great curse:

For, by the sacred radiance of the sun,
The mysteries of Hecate, and the night;
By all the operation of the orbs
From whom we do exist, and cease to be.

(I.i.111-14)

Lear's curses are all delivered in the period of his delusion, when
he has cut himself off from God, and thus their pagan contexts
are thematically appropriate. There are two concepts of nature at
war with one another in *King Lear*. One is the orthodox nature of
Hooker's Christian humanism, of Cordelia, Kent and Edgar; the
other is the nature of Renaissance scepticism, of Iago, and now of
Edmund, Goneril and Regan. While Lear is cut off from God by
his sins, he swears by the nature of Edmund; at the end of the
play he is won back to that of Cordelia.

The discord unleashed by Lear's wrong moral choice is to be
most effectively symbolized in the storm scenes which show the
extension of man's corruption to the plane of physical nature. It is
already evident, however, in the second scene of the play, where
we find it breaking out on a lower level of the social scale, in the
household of Gloucester. Goneril and Regan have not yet begun
to act against their father, and Edmund's plan is merely in its
incipient stage, but the chaos falling upon all nature is already
described by Gloucester:

These late eclipses in the sun and moon portend no good to us:
though the wisdom of nature can reason it thus and thus, yet nature
finds itself scourged by the sequent effects: love cools, friendship
falls off, brothers divide: in cities, mutinies; in countries, discord;

in palaces, treason; and the bond cracked 'twixt son and father. This villain of mine comes under the prediction; there's son against father: the king falls from bias of nature; there's father against child. We have seen the best of our time: machinations, hollowness, treachery, and all ruinous disorders, follow us disquietly to our graves.

(I.ii.112-24)

The celestial portents by which Shakespeare usually signifies the violation of natural order have already appeared in 'these late eclipses in the sun and moon'. The 'sequent effects' of this corruption in the physical universe extend to all the other levels of creation: in cities, countries, palaces and the individual family, where 'brothers divide' and 'the bond' is 'cracked 'twixt son and father'. This is the bond which Cordelia had asserted and Lear rejected. It is not, however, because of the 'late eclipses' that 'the king falls from bias of nature'; it is Lear's initial falling from this bias which has caused all the corruptions, both social and natural, which Gloucester enumerates.

In placing Lear's sinful moral choice before the beginning of the play's action, Shakespeare departs from the pattern he had developed in *Othello*. With his emphasis upon the seduction process, in that play he had centred the dramatic action about the long seduction scene in the third act. The first two acts had built up to this central episode; the last two had been a working out of its consequences. Such a formula had produced a tighter play than was now possible in *King Lear*, with its different emphasis. The seduction process is now omitted, and the play opens with the hero already fallen. In the first two acts Shakespeare shows us the equivalent of the final acts of *Othello*: the results of the hero's moral choice and the evil it unleashes throughout creation, and while doing so Shakespeare develops the parallel career of Gloucester. With the third act begins Lear's regeneration, which is not completed until his death in a moment of insupportable ecstasy.[1] At the same time, in a lower note, is developed the regeneration of Gloucester, of whose similar death we are told by Edgar.

The characters are divided unequivocally into good and evil. The villainy of Edmund, Cornwall, Oswald, Goneril and Regan darken our view of humanity, while the selfless devotion of Cordelia, Edgar, Kent and the Fool show the potentialities for good within the human spirit. The evil of the world is contrasted dra-

[1] This joyful death was first suggested by Bradley, *Shakespearean Tragedy*, p. 291.

matically with man's inherent goodness in spite of it. Between the
two opposing forces hover Gloucester and Lear, sharing good
and evil, and much like the central figures of the old morality
plays. Each must make his way from the one side to the other,
destroying the forces of evil within himself and allowing good to
triumph. Gloucester's regeneration will be climaxed by his death
in the arms of Edgar, and Lear's by his reunion with Cordelia.

The two sets of characters embody two distinctive philosophies
of life. Edgar, Cordelia, Kent and the Fool represent a Christian
humanist view of life which sees all of nature as a harmonious
order controlled by a benevolent God, and which allows for the
natural bonds of filial affection, loyalty, duty, obligation to family
and state, kindness to fellow man; as its greatest good it deifies
love, the love of man for man which can unite humanity to an
ever-loving God. Opposed to this stands the doctrine of Renaissance scepticism. Edmund is its chief symbol, and Goneril, Regan,
Cornwall and Oswald live like him by its precepts.[1] Edmund sees
nature as a Godless mechanism, governed by impersonal laws.
The universe is without divine purpose or guidance; man and
beast are alike. Edmund denies the system of correspondences
between the mind of man and the phenomena of nature which
was so integral a part of the Elizabethan doctrine of order and
degree:

> This is the excellent foppery of the world, that, when we are sick
> in fortune, – often the surfeit of our own behaviour, – we make
> guilty of our disasters the sun, the moon, and the stars: as if we were
> villains by necessity; fools by heavenly compulsion; knaves, thieves,
> and treachers, by spherical predominance; drunkards, liars, and
> adulterers, by an enforced obedience of planetary influence; and all
> that we are evil in, by a divine thrusting on: an admirable evasion of
> whoremaster man, to lay his goatish disposition to the charge of a
> star.
>
> (I.ii.128-38)

Human society in Edmund's view is debased. The mind to Edmund is an independent entity by which he can, to some extent,
control nature. He may do this by means of reason, but this is not

---

[1] See R. C. Bald, ' "Thou, Nature, Art My Goddess": Edmund and Renaissance
Free-Thought', *J. Q. Adams Memorial Studies* (Washington, D.C., 1948), pp. 337-49;
S. L. Bethell, *Shakespeare and the Popular Dramatic Tradition*, pp. 58-59; Whitaker,
Shakespeare's Use of Learning, p. 306; Heilman, *This Great Stage*, pp. 115-30.

the reason of orthodox Elizabethan doctrine, an attuning of one's will to the will of God. Edmund's reason is the ability to manipulate nature and other men for his own advantage. Like the intellect of Iago, it is utterly selfish in that it recognizes only the dominance of individual will. This is the nature who is his goddess, and to whom his services are bound (I.ii.1-2). It is fitting that Edmund should be a bastard, for, conceived outside of God's harmonious order with its moral standards, he can deny all benevolent human feelings which are a part of it, proceeding directly from the love of God. These are loyalty, the bonds of family, and that primogeniture which to Elizabethan and Jacobean Englishmen was the basis of social order.

Justice becomes a principal issue of the play, for Edgar invokes what Edmund denies, a belief in a benevolent God who visits upon men their just deserts. Similarly Edgar and Cordelia stand for the perfection of nature and the magnificence of individual man, while Edmund stands for the corruption and ugliness of nature and the cheapness of human life. On all of these important issues, the double action of the play shows Lear and Gloucester rejecting the philosophy of Edmund and learning to embrace that of Edgar.

III

Lear's division of his kingdom alone would at once alienate a Jacobean audience, for they feared nothing so much as the prospect of a divided England. The cruelty and injustice of his treatment both of Kent and Cordelia are obvious. The 'Idle old man, / That still would manage those authorities / That he hath given away' (I.iii.16-18) arouses little affection in Goneril's house, and her conduct scarcely justifies Lear's terrible curse of sterility (I.iv. 297-311). The chilling horror of these words to an audience which took curses seriously cannot be overestimated. Goneril has as yet done little to justify this outburst, and we cannot doubt – in extenuation of her conduct – that she had already received from her paternal guest 'not alone the imperfections of long-engraffed condition, but therewithal the unruly waywardness that infirm and choleric years bring with them' (I.i.300-2). In short, when Lear storms out on the heath at the end of the second act, an audience viewing the play for the first time would feel that however unkind his treatment, it has not been so unkind as what he has meted out to others. Lear never loses the sympathy of the audience, but affection for him is maintained not by anything he does, but by the viciousness of Goneril and Regan themselves, by the pathos of Lear's remorse for his treatment of Cordelia, which grows steadily under the cruel, yet loving jibes of the Fool, and by the bluff loyalty of the disguised Kent, contrasted with the obsequious and effeminate villainy of Oswald. We are moved by the spectacle of an aged man, unaware of his own violations of order which the audience so plainly sees, striving for patience while he holds back his tears (II.iv.274-81). We must not, however, allow the pathos of these lines to obscure their ironic underscoring of Lear's lack of self-knowledge, his as yet total unawareness that he is responsible for his own misfortunes.

Lear glories in the savagery of nature, not knowing that the storm is nature's reflection of his own sin. It is part of his tragic delusion that he sees the forces of nature as hostile to human life:

> Blow, winds, and crack your cheeks! rage! blow!
> You cataracts and hurricanoes, spout
> Till you have drench'd our steeples, drown'd the cocks!
> You sulphurous and thought-executing fires,
> Vaunt-couriers to oak-cleaving thunderbolts,
> Singe my white head! And thou, all-shaking thunder,
> Smite flat the thick rotundity o' the world!
> Crack nature's moulds, all germens spill at once,
> That make ingrateful man!
>
> (III.ii.1-9)

In his delusion Lear sees the forces of nature as agents of the evil within man, as

> servile ministers,
> That have with two pernicious daughters join'd
> Your high engender'd battles 'gainst a head
> So old and white as this.
>
> (III.ii.21-24)

There is no justice in the world, but the brute forces of nature will execute a kind of poetic justice out of their destructive impulses which make no distinction among various kinds of human life. The forces of wind and rain thus become powerful summoners who can execute justice upon a corrupt society:

> Let the great gods,
> That keep this dreadful pother o'er our heads,
> Find out their enemies now. Tremble, thou wretch,
> That hast within thee undivulged crimes,
> Unwhipp'd of justice: hide thee, thou bloody hand;
> Thou perjured, and thou simular man of virtue
> That art incestuous: caitiff, to pieces shake,
> That under covert and convenient seeming
> Hast practised on man's life: close pent-up guilts,
> Rive your concealing continents, and cry
> These dreadful summoners grace.   (III.ii.49-59)

His own corruption, however, Lear still cannot perceive, and then follows the irony of 'I am a man / More sinn'd against than sinning' (59-60).

And yet, while Lear dwells on the baseness of men and the corruption of nature, at the same time his sufferings cause him to feel a sympathy and love for his fellow men which before he had not known. Thus the two motifs run side by side throughout the heath scenes in a kind of grotesque counterpoint. The piteous suffering of the Fool arouses Lear's first sign of human feeling:

> Poor fool and knave, I have one part in my heart
> That's sorry yet for thee.
>
>   (III.ii.72-73)

And it is the Fool he ushers first into the protection of the hovel:

> In, boy; go first. You houseless poverty,—
> Nay, get thee in. I'll pray, and then I'll sleep.
>
>   (III.iv.26-27)

Here then, counterpoised against his violent rejection of nature and his fellow men is an acknowledgement of God, and it is followed up by a welling up of pity for the sufferings of humanity:

> Poor naked wretches, wheresoe'er you are,
> That bide the pelting of this pitiless storm,
> How shall your houseless heads and unfed sides,
> Your loop'd and window'd raggedness, defend you
> From seasons such as these? O, I have ta'en
> Too little care of this! Take physic, pomp;
> Expose thyself to feel what wretches feel,
> That thou mayst shake the superflux to them,
> And show the heavens more just.
>
>   (III.iv.28-36)

With the appearance of Edgar as Poor Tom, Lear goes mad,[1] and this madness, like Hamlet's 'antic disposition', is a symbol of his alienation from the natural order. In the mad scenes the twin motifs of scorn for humanity and an awakening feeling of kinship with humanity continue to play against one another. Edgar's function as Poor Tom is to serve as a visible symbol of man as Lear in his delusion sees him, reduced to the level of a beast:

> Is man no more than this? Consider him well. Thou owest the worm no silk, the beast no hide, the sheep no wool, the cat no perfume. Ha! here's three on's are sophisticated! Thou art the thing itself: unaccommodated man is no more but such a poor, bare, forked animal as thou art. Off, off, you lendings!
>
> (III.iv.107-12)

This is the lowest point of delusion that Lear reaches, as he tries to tear off his clothes and reduce himself to the level of 'unaccommodated man' who is no more than a mad, naked beast. But even as Lear speaks, Gloucester appears bearing his torch, a light from the world of men who are not beasts, a sign of human kindness and self-sacrifice. The old man who can risk his life to succour his king in the storm is Shakespeare's symbolic reminder that man is more than beast, that he shares, in spite of evil in the world, in the harmony of nature and the love of God which the mad Lear denies.

With such touches of human warmth Shakespeare tempers the savagery of Lear's outbursts, for as his madness progresses he grows wilder and wilder in his indictment of God and man. While his madness is a collapse of the reason which differentiates man from beast, it is also a purgatorial state. In it we continue to find the twin motifs of Lear's rejection of humanity (a collapse of reason) and his recognition of his own fellowship with humanity (the lesson of purgatory). Thus, while the mock trial of Goneril and Regan (III.iv) is a grotesque parody of justice, it is also a posing of questions which Lear had never before asked, and to which he must learn the answers. There is a double implication also in Lear's denial of authority:

[1] Bradley, *Shakespearean Tragedy*, p. 288, recognized the beginning of Lear's madness in his 'Hast thou given all to thy two daughters? / And art come to this?' (III.iv.49-50), showing for the first time that peculiar dominance of a fixed idea which is the surest sign of his madness.

LEAR: What, art mad? A man may see how this world goes with no
    eyes. Look with thine ears: see now yond justice rails upon yond
    simple thief. Hark, in thine ear: change places; and handy-dandy,
    which is the justice, which is the thief? Thou hast seen a farmer's
    dog bark at a beggar?
GLOUCESTER: Ay, sir.
LEAR: And the creature run from the cur? There thou mightst be-
    hold the great image of authority: a dog's obeyed in office.

(IV.vi.153-63)

He himself had been that dog (IV.vi.98). Now he considers the
guilt and corruption which make the punished one with the pun-
isher:

> Thou rascal beadle, hold thy bloody hand!
> Why dost thou lash that whore? Strip thine own back;
> Thou hotly lust'st to use her in that kind
> For which thou whipp'st her. The usurer hangs the cozener.
> Through tatter'd clothes small vices do appear;
> Robes and furr'd gowns hide all. Plate sin with gold,
> And the strong lance of justice hurtless breaks;
> Arm it in rags, a pigmy's straw does pierce it.

(IV.vi.164-71)

In denying authority, Lear is again denying his own position as a
king appointed by and responsible to God, the source of all authority. These are speeches of cynicism and despair, but they exhibit
also an awareness of the imperfection of man, that all men are
sinners, and that in spite of the authority he had wielded as king,
Lear had shared too in the common guilt of humanity: he was not
'ague proof' (IV.vi.107). The denial of authority is the sin of pride,
for it is a denial of God; but Lear's awareness of his own insufficiency is at the same a rejection of pride. Thus can grow the
humility necessary for redemption.

As the play more and more probes the question of human
power, it becomes increasingly a play about lust. This becomes
the symbol of animal power wielded by man; lust reduces man to
the level of the beast.[1] At the height of his madness, Lear, like

---

[1] Whitaker, *Shakespeare's Use of Learning*, pp. 311-12, has indicated that Lear's
generalization of lust to include all sinful appetite is in accord with a general Christian
tradition which saw lust as typifying the 'revolt of man's sinful flesh against God's
ordered nature'.

Iago, denies the existence of human love: he sees animal lechery as man's controlling emotion:

> Thou shalt not die: die for adultery! No:
> The wren goes to't, and the small gilded fly
> Does lecher in my sight.
> Let copulation thrive; for Gloucester's bastard son
> Was kinder to his father than my daughters
> Got 'tween the lawful sheets.
> To't, luxury, pell-mell! for I lack soldiers.
> Behold yond simpering dame,
> Whose face between her forks presages snow;
> That minces virtue, and does shake the head
> To hear of pleasure's name;
> The fitchew, nor the soiled horse, goes to't
> With a more riotous appetite.
>
> (IV.vi.113-25)

The delusion in these lines is emphasized by the reference to 'Gloucester's bastard son', for the audience by this time knows well that he has not been 'kinder to his father than my daughters / Got 'tween the lawful sheets'. Edmund's career can only reinforce for the audience their sense of the perversion of values in Lear's outburst. Yet this bitter indictment of humanity is echoed by Gloucester's 'O, let me kiss that hand' (IV.vi.134).

When Lear awakens from his sleep he is a regenerated soul. There is a new humility in his words to Cordelia, and new awareness of his own nature as a man:

> Pray, do not mock me:
> I am a very foolish fond old man,
> Fourscore and upward, not an hour more nor less;
> And, to deal plainly,
> I fear I am not in my perfect mind.
> Methinks I should know you, and know this man;
> Yet I am doubtful: for I am mainly ignorant
> What place this is; and all the skill I have
> Remembers not these garments; nor I know not
> Where I did lodge last night. Do not laugh at me;
> For, as I am a man, I think this lady
> To be my child Cordelia.   (IV.vii.59-70)

The dominant note of the passage is Lear's awareness of his own ignorance aud imperfection. Now he is ready to renounce the power and pomp he had once craved to enjoy without responsibility. His only value is the love which in his madness he had denied, but which he now sees reflected in Cordelia:

> No, no, no, no! Come, let's away to prison:
> We two alone will sing like birds i' the cage:
> When thou dost ask me blessing, I'll kneel down
> And ask of thee forgiveness: so we'll live,
> And pray, and sing, and tell old tales, and laugh
> At gilded butterflies, and hear poor rogues
> Talk of court news; and we'll talk with them too,
> Who loses and who wins; who's in, who's out;
> And take upon's the mystery of things,
> As if we were God's spies: and we'll wear out,
> In a wall'd prison, packs and sects of great ones,
> That ebb and flow by the moon.

                                        (V.iii.8-19)

The things of the world are evanescent vanities he will gladly forgo for the reality of love. He has attained an ideal of Christian stoicism through acceptance of human love, which is a reflection of the love of God and of the perfection and harmony of the universe – of all which in his madness he had denied. After such renunciation, which sets its seal upon the after-life of heaven, there is no possibility other than death, and in this instance a reunion in heaven for Lear with the Cordelia who has preceded him there. If Lear's final belief, as his heart breaks, that Cordelia lives is contrary to fact, this is of small significance, for Shakespeare's audience could not doubt that she dwelt, in fact, where her father soon would join her.

IV

We are not to suppose that the fate which overtakes Gloucester is mere retribution for lechery, for his sin goes deeper than that. Gloucester violates the laws of primogeniture, as surely as Lear violates the duties of kingship. Gloucester's sin is thus also a denial of God's law and of the harmonious order of the universe, although on a plane slightly lower than that of Lear; the two sins together work the universal collapse of order with which the play is concerned.[1]

---

[1] The Gloucester sub-plot is Shakespeare's addition to the Lear story of generically unrelated matter from an alien source, the *Arcadia* of Sir Philip Sidney. The political and philosophical implications of Sidney's work were an important in-

The key to Gloucester's sin is in the opening scene of the play: 'But I have, sir, a son by order of law, some year elder than this, who yet is no dearer in my account' (I.i.19-21), he says to Kent. Edmund tells us a little later that 'Our father's love is to the bastard Edmund / As to the legitimate' (I.ii.17-18). That Gloucester should make no distinction in his love for his two sons might seem commendable to a modern audience, but to a Jacobean one it would have had different implications. In negating the difference between legitimate and illegitimate – and it must be noted that Shakespeare makes Edgar the elder as well as the legitimate son – Gloucester is denying the laws of society, and like Lear he is rejecting the bond of nature of which those laws are a reflection, for the doctrine of Natural Law, formulated in the Middle Ages and preserved in the orthodoxy of Hooker, saw all human law as an emanation of the eternal law of God. This negation by Gloucester of the difference between his sons causes Edmund, as his soliloquy indicates (II.ii.1-22), to conceive his plot against Edgar, as it causes Gloucester to succumb to his bastard son's machinations. This illogic, which reflects the illogic of Lear, springs from Gloucester's acceptance of his bastard son as equal to his legitimate. Once the order of nature is broken, every kind of illogic must follow.

Gloucester must suffer for his violation of order, just as Lear suffers for his, and through suffering he must undergo a like purgation, come to a state of Christian stoicism, and die joyfully. Gloucester's blinding is thematically appropriate, for Shakespeare wishes to emphasize the physical aspects of his purgation, just as he emphasizes the mental anguish of Lear. Gloucester was truly blind when he had his eyes; he learns to see when he has lost them:

> I have no way, and therefore want no eyes;
> I stumbled when I saw: full oft 'tis seen,
> Our means secure us, and our mere defects
> Prove our commodities.

> (IV.i.20-23)

fluence upon the entire play of *King Lear*, and they may have first suggested to Shakespeare the means of transforming the fairy-tale motifs of his main source, the old *Leir* play, into a tragedy with wide cosmic implications. The dominant theme, not only of the King of Paphlagonia episode which Shakespeare borrowed, but of the entire *Arcadia*, was that of royal responsibility and authority. This concern in Sidney's work coincided with the implications Shakespeare saw in the Lear story. See Fitzroy Pyle, ' "Twelfth Night", "King Lear" and "Arcadia" ', *MLR*, XLIII (1948), 449-55.

His blindness offers the same way to regeneration as Lear's torment and madness in the storm. In typical Shakespearian fashion,
the brutality of the blinding is tempered by the humanity of the
servants' conversation which follows immediately afterwards, and
the stabbing of Cornwall seems to represent an intervention of
divine justice. While Shakespeare shows the sins of Gloucester he
displays in him also feelings of kinship with humanity, so as not
to alienate the audience from him, and so as to prepare for his
final redemption.

We admire Gloucester as he goes out into the storm to help his
king, but even here Shakespeare leaves his motives ambivalent:
'these injuries the king now bears will be revenged home; there's
part of a power already footed: we must incline to the king' (III.
iii.11-14). Is it kindness or policy which motivates him? Probably
both, but the policy is a foolish one which loses him his eyes, and
the kindness helps to redeem him as a man.

As Gloucester wanders blind towards Dover he suffers the same
purgation Lear suffers in his madness, and in the scenes of Gloucester's blindness we find the same twin motifs which run through
Lear's mad scenes: on the one hand a despair which rejects the
order of God, denies justice and sees humanity as utterly debased;
and on the other a welling up of love for his fellow men. At the
very lowest point of his progression Gloucester speaks words
which have been often misinterpreted and quoted out of context:

> As flies to wanton boys, are we to the gods,
> They kill us for their sport.

> (IV.i.38-39)

This is not Shakespeare's philosophy or the intellectual statement
of the play; it is the very opposite. These lines correspond in
the scheme of Gloucester's regeneration to Lear's tearing off his
clothes before Poor Tom in the scheme of his. This is the low
point from which Gloucester must emerge, just as Lear emerges
from his, and Gloucester's recovery is effected by the old man
who leads him and by Edgar, who teaches him the meaning of
love and of resignation to divine will.

The humane feelings in Gloucester appear immediately after
these words of despair, when he asks the old man to find raiment
to clothe the naked beggar before him, whom he does not know
really is his son:

> do it for ancient love;
> And bring some covering for this naked soul,
> Who I'll entreat to lead me.
>
> (IV.i.45-47)

The clothes which Lear would tear off and with which Gloucester now would cover his son are the symbols of humanity and love which set man apart from the lower animals.

A feeling for the ills of humanity such as he never had experienced before now wells up in Gloucester:

> Here, take this purse, thou whom the heavens' plagues
> Have humbled to all strokes: that I am wretched
> Makes thee the happier: heavens, deal so still!
> Let the superfluous and lust-dieted man,
> That slaves your ordinance, that will not see
> Because he doth not feel, feel your power quickly;
> So distribution should undo excess,
> And each man have enough.
>
> (IV.i.67-74)

That this speech corresponds to Lear's 'Poor naked wretches', etc., was first noted by Samuel Johnson. The two speeches afford deliberate echoes of one another to stress parallel points in the regenerations of Lear and Gloucester.

Gloucester's attempted suicide has been censured as absurd, but we must remember that here again Shakespeare is not presenting scientific fact. This episode is a ritual element designed to portray an underlying idea. It is the final step in Gloucester's purgation, for out of his supposed rescue from death he learns what he must know in order to be redeemed, that 'the clearest gods, who make them honours / Of men's impossibilities, have preserved thee' (IV.vi.73-74). He comes to recognize the justice of the divine order and thus to bear his lot on earth as every man must:

> I do remember now: henceforth I'll bear
> Affliction till it do cry out itself
> 'Enough, enough' and die.
>
> (IV.vi.76-78)

In his 'O, let me kiss that hand' (IV.vi.134), which follows soon afterward as he comes upon the mad Lear, there is recognition of the essential nobility of man. The final stage of Gloucester's regeneration is recounted by Edgar:

K

                              and in this habit
          Met I my father with his bleeding rings,   (*eyes*)
          Their precious stones new lost; became his guide,
          Led him, begg'd for him, saved him from despair;
          Never, – O fault! – reveal'd myself unto him,
          Until some half-hour past, when I was arm'd:
          Not sure, though hoping, of this good success,
          I ask'd his blessing, and from first to last
          Told him my pilgrimage: but his flaw'd heart,
          Alack, too weak the conflict to support!
          'Twixt two extremes of passion, joy and grief,
          Burst smilingly.

                                              (V.iii.188-99)

Gloucester is regenerated through the love of Edgar, and he dies
happily, thus paralleling the progression of Lear.

                               V

Edgar sums up an important theme of the play in his final words
to his brother:

          The gods are just, and of our pleasant vices
          Make instruments to plague us:
          The dark and vicious place where thee he got
          Cost him his eyes.

                                              (V.iii.170-3)

This speech bothered Bradley (p. 305), who thought it in very
poor taste that Edgar should remind his dying brother of his
bastardy. But Edgar is not a real person; he is a dramatic device
which Shakespeare uses to perform certain specific functions within his larger design.[1] His speech here is not designed to throw light
upon his character, but to assert forcefully at the end of the play
the justice and order which Gloucester and Lear had at first denied
and then come to accept.

    Edgar is adapted to various purposes in different parts of the
play. As Poor Tom he serves as a symbol of man reduced to the
level of the beast; that he is in disguise symbolically underlines
that in reality man is not so. There is no need to search for other
reasons for his assumption of this particular disguise. Shakespeare
wishes merely to provide a visual symbol of man as Lear in his

    [1] See Leo Kirschbaum, 'Banquo and Edgar: Character or Function', *Essays in
Criticism*, VII (1957), 9.

delusion conceives him to be. As he leads his blind father, Edgar takes on a different role. Here he becomes a symbol of the very opposite of Poor Tom – of human devotion, of those qualities which raise man above the level of the beast and link him to God. As such he is able to teach his father the lessons necessary for his redemption.

Finally, in his combat with Edmund, Edgar becomes a symbol of divine justice triumphing over evil to reassert the harmony of God's natural order. The blast of his trumpet as he goes into combat is a symbolic echo of the last judgement. There is little logic in Edgar's behaviour from first to last, and that there is but slight psychological consistency in his character is an irrelevant consideration in the total design of Shakespeare's play.

Similarly, Cordelia cannot be judged by any standard of psychological verisimilitude. The tendency to censure her for her conduct in the opening scene comes from a failure to perceive that she is not a real person, that her function here is a thematic one, to emphasize the nature of the bond which Lear rejects, and not to humour a foolish father, as a real daughter might have done. She serves, like the earlier Desdemona, as a symbol of love and self-sacrifice, a reflection of the love of God.[1]

The Fool is used as a reminder both to Lear and the audience of the folly of Lear's initial behaviour, but more than that, he serves to mirror the basic conflict of the play, that between the forces of Edmund and those of Edgar. The Fool's reason prompts him to follow the path of the evil force, to desert Lear and fend for himself, but something within him keeps him loyal to Lear in spite of all. He stands also between good and evil, but he chooses good not by reason, for he is a fool, but because of the intuitive promptings of his heart. He stands for those forces linking man to God which are a part of man's inherent being and which cannot be subjected to the imperfect analysis of human reason. Next to his folly, the reason of Edmund becomes grotesque and absurd.[2]

---

[1] She has been called, in fact, a symbol of Christ, who must die to make possible her father's redemption, by Parker, pp. 141-2, Bethell, pp. 59-61, and Siegel, p. 186.

[2] See the excellent discussion in Enid Welsford, *The Fool: His Social and Literary History* (New York, 1935), pp. 253-69. Miss Welsford has pointed out to me that whereas at the beginning of the play the good characters are disorganized and separate from one another and the evil characters are closely joined in a compact group, at the end of the play the evil characters are dispersed and the good characters have come together. This should be reflected in the staging of the play.

In the Fool's shivering and whimpering on the heath a further note of pathos is added to the play, and we are never permitted to forget that his piteous suffering too is caused by Lear's initial sin. The Fool is not a psychologically consistent character. Like Cordelia and Edgar he is a dramatic device used to perform specific thematic functions. As an object of Lear's affection he throws light upon Lear. When he taunts his master on the heath, he is a dramatic symbol of the conflict within Lear's own mind. He drops out of the play when Shakespeare no longer needs him, but in Lear's final 'And my poor fool is hang'd' (V.iii.305), which refers obviously to Cordelia, we are told also the fate of the Fool, for it appears that both parts were played by the same boy actor, and we can assume that the Jacobean audience would have recognized in Lear's arms the body not only of his redeeming daughter, but that of his redeeming Fool as well. That he too must die is an additional price of Lear's redemption.

King Lear asserts the perfection of God's harmonious order and the inevitable triumph of justice, with the forces of evil preying upon and destroying themselves. In the process they subvert the good, but finally good must be victorious. In such a world man must subject his will to the will of God, patiently enduring whatever may come, with only faith in the perfection of the divine plan to sustain him, for as Edgar instructs his father:

> Men must endure
> Their going hence, even as their coming hither:
> Ripeness is all.
>
> (V.ii.9-11)

More specifically, in this play, Shakespeare affirms the possibility of human salvation, and he does this by placing in an imaginative setting the regeneration from evil of two aged men. In the vagueness of the place setting Shakespeare creates the feeling that the stage of *Lear* is the entire world, and in the double action he reminds us forcefully that the life-journey of Lear may be the life-journey of everyman.

CHAPTER SEVEN

The Operation of Evil:
Timon of Athens and *Macbeth*

There is no shallow optimism in Shakespeare's tragic vision, for the very possibility of human salvation which he affirmed in *King Lear* implied also the reality of damnation, and to this reality he turned in the plays which followed. *Timon of Athens* and *Macbeth* still assert a just moral order and a benevolent God, but they concentrate more fully than before upon the operation of evil within that order, and particularly in *Macbeth*, on the power of evil itself to generate opposing forces of good. These two plays are similar in that they stem from the same concern with damnation. If they are different in execution, it may be that Shakespeare found his manner of treating the damnation theme in *Timon* to be unsatisfactory, that he abandoned the play[1] and then went on to probe the same problem along different lines in *Macbeth*. Bradley, I believe, showed a keener poetic instinct than most recent commentators when he held that *Timon* was written immediately after *Lear*, in late 1605 or 1606, and that it was followed closely by *Macbeth*.[2]

From the incomplete draft of a play which has come down to us,

---

[1] That *Timon* is an unfinished play has been argued effectively by Una M. Ellis Fermor, 'Timon of Athens: An Unfinished Play', *RES*, XXII (1946), 96-108. W. W. Greg, *The Editorial Problem in Shakespeare* (Oxford, 1951), p. 149, argues that the Folio text was set up from 'foul papers that had never been reduced to order'. See also Chambers, *William Shakespeare*, I, 482; Terrence Spencer, 'Shakespeare Learns the Value of Money', *Shakespeare Survey 6* (Cambridge, 1953), pp. 75-78; H. S. Wilson, *On the Design of Shakespearian Tragedy*, pp. 138-53.

[2] *Shakespearean Tragedy*, p. 246. 'The play,' Bradley writes, 'bears so strong a resemblance to *King Lear* in style and in versification that it is hard to understand how competent judges can suppose that it belongs to a time at all near that of the final romances, or even that it was written so late as the last Roman plays. It is more likely to have been composed immediately after *King Lear* and before *Macbeth*.'

we can discern the governing plan. Timon, like Lear, is brought by evil to a denial of God and his moral order and to a negation, like that of Lear upon the heath, of the difference between man and beast. He reduces himself to the 'unaccommodated man' which Lear had seen in Poor Tom, and which now is symbolized in Apemantus. Timon is offered by his simple servant, Flavius, the possibility of redemption just as Lear was offered it by Cordelia, but unlike Lear, Timon rejects this offer and dies the beast he actually has become. Alcibiades, like Gloucester, undergoes a parallel progression, but unlike Timon he accepts the proffered chance of redemption. By this sub-plot Shakespeare may have tried to effect for his audience the kind of tragic reconciliation which the fate of Timon alone could not evoke. It is largely because the sub-plot was left so incomplete, with important details inadequately explained, that the play remains unsatisfying.[1]

The action was designed to stress the scenes of Timon's misanthropic fury beside his cave, and this part of the play is in its most complete state. Shakespeare did not fill in details of the sub-plot which might have made the parallel between Timon and Alcibiades more clear, and he did not develop a reason for Timon's degeneration which would be dramatically as satisfying as his explanation of the suffering of Lear. It is idle, perhaps, to speculate upon why Shakespeare abandoned the play, but it may have been in part his realization that the redemption of a secondary character

---

[1] The sources of *Timon* have long posed a vexing problem. The story appears in Lucian's dialogue, *Timon the Misanthrope*, in Plutarch's life of Antony and in an academic play, written probably at Cambridge, which had come to be performed by London schoolboys. See J. Q. Adams, 'The Timon Plays' *JEGP*, IX (1910), 506-24. The story may be found also in the *Silva* of Pedro Mexia, in various French accounts and in several English ones including William Painter's *Palace of Pleasure*. R. W. Bond, 'Lucian and Boiardo in "Timon of Athens" ', *MLR*, XXVI (1931), 52-62, considers Shakespeare's chief source to have been the Italian *Timone* of Matteo Boiardo. A lost source-play has been argued most recently by Georges Bonnard, 'Note sur les Sources de *Timon of Athens*', *Etudes Anglaises*, VII (1954), 56-69. For a comprehensive survey of the problem see J. C. Maxwell, ed., *Timon of Athens* (Cambridge, 1957), pp. ix-xi, and Willard Farnham, *Shakespeare's Tragic Frontier* (Berkeley, 1950), pp. 50-67. I would suggest that Shakespeare found in some earlier Timon play, now lost, a dramatic situation which might be used to pose the problem of an 'unregenerate Lear'. Again he sought for a sub-plot which, like the Gloucester sub-plot of *Lear*, might give his theme a universal range. This he found in Plutarch's life of Alcibiades. *Timon* may have involved a combination of sources not unlike Shakespeare's earlier use of Sidney's *Arcadia* to reshape and illuminate a theme in the older *Leir*, although there is some difference in that the connexion of Alcibiades with Timon already had been made by Plutarch.

after the damnation of his hero could not effect for his audience
the feeling of reconciliation at which he aimed. Shakespeare may
have come to realize that in order to assert a benevolent and purposive order in the universe while at the same time he destined his
hero to damnation, he must cast his action on a wider canvas.
He must show the corrupting force of evil, but he must show at
the same time that out of evil itself good may be generated; in
spite of one man's damnation, order may be restored to the whole.
Damnation itself must be portrayed as the source of a good which
might encompass the whole of creation. Such a scheme he attempted in *Macbeth*.

II

Timon's love for his fellow men is based not upon a calculating
reason, but upon an unthinking openness of heart.[1] It is all-giving,
and it makes no distinctions among men. What Timon gives, he
gives 'freely ever; and there's none / Can truly say he gives, if he
receives' (I.ii.10-11). He is guilty of no such sin as that of Lear in
dividing his kingdom. Timon's greatest crime in the first two acts
is merely folly in worldly matters, a folly which proceeds from
indulgence in human feeling to the exclusion of reason. In this
Timon looks forward to Antony as much as he looks back to
Lear. The function of Flavius in the first two acts is to remind the
audience of Timon's folly, to point out that his prodigal gener-
osity can lead only to disaster. The society which turns upon
Timon is the ordinary society which will turn upon any man of
similar folly; he experiences the ordinary evil of the world. It is
wrong to see this play as evidence of some kind of disillusionment
with society which Shakespeare came to suffer.

Timon is a fool in worldly matters, but he is not evil. He is
rather, as Flavius tells us, 'Undone by goodness! Strange, unusual
blood, / When man's worst sin is, he does too much good!' (IV.
ii.38-39). He suffers like Othello and Lear from an inability to distinguish appearance from reality, but we cannot doubt his own
statement that 'No villainous bounty yet hath pass'd my heart; /
Unwisely, not ignobly, have I given' (II.ii.182-3). The dominant

---

[1] This has been best argued by G. Wilson Knight, *The Wheel of Fire*, pp. 207-39.
Willard Farnham, *Shakespeare's Tragic Frontier*, pp. 39-77, reflects the more common
notion when he describes Timon as a deeply flawed character whose 'love' of
humanity is not love at all, but a selfishness which easily turns to hatred. There is
nothing in the play to support such a view.

motif of the opening scene is worldly magnificence, the fulfilment
of life, with the Poet, Painter, Jeweller and Merchant all coming
to lay their services before Timon.[1] They represent the good things
of life which Timon's love evokes. The tragedy lies not in his
prodigality – for the play is not a puritan lesson in the virtue of
thrift – but in the corruption of such love, and thus the destruction of the human felicity it nurtures. Timon's munificence is the
symbol of the human excellence he comes to forfeit.

In *Timon*, as in *Lear*, the secondary characters are divided clearly
between good and evil, and the lightness with which they are
sketched shows us that Shakespeare first conceived of them as
symbols of particular moral positions. On the one hand are the
flattering lords, Ventidius, Lucius, Lucullus and Sempronius. They
do not represent the terrible demonic forces of Goneril, Regan or
Edmund, but stand rather for the self-seeking pettiness of ordinary society, and as such they lack the Satanic grandeur which lends
a note of the heroic to Edmund and Iago. They are beneath
Oswald in their loathsomeness. These are the beasts who 'dip their
meat in one man's blood' (I.ii.42).

But these lords are not all of humanity. On the other hand, in
a neat parallel of four, stand Timon's faithful servants, Flavius,
Flaminius, Lucilius and Servilius. Their loyalty is one of the play's
major themes, an essential element in the total complex. The symbolic functions of both lords and servants are made clear in the
first four scenes of the third act. In each of these scenes we are
shown first a selfish rejection of Timon by one of the sycophantic
lords and then the contrasting fidelity of one of the servants, usually with such a comment as that of the servant Flaminius when
Lucullus has shown his inhumanity:

> Let molten coin be thy damnation,
> Thou disease of a friend, and not himself!
> Has friendship such a faint and milky heart,
> It turns in less than two nights? O you gods,
> I feel my master's passion! this slave,

[1] See Knight, *The Wheel of Fire*, pp. 207-11. The initial nobility of Timon has been
recognized also by A. S. Collins, '*Timon of Athens*, A Reconsideration', *RES*, xxii
(1946), 99-101; H. S. Wilson. *On the Design of Shakespearian Tragedy*, p. 140; and
R. P. Draper, 'Timon of Athens', *SQ*, viii (1957), 195-200. E. C. Pettet, '*Timon of
Athens:* The Disruption of Feudal Morality', *RES*, xxiii (1947), 321-36, sees Timon
as an embodiment of the feudal ideal of bounty, and the theme of the play as the
destruction of this ideal by the new practice of usury.

Unto his honour, has my lord's meat in him:
Why should it thrive and turn to nutriment,
When he is turn'd to poison?
O, may diseases only work upon't!
And, when he's sick to death, let not that part of nature
Which my lord paid for, be of any power
To expel sickness, but prolong his hour!

                                                        (III.i.55-66)

This foreshadows the hatred of humanity into which Timon himself is soon to fall; the servant feels his master's passion, and the audience begins to feel it too. Our detestation for Lucullus makes us share the outrage of Flaminius, and thus is built up sympathy for Timon, a participation in his own sense of injustice. We sorrow at his degeneration into beast, as we can never sorrow for the death of Goneril or Regan.

Servants and lords together represent mankind, much like the characters of *King Lear*, although here they are drawn more narrowly and in more specific terms. Lear attains salvation because he learns through suffering to recognize the goodness of Cordelia in spite of the evil of Goneril, and in his death he is united with this goodness and with God. Timon is damned because although he comes to perceive that Flavius is 'one honest man' (IV.iii.504), rather than embrace this goodness, he attempts to destroy it as unnatural, and in doing so he forfeits his own humanity. Timon rejects the godlike qualities of man; he is cut off from his fellow men and from God by the watery tomb whose construction he himself decrees.

Alcibiades is wronged by the Athenian senate as fully as Timon is wronged by his false friends. The two themes are linked in that both men suffer the effects of unnatural ingratitude; Alcibiades has given Athens his blood, Timon his money; each is rejected in return. Alcibiades, however, has been the man of action, unlike Timon the man of feeling, and his perversion of values appears in a lust for revenge. He learns at the end what Timon never learns, that good may exist in spite of evil, and he is redeemed from the fury which has possessed him. The reasons for his banishment from Athens are left unclear, although we know that it has resulted from his defence of a friend, and by this emphasis upon friendship his fate is linked to that of Timon; both suffer because of their love of their fellow men. Imperfect as the details of the sub-plot may be, it is obvious that Alcibiades was designed both as contrast and as parallel to Timon: to illustrate the similar effect of the world's evil upon a different kind of personality and thus lend a universal range to the theme.

Apemantus is used for several purposes. As the man-hating cynic in the opening scenes of the play, he is man reduced to beast by his rejection of the humanity which is God's noblest creation. As such he is used to set off the opposite qualities of the magnanimous Timon. The cynicism of Apemantus is pride in the medieval theological sense; his scorn for humanity is a denial both of his brotherhood to man and of the fatherhood of God. Timon's acceptance of Apemantus foreshadows his own degeneration into similar sin. Apemantus at the beginning of the play is used also to make clear to the audience the beast-like qualities of Timon's other guests. His dual role of beast symbol and beast excoriator may offend psychological consistency, but we are not to think of Apemantus as a realistic portrait from life. In his scorn for Timon's flatterers, Apemantus stands also for a kind of justice, and he appears as a friend to Timon:

> I scorn thy meat; 'twould choke me, for I should ne'er flatter thee.
> O you gods, what a number of men eat Timon, and he sees 'em not!
> It grieves me to see so many dip their meat in one man's blood; and
> all the madness is, he cheers them up too.

> (I.ii.39-43)

All of these diverse roles are performed when Apemantus visits Timon before his cave. In one role he makes clear to the audience the pride which, like his own, is the basic ingredient of Timon's misanthropy:

> If thou didst put this sour-cold habit on
> To castigate thy pride, 'twere well: but thou
> Dost it enforcedly.

> (IV.iii.239-41)

Timon's suffering is not the purifying agony which had led to Lear's redemption. 'Thou shouldst desire to die, being miserable' (248), says Apemantus, and we know that Timon has come to glory in his own delusion. He will not die so long as he can curse humanity and plot revenge against it. 'Art thou proud yet?' Apemantus asks, and Timon replies, 'Aye, that I am not thee' (IV.iii. 276-7), underscoring ironically for the audience his self-delusion in not knowing that he already is like Apemantus. When Timon stones Apemantus and the two revile one another (IV.iii.370-5), they are united in their common rejection of God and man. Timon will use his new-found gold 'that beasts / May have the world in empire!' (IV.iii.392-3).

Timon's hatred of humanity is contrasted with that of Apemantus. Since Apemantus has been born a dog, his hatred is natural, whereas for Timon, who was born with human feelings, such hatred is a gross perversion of nature. This contrast accents the greater horror of Timon's fall, that one born in Godlike magnificence should come to the false estimate of humanity to which the logic of a dog might naturally lead him.

III

One of the flaws in the play is that Timon's degeneration into beast is inadequately explained. We see his open-minded nobility in the first two acts, and the ruin which this will bring him. At the end of the second act he is ruined, but he still trusts in the goodness of humanity. The first four scenes of the third act show Timon testing his friends, with their animal natures contrasted to the simple human qualities of Timon's servants. The fifth scene introduces the Alcibiades sub-plot, and in the last scene we see the already misanthropic Timon serving his mock banquet to those he now detests:

> Most smiling, smooth, detested parasites,
> Courteous destroyers, affable wolves, meek bears,
> You fools of fortune, trencher-friends, time's flies,
> Cap and knee slaves, vapours, and minute-jacks!
> Of man and beast the infinite malady
> Crust you quite o'er!
>
> (III.vi.104-9)

Poorly explained as the transition is, we can nevertheless perceive in the design of the play that Timon has been presented with a moral choice not unlike that of Othello. He has already made his choice when he serves his banquet of water. In his misfortune he had been shown both the God-like and the bestial elements in man, but he has chosen to accept the latter as the stamp of God's creation. The choice he might have made is in the Senator's words to Alcibiades:

> He's truly valiant that can wisely suffer
> The worst that man can breathe, and make his wrongs
> His outsides, to wear them like his raiment, carelessly,
> And ne'er prefer his injuries to his heart,
> To bring it into danger. (III.v.31-35)

Instead of accepting his misfortunes patiently as God's will in an harmonious universal order – as Lear and Gloucester learn to accept theirs – Timon denies the existence of all moral law and negates the difference between man and beast. This is his wrong moral choice, and unlike Othello he never learns how wrong it is.

Timon's speech as he leaves Athens for ever (IV.i.1-41) – a symbolic severing of the bond which ties him to humanity – is cast by Shakespeare as a systematic repudiation of Elizabethan morality, of the great ethical system mirrored in Hooker's *Of the Laws of Ecclesiastical Polity*, with its concept of order, degree, and its correspondences linking man to God. Timon would destroy chastity, the reflection in Christian terms of the innocence of God, and he would subvert all of the normal relations within family and state:

> Matrons, turn incontinent!
> Obedience fail in children! slaves and fools,
> Pluck the grave wrinkled senate from the bench,
> And minister in their steads! to general filths
> Convert o' the instant, green virginity,
> Do't in your parents' eyes! bankrupts, hold fast;
> Rather than render back, out with your knives,
> And cut your trusters' throats! bound servants, steal!
> Large-handed robbers your grave masters are,
> And pill by law. Maid, to thy master's bed;
> Thy mistress is o' the brothel! Son of sixteen,
> Pluck the lined crutch from thy old limping sire,
> With it beat out his brains! (IV.i.3-15)

Those natural human feelings which reflect the will of God in the great system of natural law, and which preserve order and degree in society, Timon would destroy:

> Piety, and fear,
> Religion to the gods, peace, justice, truth,
> Domestic awe, night-rest, and neighbourhood,
> Instruction, manners, mysteries, and trades,
> Degrees, observances, customs, and laws,
> Decline to your confounding contraries,
> And let confusion live! (IV.i.15-21)

Not only would he subvert state, family, and the physical earth itself, but upon the human body he calls for the visitation of horrible disease:

> Plagues, incident to men,
> Your potent and infectious fevers heap
> On Athens, ripe for stroke! Thou cold sciatica,
> Cripple our senators, that their limbs may halt
> As lamely as their manners! Lust and liberty
> Creep in the minds and marrows of our youth,
> That 'gainst the stream of virtue they may strive,
> And drown themselves in riot! Itches, blains,
> Sow all the Athenian bosoms; and their crop
> Be general leprosy!
>
> (IV.i.21-30)

As in *King Lear* Shakespeare extends the range of his tragedy beyond the soul of individual man and on to its corresponding planes in the scheme of creation: the state and the physical universe itself. The corruption of Timon is echoed in his desire for the corruption of the total cosmos. The upheaval in nature receives no such powerful emphasis as the storm scenes of Lear, but before Timon's cave are paraded symbols of human disease in the whores who visit him, of the collapse of law in the robbers who seek his gold, and of rebellion plunging the state into civil war in the avenging army of Alcibiades. The redemption of Alcibiades is drawn also in political as well as personal terms, for it brings an end not only to the troubled passions within him, but also to the political chaos in Athens.

Timon ends his terrible incantation with an acceptance of the beast as nobler than man, with a rejection of the gods, and a total severance of his bond to his fellow men:

> Timon will to the woods; where he shall find
> The unkindest beast more kinder than mankind.
> The gods confound – hear me, you good gods all –
> The Athenians both within and out that wall!
> And grant, as Timon grows, his hate may grow
> To the whole race of mankind, high and low!
> Amen.
>
> (IV.i.35-41)

From this scene of terrible rejection, Shakespeare turns to Timon's servants, and through them he asserts a contrary position. Flavius in his kindness and humility affirms the goodness of man which Timon has just denied. To his fellow servants he gives his own poor fortune, and he resolves to follow his master in misery:

> Good fellows all,
> The latest of my wealth I'll share amongst you.
> Wherever we shall meet, for Timon's sake,
> Let's yet be fellows; let's shake our heads, and say,
> As 'twere a knell unto our master's fortunes,
> 'We have seen better days'. Let each take some;
> Nay, put out all your hands. Not one word more:
> Thus part we rich in sorrow, parting poor.
>
> . . . .
>
> Alas, kind lord!
> He's flung in rage from this ingrateful seat
> Of monstrous friends, nor has he with him to
> Supply his life, or that which can command it.
> I'll follow and inquire him out:
> I'll ever serve his mind with my best will;
> Whilst I have gold, I'll be his steward still.
>
> (IV.ii.22-50)

Here then is a servant who will not betray his master. Flavius stands as evidence that the unnatural chaotic world which Timon sees is the product of his own madness and delusion.

Timon's misanthropic tirades, like the speeches of the mad Lear upon the heath, represent a perversion born out of delusion. Timon exults in the animal nature of man, and like Lear he expresses this nature in terms of brute sexual fury. The theme of sinful sexuality, the polar contrary of love, had been introduced earlier, with the Fool's dwelling upon syphilis (II.ii.71-72). Alcibiades in his visit to Timon's cave is accompanied by two whores, who provide symbols of love reduced to lust and who offer scope for Timon's concern with animal sexuality. He calls upon Timandra to corrupt the innocent youth of Athens:

> Be a whore still: they love thee not that use thee;
> Give them diseases, leaving with thee their lust.
> Make use of thy salt hours: season the slaves
> For tubs and baths; bring down rose-cheeked youth
> To the tub-fast and the diet.
>
> (IV.iii.82-86)

This is in marked contrast to the kind of love which Timon had represented in the first two acts. Perverted love degenerates into the animal brutality of lust.

Timon would establish the horror of war as the normal condition of human life. For this theme also the appearance of Alcibiades offers occasion:

> Follow thy drum;
> With man's blood paint the ground, gules, gules:
> Religious canons, civil laws are cruel;
> Then what should war be?
>
> (IV.iii.58-61)

The sun, symbol of light and of the generation of life, Timon would blot out and render sterile like the moon: 'O blessed breeding sun, draw from the earth / Rotten humidity; below thy sister's orb / Infect the air!' (IV.iii.1-3). The earth itself is a 'damned earth, / Thou common whore of mankind' (IV.iii.41-42). The long third scene of Act IV is devoted to Timon's repeated expressions of his perverted values, his confusion of order in nature, in society, and in the body of man. These speeches are the marks of Timon's delusion. They are even more savage in their fury than those of the mad Lear, and they are unmarked by the contrasting motif of human love and sympathy which we have noted in Lear's outbursts, and which make possible his redemption.

Timon has other visitors in his exile. To the banditti who come to rob him he gives gold and he urges them 'to Athens go, / Break open shops; nothing can you steal, / But thieves do lose it' (IV. iii.449-51). This shows that Timon stands for the perversion of justice. All nature to him reflects a pattern of injustice with which human thievery may accord:

> I'll example you with thievery:
> The sun's a thief, and with his great attraction
> Robs the vast sea: the moon's an arrant thief,
> And her pale fire she snatches from the sun:
> The sea's a thief, whose liquid surge resolves
> The moon into salt tears: the earth's a thief,
> That feeds and breeds by a composture stolen
> From general excrement: each thing's a thief:
> The laws, your curb and whip, in their rough power
> Have uncheck'd theft.
>
> (IV.iii.438-47)

The visit of the Poet and the Painter emphasizes Timon's rejection of the former values by which he had lived, for his praise and support of the artists at the play's beginning is recalled. Art, the revelation of true reality, he now sees only as deceitful false appearance. With the banishment of the Poet and the Painter, the former Timon is gone forever.

The most significant of Timon's visitors is his faithful steward, Flavius, for their meeting provides the crucial test in which a fallen Timon is offered the chance of redemption. When he rejects it, we know that his damnation is assured. Flavius comes upon the scene proclaiming the goodness and fidelity for which he stands, and at the same time recapitulating the progression of Timon to this point:

> O you gods!
> Is yond despised and ruinous man my lord?
> Full of decay and failing? O monument
> And wonder of good deeds evilly bestow'd!
> What an alteration of honour
> Has desperate want made!
> What viler thing upon the earth than friends
> Who can bring noblest minds to basest ends!
> How rarely does it meet with this time's guise,
> When man was wish'd to love his enemies!
> Grant I may ever love, and rather woo
> Those that would mischief me than those that do!
> Has caught me in his eye: I will present
> My honest grief unto him; and, as my lord,
> Still serve him with my life. My dearest master!
>
> (IV.iii.464-78)

When Timon who has 'forgot all men' refuses to recognize him, Flavius weeps and pleads that, 'The gods are witness, / Ne'er did poor steward wear a truer grief / For his undone lord than mine eyes for you' (IV.iii.486-8). Now Timon recognizes the faithful honest man which Flavius is:

> Had I a steward
> So true, so just, and now so comfortable?
> It almost turns my dangerous nature mild.
> Let me behold thy face. Surely, this man
> Was born of woman.

Forgive my general and exceptless rashness,
You perpetual-sober gods! I do proclaim
One honest man – mistake me not – but one;
No more, I pray, – and he's a steward.

(IV.iii.497-505)

Flavius demonstrates by his very existence the goodness of humanity which Timon has denied. Timon sees this goodness in one
man, and this awareness almost turns his 'dangerous nature mild',
but he will not accept the implications of what he sees. He beholds
only a single isolated instance which he actually regrets to find,
for 'How fain would I have hated all mankind!' (506). Flavius cannot change the concept of humanity which is Timon's delusion:
'but all, save thee, / I fell with curses' (507-8).

When Flavius convinces Timon that 'That which I show,
heaven knows, is merely love, / Duty and zeal to your unmatched
mind, / Care of your food and living' (522-4), Timon still cannot
learn what might bring him redemption: that the goodness of
Flavius is as much a part of God's order as is the evil which has
driven him from Athens. Rather than embrace this goodness as
an affirmation of God, Timon attempts to destroy it as unnatural:

Thou singly honest man,
Here, take: the gods out of my misery
Have sent thee treasure. Go, live rich and happy;
But thus condition'd: thou shalt build from men;
Hate all, curse all, show charity to none,
But let the famish'd flesh slide from the bone,
Ere thou relieve the beggar; give to dogs
What thou deny'st to men; let prisons swallow 'em,
Debts wither 'em to nothing; be men like blasted woods,
And may diseases lick up their false bloods!
And so farewell and thrive.

(IV.iii.530-40)

Flavius may be viewed as a Christ symbol offering salvation. Not
only does Timon reject this offer, but he would reduce the saviour
himself to his own bestial level.

In the final act we are shown the death of Timon and the contrasting redemption of Alcibiades. Timon rejects the offer of the
Athenian senators to atone for the injuries society has done him.
Their mission to Timon's cave prepares the audience for Alcibiades' march against Athens which will bring the play to its

L

climax. The delight which Timon takes in the coming destruction
of his city prepares for and sets off the contrasting regeneration of
Alcibiades which will assure the salvation of Athens as well.

It is the same perverted Timon who addresses the Senators who
come to visit him:

> If Alcibiades kill my countrymen,
> Let Alcibiades know this of Timon,
> That Timon cares not. But if he sack fair Athens,
> And take our goodly aged men by the beards,
> Giving our holy virgins to the stain
> Of contumelious, beastly, mad-brained war,
> Then let him know, and tell him Timon speaks it,
> In pity of our aged and our youth,
> I cannot choose but tell him, that I care not,
> And let him take't at worst; for their knives care not,
> While you have throats to answer: for myself,
> There's not a whittle in the unruly camp
> But I do prize it at my love before
> The reverend'st throat in Athens. So I leave you
> To the protection of the prosperous gods,
> As thieves to keepers.
>
> (V.i.172-87)

There is an ironic foreshadowing in the final lines, for the Gods
will in fact preserve Athens, and this preservation will be a repudiation of Timon's rejection of them. Timon then announces his
own coming death. He will blot out the sun, and in his watery
tomb be isolated for ever from humanity:

> Come not to me again: but say to Athens,
> Timon hath made his everlasting mansion
> Upon the beached verge of the salt flood;
> Who once a day with his embossed froth
> The turbulent surge shall cover: thither come,
> And let my grave-stone be your oracle.
> Lips, let sour words go by and language end:
> What is amiss plague and infection mend!
> Graves only be men's works and death their gain!
> Sun, hide thy beams! Timon hath done his reign.
>
> (V.i.217-26)

Timon himself has become a symbol of death, as his invitation to
the Athenians to hang themselves from his tree may attest. He

dies in total negation of the goodness of life which in the opening
scenes of the play he had represented. Shakespeare's final comment is in the words of the common soldier who discovers
Timon's tomb: 'Some beast rear'd this; there does not live a man'
(V.iii.4).

To Alcibiades the Athenian senators, representatives of humanity in the large, have made the same offer of atonement for their
sins which they had made to Timon:

> Noble and young,
> When thy first griefs were but a mere conceit,
> Ere thou hadst power or we had cause of fear,
> We sent to thee, to give thy rages balm,
> To wipe out our ingratitude with loves
> Above their quantity.
>
> (V.iv.13-18)

Ingratitude and love are both parts of God's order; in the normal
scheme of things, love will triumph if man will let it do so. The
second senator draws the parallel between the cases of Timon and
Alcibiades and reminds the audience that all humanity is not debased by the evil which is but a part of it:

> So did we woo
> Transformed Timon to our city's love
> By humble message and by promised means:
> We were not all unkind, nor all deserve
> The common stroke of war.
>
> (V.iv.18-22)

This theme is repeated in a series of speeches, one following the
other in a kind of choral ritual:

> These walls of ours
> Were not erected by their hands from whom
> You have received your griefs.
>
> (V.iv.22-24)

> All have not offended;
> For those that were, it is not square to take
> On those that are, revenges: crimes, like lands,
> Are not inherited.
>
> (V.iv.35-37)

In the repeated idea that Athens now is peopled with new men, that the old who sinned against Timon and Alcibiades have long been dead, we have the same feeling of rebirth which we have noted at the end of *Lear*. The forces of evil have worked themselves out in the natural course of things, and society is ready for rebirth of the good. This will be reflected in the regenerated Alcibiades.

Alcibiades brings not only retribution but forgiveness. From the beginning he had stood for pity as opposed to the strictness of justice. When the first senator had said to him that 'Nothing emboldens sin so much as mercy' (III.v.3), he had replied:

> I am an humble suitor to your virtues;
> For pity is the virtue of the law,
> And none but tyrants use it cruelly.

> (III.v.7-9)

It is to this sense of pity as well as to his sense of justice that the senators now appeal:

> What thou wilt,
> Thou rather shalt enforce it with thy smile
> Than hew to't with thy sword.

> (V.iv.44-46)

> Throw thy glove,
> Or any token of thine honour else,
> That thou wilt use the wars as thy redress
> And not as our confusion, all thy powers
> Shall make their harbour in our town, till we
> Have seal'd thy full desire.

> (V.iv.49-54)

This offer Alcibiades accepts, and in this acceptance is his redemption. He will use the force of arms to assert order and justice, rather than to bring the chaos which Timon had anticipated in the sack of Athens. The guilty will be punished, but the innocent will know a new felicity, and order will be restored:

> Then there's my glove;
> Descend, and open your uncharged ports:
> Those enemies of Timon's and mine own
> Whom you yourselves shall set out for reproof
> Fall and no more: and, to atone your fears

> With my more noble meaning, not a man
> Shall pass his quarter, or offend the stream
> Of regular justice in your city's bounds,
> But shall be render'd to your public laws
> At heaviest answer.
>
> (V.iv.54-63)

> Bring me into your city,
> And I will use the olive with my sword,
> Make war breed peace, make peace stint war, make each
> Prescribe to other as each other's leech.
>
> (V.iv.81-84)

Athens is saved by a man who, like Timon, has suffered through man's inhumanity but has come to see that there is nobility in God's creation in spite of evil. This evil he will oppose as every new generation must, and he will do so by the exercise of justice. The play closes upon the note of ancient evil destroyed and of good reborn. Alcibiades reads Timon's epitaph with the hope that the sea may 'weep for aye / On thy low grave, on faults forgiven' (78-79). In his recognition of the goodness of man there is room for forgiveness even of Timon's monstrous sin. This is Shakespeare's attempt at tragic reconciliation. If it is not entirely successful, it may be because the regeneration of Alcibiades is not so fully developed as the degeneration of Timon. It appears as a mere appendage to the play, weak and anti-climactic after Timon's powerful renunciation of God and man, upon which Shakespeare has lavished his greatest poetic skill. We remember at the end Timon's defiance rather than Alcibiades' submission. The final scene, in short, does not offer a real emotional equivalent for its intellectual content, and this content is basic to the total structure of the play.

IV

Macbeth is a closely knit, unified construction, every element of which supports a thematic statement.[1] The hero's life-journey is cast into a symbolic pattern to reflect a view of evil's operation in the world, and the other characters are designed to set off the

---

[1] That *Macbeth* was written in 1606 and performed for the first time on August 7 of that year at Hampton Court before James I and King Christian of Denmark is virtually certain. See Henry N. Paul, *The Royal Play of Macbeth* (New York, 1950). On the sources see also Kenneth Muir, *Shakespeare's Sources*, 1, 167-86.

particular concerns implicit in the action of the hero. For the basic structure of the play, Shakespeare returned to *Richard III*. Macbeth accepts evil in the third scene of the play, and there is also a suggestion that he has partly succumbed to it even before the action begins.[1] In the second act he commits the deed to which his choice of evil has led him. For the final three acts, as he rises higher in worldly power, like Richard III he sinks deeper into evil, until at the end he is utterly destroyed.

Macbeth is not like Richard a scourge of God whose evil course is a necessary element in a larger merciful divine scheme. He is rather, like Othello, a man of potential goodness, in whose fall we are made to feel our common frailty and our fellowship with him in sin. His soliloquies inform the supreme illusion of reality in his characterization, and we see him not as an abstract symbol of evil in whose destruction we may rejoice, but rather as a fellow human in whose fall there is terrible waste and a view of the fate of which we ourselves are capable. There is also in the fall of Macbeth a heroic quality, for we admire the greatness of the man in spite of all, and we sense the courage of his devotion to his sinful moral choice, demonic though that devotion may be. In this there is a suggestion of the paradox which Shakespeare is to develop in his final Roman plays.

Shakespeare's movement from *Othello* to *Lear* had, in part, been from the range of a circumscribed domestic tragedy to one embracing the entire scheme of creation. *Macbeth* is a large universal tragedy like *Lear*, but it also includes the domestic qualities of *Othello*; these are most evident in the relation between Macbeth and his wife, whose tragedy we feel more intensely than we can the political tragedy which falls upon Scotland. This domestic tragedy is carefully subordinated to the larger conception of which it is but a part. To make clear the cosmic scope of *Macbeth* Shakespeare further developed the technique he had used in *Lear*. The tragedy is cast simultaneously on the planes of man, the state, the family and the physical universe; each is thrown into chaos by the sin of Macbeth, and evil is allowed to work itself out on each of these corresponding planes.

Although there is no redemption for the fallen hero as in *King*

---

[1] In Banquo's 'why do you start; and seem to fear / Things that do sound so fair?' (I.iii.51-52) there is the implication that the prophecy of the witches merely seconds an idea already in Macbeth's mind.

Lear, Shakespeare's final statement is not one of despair, for the play asserts divine order and purpose. There can be little doubt of the final damnation of 'this dead butcher and his fiend-like queen' (V.viii.69), but the audience comes to feel that Macbeth is destroyed by counter-forces which he himself, through his very dedication to evil, sets in motion. The very violence of his tyranny causes Macduff and Malcolm to oppose him. His very trust in the witches, which starts him on his evil course, leads also to his final destruction. The total emotional and intellectual impact of the play reveals good through divine grace emerging out of evil and triumphant at the end with a promise of rebirth.

Othello and Lear in their falls parallel the fall of Adam, and like Adam they are able to learn from their disasters the nature of evil and thus attain a victory in defeat. The destruction of Macbeth reflects the fall of Satan himself, and the play is full of analogies to make this parallel clear.[1] Like Satan, Macbeth is aware from the first of the evil he embraces, and like Satan he will not renounce his free-willed moral choice once it has been made. It is fitting that this evil be symbolized by ambition, for this was the sin of Satan. For Shakespeare, as it had been for Aquinas, ambition was an aspect of pride, a rebellion against the will of God and the order of nature.[2] Macbeth, through love of self, sets his own will against divine will, chooses a lesser finite good – kingship and power – rather than the infinite good of God's order.

The ambitious man will strive to rise higher on the great chain of being than the place God has appointed him. To do so he must break the bond which ties him to God and to the rest of humanity. It is of this bond that Macbeth speaks immediately before the murder of Banquo:

> Come, seeling night,
> Scarf up the tender eye of pitiful day;
> And with thy bloody and invisible hand
> Cancel and tear to pieces that great bond
> Which keeps me pale!
>
> (III.ii.48-52)

---

[1] See P. N. Siegel, *Shakespearean Tragedy and the Elizabethan Compromise*, p. 145; M. D. H. Parker, *The Slave of Life*, pp. 163-4; J. Dover Wilson, ed., *Macbeth* (Cambridge, 1947), p. lxvi.

[2] See W. C. Curry, *Shakespeare's Philosophical Patterns* (Baton Rouge, 1937), p. 112; Parker, *The Slave of Life*, p. 150.

This is the bond which ties Macbeth to humanity and enjoins him
to obey the natural law of God which he has already broken in
his murder of Duncan, but which still keeps him pale, in the un-
diminished terror of the act he has already committed and of that
he is about to commit. It is the bond of nature which Cordelia had
invoked and Lear rejected. Macbeth is aware of the implications
of this bond as Lear in his folly is not; he is calling upon the
Satanic forces of darkness to sever it and thus enable him again to
defy the laws of man and God, to murder his friend and his guest.

That Macbeth's crime is opposed to the order and harmony of
the universe is supported by the imagery of planting and hus-
bandry, of feasting and conviviality, by the pleasant evocation of
the calmness and beauty of nature as Duncan and Banquo enter
the dread castle walls (I.iv.1-9).[1] Duncan himself stands for the
fruitful aspects of nature; he is like Timon the source of the goodness of life, of all that Macbeth may hope to attain:

> I have begun to plant thee, and will labour
> To make thee full of growing.

(I.iv.28-29)

The murder of Duncan strikes at all which makes life good, fruitful, beautiful. Macbeth cuts off the source of his own being, and
this is echoed in Lady Macbeth's 'Had he not resembled / My
father as he slept, I had done 't' (II.ii.13-14), for this line, upon
which so many fantastic theories have been spun, is not primarily
a literal statement; it is choral commentary to emphasize the father
symbolism with which Duncan is endowed.

Macbeth's sin, like Satan's, is a deliberate repudiation of nature,
a defiance of God. All of the natural forces which militate against
the deed are evoked by Macbeth himself:

> He's here in double trust;
> First, as I am his kinsman and his subject,
> Strong both against the deed; then, as his host,
> Who should against his murderer shut the door,
> Not bear the knife myself. Besides, this Duncan
> Hath borne his faculties so meek, hath been

---

[1] G. Wilson Knight, *The Imperial Theme*, pp. 125-53; L. C. Knights, 'How Many
Children Had Lady Macbeth?' in *Explorations* (New York, 1947), pp. 36-38;
Cleanth Brooks, 'The Naked Babe and the Cloak of Manliness', in *The Well Wrought
Urn* (New York, 1947), pp. 43-44; Speaight, *Nature in Shakespearian Tragedy*, pp.
44-48.

> So clear in his great office, that his virtues
> Will plead like angels, trumpet-tongued, against
> The deep damnation of his taking-off;
> And pity, like a naked new-born babe,
> Striding the blast, or heaven's cherubim, horsed
> Upon the sightless couriers of the air,
> Shall blow the horrid deed in every eye,
> That tears shall drown the wind. I have no spur
> To prick the sides of my intent, but only
> Vaulting ambition, which o'erleaps itself
> And falls on the other.
>
> (I.vii.12-28)

Macbeth knows that by defying God's natural order he forfeits his own claim to manhood:

> I dare do all that may become a man;
> Who dares do more is none.
>
> (I.vii.46-47)

Because he willingly embraces damnation, the way of redemption is closed to him, and he must end in destruction and despair. In denying nature Macbeth cuts off the source of redemption. Once he has given his 'eternal jewel' to the 'common enemy of man', he must abide by the contract he has made. This is a tragedy about damnation in Christian terms; Macbeth and the audience are always aware of this.

V

The characters of *Macbeth* are infused with an illusion of reality which serves to embody their thematic functions in specific emotional terms, but they are not shaped primarily by the demands of psychological verisimilitude. All that we need to know about the witches is that they are a convenient dramatic symbol for the force of evil in the world. To question the motives of Banquo in not revealing his knowledge of the witches, or to wonder where Lady Macbeth has sequestered the children whose brains she is willing to dash out is fruitless, for these characters function primarily as dramatic vehicles governed by the over-all demands not of fact or psychology, but thematic design.

As symbols of evil the witches are cast in traditional terms. They are contrary to nature, women with the beards of men; their incantation is a Black Mass, and the broth they stir consists of the disunified parts of men and animals, creation in chaos. They deliberately wait for Macbeth and Banquo, as evil waits for all men. They do not, however, suggest evil to man; they suggest an object which may incite man's own inclination to evil which is the fruit of original sin, and they do this by means of prophecy. The good man, like Banquo, can resist their appeal, for man shares in the grace of God, as well as in original sin.

The witches hold forth the promise of worldly good, as evil must, for if it were not attractive it would offer no temptation. But the promises of evil are false; seeming truths are half truths, for evil works through deception, by posing as the friend of man. Thus Eve had been seduced by Satan in the garden of Eden, and thus Othello had been seduced by 'honest' Iago. Banquo at once recognizes the Satanic origin of the witches: 'What, can the devil speak true?' (I.iii.106) and he perceives the manner in which they work:

> And oftentimes, to win us to our harm,
> The instruments of darkness tell us truths,
> Win us with honest trifles, to betray's
> In deepest consequence.
>
> (I.iii.122-6)

To make this statement about the deceptive nature of evil Shakespeare works into the texture of his play the theme of appearance versus reality. There is always confusion and uncertainty in the appearance of evil, darkness rather than light, never the clear, rational certainty of the natural order. The theme of uncertainty is set in Macbeth's opening remark: 'So foul and fair a day I have not seen' (I.iii.38). 'There's no art / To find the mind's construction in the face' (I.iv.11-12), says Duncan, and Lady Macbeth cautions her husband to 'look like the innocent flower, / But be the serpent under't' (I.v.66-67). Macbeth himself says that 'False face must hide what the false heart doth know' (I.vii.82). His own treachery is foreshadowed by that of the Thane of Cawdor, of whom Duncan says, 'He was a gentleman on whom I built / An absolute trust' (I.iv.14-15). All is falsehood, uncertainty, deception.

Only when Birnam Wood has in fact come to Dunsinane and he faces a foe not born of woman, does Macbeth himself learn that evil operates through deception:

> And be these juggling fiends no more believed,
> That palter with us in a double sense;
> That keep the word of promise to our ear,
> And break it to our hope.
>
> (V.viii.19-22)

But by this time he has committed his soul beyond retreat.

The witches offer to Banquo temptation not unlike what they offer Macbeth, and Banquo is sorely tempted, as any man must be:

> yet it was said
> It should not stand in thy posterity,
> But that myself should be the root and father
> Of many kings. If there come truth from them –
> As upon thee, Macbeth, their speeches shine –
> Why, by the verities on thee made good,
> May they not be my oracles as well,
> And set me up in hope? But hush! no more.
>
> (III.i.3-10)

The difference between Macbeth and Banquo is that Banquo 'hath a wisdom that doth guide his valour / To act in safety' (III.i.53-54). He will not perform an evil act, although evil may tempt him, and he is unwilling to dwell upon temptation, as Macbeth does, until it provoke him to sin. Banquo is ordinary man, with his mixture of good and evil, open to evil's soliciting, but able to resist it. Shakespeare is saying that in such a man, who in spite of temptation can use his reason to resist evil, the hope for the future lies. This hope is embodied in Fleance, symbolic of a future rooted in the acceptance of natural law, which inevitably must return to reassert God's harmonious order when evil has worked itself out. This is why, in terms of the play's total conceptual pattern, it is impossible for Macbeth to kill Fleance, try as he may. Evil cannot destroy the promise of ultimate good.

Banquo, humanly weak and subject to temptation, stands nevertheless 'in the great hand of God' (II.iii.133). Symbolically he represents one aspect of Macbeth, the side of ordinary humanity which Macbeth must destroy within himself before he can give his soul entirely to the forces of darkness. This is why Macbeth must murder Banquo, and it is why the dead Banquo returns to him as a reminder that, as a man, he cannot easily extinguish the human force within himself, that the torment of fear, the 'terrible dreams / That shake us nightly' (III.ii.18-19), the scorpions in his mind (III.ii.36), will continue until his own destruction. Banquo and his ghost are used to illuminate the conflict within the mind of Macbeth, the difficulty of any severance of the bond which ties man to humanity.

Macduff and Malcolm serve similar symbolic functions. Macduff is a force of divine retribution generated by Macbeth's own course of evil. Malcolm is Shakespeare's portrait of the ideal king, and his chief function is to represent a restitution of order in the state which will succeed the tyranny of Macbeth.[1] *Macbeth* is full of political considerations which come to a head in the crucial scene in which Macduff and Malcolm meet in England. This scene is designed to define the nature of tyranny, to delineate the character of the ideal king, and to prepare for the restitution of order in Scotland with the coming of such a king.

Just as Banquo stands for that side of Macbeth which would uphold the natural order and reject evil, Lady Macbeth represents the contrary side. Much nonsense has come from attempts to treat her as a real person, to analyse her motives, account for her children and in general assign to her a share in Macbeth's tragic downfall to which her dramatic function does not entitle her. The moral choice which destroys Macbeth is his alone; her function is merely to second him in this choice, to counter-act those forces within him which are in accord with nature and in opposition to evil, those very forces represented by Banquo. Macbeth is in the position of the traditional morality-play hero placed between good and evil angels. Lady Macbeth seduces him, and Banquo must be destroyed.

For this reason her speeches draw upon the corruption of nature and the reversal of normal life impulses. She calls upon the forces of darkness to support her in her purposes:

> Come, you spirits
> That tend on mortal thoughts, unsex me here,
> And fill me from the crown to the toe top-full
> Of direst cruelty! make thick my blood;
> Stop up the access and passage to remorse,
> That no compunctious visitings of nature

[1] See E. M. W. Tillyard, *Shakespeare's History Plays* (New York, 1947), p. 317. I have treated the play's political implications in *The English History Play in the Age of Shakespeare*, pp. 254-9.

> Shake my fell purpose, nor keep peace between
> The effect and it! Come to my woman's breasts,
> And take my milk for gall, you murdering ministers,
> Wherever in your sightless substances
> You wait on nature's mischief! Come, thick night,
> And pall thee in the dunnest smoke of hell,
> That my keen knife see not the wound it makes,
> Nor heaven peep through the blanket of the dark,
> To cry 'Hold, hold!'
>
> (I.v.41-56)

Woman is the normal symbol of life and nourishment: the dramatist by this reversal can emphasize the unnaturalness of the contraries to which Lady Macbeth appeals. She must become unsexed, and her milk must convert to gall. Her very need to put aside her feminine qualities informs the illusion of reality in her characterization.

The motif of the unnatural is evoked again in the savage cry:

> I have given suck, and know
> How tender 'tis to love the babe that milks me:
> I would, while it was smiling in my face,
> Have pluck'd my nipple from his boneless gums,
> And dash'd the brains out.
>
> (I.vii.54-58)

We cannot say whether she actually has children or not, for this speech is not designed to convey fact. It is a ritual statement in which Shakespeare seizes upon an unnatural image in order to emphasize that the speaker is urging Macbeth on the basis of all which is opposed to nature and God. If Shakespeare later in the play, in Macduff's 'He has no children' (IV.iii.216) seems to indicate that Macbeth is childless, it is not that he has forgotten this earlier speech. There Shakespeare wishes to emphasize the intensity of Macduff's feeling in the same ritual manner.[1] Shakespeare, morover, makes his tyrant childless, much as he had done in *Julius Caesar*, to indicate that such a man can offer no hope for a peaceful succession. Macbeth is the destroyer of life; he cannot be portrayed as its creator.

Throughout the play Lady Macbeth's femininity is held in juxtaposition to the unnatural forces which she would call into play.

---

[1] To suppose that Macduff here is referring to Malcolm rather than to Macbeth is to rob the scene of much of its emotional intensity.

In the murder scene the unnatural aspect of Lady Macbeth is dominant, but her femininity comes through in her inability to kill the king herself. When the body is discovered, she is the first to collapse. This careful juxtaposition of contraries comes to a head when she walks in her sleep in the fifth act. Here the images of blood are mingled with her feminine desire for the 'perfumes of Arabia' to 'sweeten this little hand' (V.i.56). In her death by suicide there is further emphasis upon the theme which dominates the play: that evil inevitably must breed its own destruction.

IV

The specific act of evil occurs on two levels, the state and Macbeth's own 'single state of man' (I.iii.140); the crime is ethical and political, for Macbeth murders not only his kinsman and guest, but his king as well, and its immediate end is to replace a divinely sanctioned monarchy with a tyranny built on usurpation. Once evil is unleashed, it corrupts all of creation, not only man and the state, but the family and the physical universe as well. Shakespeare explores the process of corruption on these four interrelated planes.

That the physical universe has been thrown out of harmony is made clear in the speech of Lennox which immediately follows Duncan's murder:

> The night has been unruly: where we lay,
> Our chimneys were blown down; and, as they say,
> Lamentings heard i' the air; strange screams of death,
> And prophesying with accents terrible
> Of dire combustion and confused events
> New hatch'd to the woeful time: the obscure bird
> Clamour'd the livelong night: some say, the earth
> Was feverous and did shake.
>
> (II.iii.59-66)

This confusion in nature is stressed again in the brief exchange between Ross and a nameless old man. The strange phenomena which Ross describes are all perversions of physical nature which indicate that one man's crime has thrown the entire universe out of harmony:

> Thou seest, the heavens, as troubled with man's act,
> Threaten his bloody stage: by the clock, 'tis day,
> And yet dark night strangles the travelling lamp:

> Is't night's predominance, or the day's shame,
> That darkness does the face of earth entomb,
> When living light should kiss it?
>
> (II.iv.4-9)

The order of nature is reversed, the sun blotted out. On the animal plane, a falcon is killed by a mousing owl, and most horrible of all:

> And Duncan's horses – a thing most strange and certain –
> Beauteous and swift, the minions of their race,
> Turn'd wild in nature, broke their stalls, flung out,
> Contending 'gainst obedience, as they would make
> War with mankind.
>
> (II.iv.14-18)

Man by his sin has forfeited his dominion over nature; horses turn against their natural master, and 'they eat each other'.

This corruption in nature contains within itself the means of restoring harmony; in the working out of evil is implicit a rebirth of good. Shakespeare uses the very perversion of nature, in the form of a moving forest and a child unborn of mother to herald the downfall of the tyrant and thus to restore the physical universe to its natural state of perfection. That the forest does not really move, and that Macduff was only technically so born are of no significance, for Shakespeare is giving us not scientific fact but thematic symbol.

Upon the state, Macbeth unleashes the greatest political evils of which Shakespeare's audience could conceive, tryanny, civil war, and an invading foreign army. The tyranny of Macbeth's reign, in which:

> each new morn
> New widows howl, new orphans cry, new sorrows
> Strike heaven on the face, that it resounds
> As if it felt with Scotland and yell'd out
> Like syllable of dolour.
>
> (IV.iii.4-8)

is set off by the initial description of the gentility and justice of Duncan's previous rule, with a king still firm enough to overcome the threats both internal and external with which the opening scenes of the play are concerned. Holinshed, on the contrary, had stressed Duncan's 'feeble and slothful administration' and he had, by way of contrast, praised Macbeth for the excellence of at least the first ten years of his reign.

The disorder in the state, as it works out its course, is also the source of its own extinction and the restoration of political harmony. The very tyranny of Macbeth arouses Macduff against him, causes Malcolm to assert the justice of his title, and perhaps most significantly, causes the saint-like English king, Edward the Confessor, to take arms against Macbeth. In Act IV, Scene ii is described King Edward's curing of scrofula by touch. This is Shakespeare's means of underscoring the saintliness of Edward and of illustrating that he is an emissary of God, an instrument of supernatural Grace, designed to cleanse the unnatural evil in the state, just as he removes evil from individual man. Macbeth's very tyranny has made him 'ripe for shaking, and the powers above / Put on their instruments' (IV.iii.237-8).

The family relationship between Macbeth and his wife steadily deteriorates. At the beginning of the play they are one of the closest and most intimate couples in all literature. She is 'my dearest partner in greatness' (I.v.10-11), and much as it harrows him to think of its implications, he sends her immediate word of the witches' prophecy, so that she may not 'lose the dues of rejoicing' (I.v.11-12). The very terror of the murder scene emphasizes the closeness of the murderers. But as the force of evil severs Macbeth from the rest of humanity, it breaks also the bond which ties him to his wife. He lives more and more closely with his own fears into which she cannot intrude, as the banquet scene illustrates. She cannot see the ghost which torments her husband.

The gradual separation of man and wife first becomes apparent just before the murder of Banquo. No longer does Macbeth confide in her: 'Be innocent of the knowledge, dearest chuck, / Till thou applaud the deed' (III.ii.45-46). At the play's beginning they plan the future together; at the end each dies alone, and when the news of her death comes to Macbeth, he shows little concern:

> She should have died hereafter;
> There would have been a time for such a word.
>
> (V.v.17-18)

This theme of family disintegration is repeated in Macduff's desertion of his wife and children.[1]

---

[1] Knight, *The Wheel of Fire*, p. 144, misses the symbolic import of this otherwise unexplainable event when he calls it merely part of the deliberate illogic with which Shakespeare infuses the play. Dover Wilson (p. xxxix) offers it merely as evidence of Shakespeare's shortening of a longer play.

On the disintegration of Macbeth the man, Shakespeare lavishes his principal attention. He is careful to paint his hero in the opening scenes as a man of great stature, the saviour of his country, full of the 'milk of human kindness'. Macbeth has natural feelings which link him to his fellow men and cause him to view with revulsion the crime to which ambition prompts him. Once the crime is committed these feelings are gradually destroyed, until at the end of the play he is, like Timon of Athens, unnatural man, cut off from humanity and from God. As his link with humanity weakens, so also does his desire to live, until at last he sinks into total despair, the medieval sin of *Acedia*, which is the surest evidence of his damnation.

Macbeth's extraordinary powers of imagination[1] are not the cause of his destruction; they could not be so viewed within any meaningful moral system. It is to indicate Macbeth's strong moral feelings that Shakespeare endows his hero with ability to see all of the implications of his act in their most frightening forms before the act itself is committed. Imagination enables Macbeth emotionally to grasp the moral implications of the deed he contemplates, to participate imaginatively, as does the audience, in the full horror of the crime. Macbeth is fully aware of God's moral system with its 'even-handed justice', which 'Commends the ingredients of our poison'd chalice / To our own lips' (I.vii.10-12). His soliloquy in contemplation of Duncan's murder (I.vii.1-28) is designed to underscore his feelings of kinship with the moral order before he commits his crime.

As he prepares to enact the deed he dreads, he calls in another soliloquy for the suppression of these feelings within him. In a devilish incantation he calls for darkness and the extinction of nature, conjuring the earth itself to look aside while he violates the harmonious order of which he and it are closely related parts:

> Now o'er the one half-world
> Nature seems dead, and wicked dreams abuse
> The curtain'd sleep; witchcraft celebrates
> Pale Hecate's offerings, and wither'd murder,
> Alarum'd by his sentinel, the wolf,
> Whose howl's his watch, thus with his stealthy pace,

[1] These have been much commented on. See Bradley, *Shakespearean Tragedy*, pp. 353-6; Paul, *The Royal Play of Macbeth*, pp. 44-74; John Arthos, 'The Naive Imagination and the Destruction of Macbeth', *ELH*, XIV (1947), 114-26.

M

> With Tarquin's ravishing strides, towards his design
> Moves like a ghost. Thou sure and firm-set earth,
> Hear not my steps, which way they walk, for fear
> Thy very stones prate of my whereabout,
> And take the present horror from the time,
> Which now suits with it.   (II.i.49-60)

The figure of the wolf is appropriate, for here Macbeth allies himself with the destroyer of the innocent lamb, symbolic of God, just as he allies himself with the ravisher Tarquin, the destroyer of chastity, symbolic in the Renaissance of the perfection of God.

That Macbeth cannot say 'amen' immediately after the murder is a sign of his alienation from God. He will sleep no more, for sleep is an aspect of divine mercy which offers man escape from worldly care. Steadily Macbeth moves farther and farther from God and his fellow men, and his bond with nature is weakened. After the murder of Duncan he is committed to an unnatural course from which he cannot retreat:

> For mine own good,
> All causes shall give way: I am in blood
> Stepp'd in so far that, should I wade no more,
> Returning were as tedious as go o'er.
>   (III.iv.135-8)

He has become the centre of his own little world, for which 'all causes shall give way'. Now Macbeth is ready to seek the witches out, and their words lead him to the most horrible excess of all, the wanton murder of Macduff's family. At the beginning of the play, evil had come to Macbeth unsought; he had followed its promptings in order to attain definite ends, and not without strong misgivings. At the end he embraces evil willingly and without fear, for no other purpose than the evil act itself.

The divided mind and the fear felt by the early Macbeth were the signs of his kinship with man and God, but by the fifth act:

> I have almost forgot the taste of fears:
> The time has been, my senses would have cool'd
> To hear a night-shriek; and my fell of hair
> Would at a dismal treatise rouse and stir
> As life were in't: I have supp'd full with horrors;
> Direness, familiar to my slaughterous thoughts,
> Cannot once start me.
>   (V.v.9-15)

With the loss of human fear,[1] Macbeth must forfeit also those human qualities which make life liveable: 'that which should accompany old age, / As honour, love, obedience, troops of friends' (V.iii.24-25). There is nothing left for him but the despair of his 'To-morrow and to-morrow' speech (V.v.19-28). Even with this unwillingness to live, in itself a denial of the mercy of God, Shakespeare will not allow to Macbeth the heroic gesture of suicide which he grants to Brutus and Othello. Macbeth will not 'play the Roman fool' (V.viii.1). His spiritual destruction must be reflected in an ignominious physical destruction, and the play ends with the gruesome spectacle of the murderer's head held aloft in triumph. One man has been damned. But when we reflect upon the play in its totality we see that in spite of this there is order and meaning in the universe, that good may be reborn out of evil. We experience that feeling of reconciliation which is the ultimate test of tragedy.

[1] Macbeth's fears have been made much of by critics. For Lily B. Campbell, *Shakespeare's Tragic Heroes*, pp. 208-39, the play is a study in the pathology of fear. For H. S. Wilson, *On the Design of Shakespearian Tragedy*, p. 20, '*Macbeth* is the story of a great man who was afraid'. Macbeth's fears are significant chiefly as a dramatic device to stress his human ties, and thus to serve the larger thematic design of the play.

CHAPTER EIGHT

The Final Paradox:
Antony and Cleopatra and *Coriolanus*

❦❧❦

In *Antony and Cleopatra* and *Coriolanus* Shakespeare returned to the theme of damnation he had probed in *Timon* and *Macbeth*, but he did so with a further question. Need the destruction of man be sordid and fearful? Could there not be in an evil choice itself some heroic quality with which we instinctively sympathize? While rationally we censure a wrong moral choice which must lead to destruction, can we not emotionally second that choice, and thus participate more fully in it than ever we could in the jealousy of Othello or the ambition of Macbeth? In these final Roman plays Shakespeare probed the paradox of a road to damnation which might be heroic and awe-inspiring.

This is not to say that these plays are un-Christian, or that they exalt a pagan morality. They are based upon Christian assumptions, that lust in the one instance and pride in the other are ways to damnation. There is never any question of the evil which the hero in each play has chosen. It is nevertheless true also that in neither of these plays does Shakespeare stress the after-life or the soul's ultimate fate. We have tragic waste and loss, but the emphasis is upon the destruction of the things of this world, of glory, honour, reputation, self-esteem.[1]

We begin in each play with a hero deeply flawed, one who has already accepted an obvious and easily identifiable type of evil. Antony and Cleopatra were symbols of lustful appetite centuries before Shakespeare approached the subject. Coriolanus is a symbol

---

[1] See J. F. Danby, *Poets on Fortune's Hill* (London, 1952), p. 149. The omission of the religious dimension is deliberate, Danby holds, 'because after *King Lear* there can be no doubt that Shakespeare knew exactly where he was in these matters. Both *Antony and Cleopatra* and *Coriolanus* follow North's Plutarch without benefit of clergy.'

of pride whose operation he exemplifies in fairly traditional terms. The remarkable fact about both plays is that while Shakespeare displays the destructive power of sin, at the same time he builds up not only sympathy for the sinners, but a kind of acquiescence in the sin itself. If Cleopatra represents the lust which destroys Antony, she is also portrayed with a magnificence and adulation reflected in the eulogies of Enobarbus, and the folly of Antony is tempered by our sense of his magnanimity. If Coriolanus is hateful in his pride, that pride itself is sprung from obvious greatness, and it is the source of a heroic grandeur which is paraded before the audience in full magnificence, with the craven tribunes as foils to set it off. The destructive power of evil and the magnificence of evil are simultaneously displayed.

Because the final statement is paradox, the audience can have no such feeling of powerful affirmation as comes at the close of *Lear* or *Macbeth*.[1] Some feeling of tragic reconciliation Shakespeare nevertheless attempted to arouse. He relied in both plays upon strong audience identification with the hero, an acquiescence in the hero's sin, and a vicarious sharing in the heroic stature of his defeat. In *Antony and Cleopatra* there is a regeneration of the heroine in the final act which Shakespeare may have intended to reflect also upon the hero to whom she has become united. In *Coriolanus* the hero dies embracing his sin to the very end, but in his death there is heroic altruism and self-sacrifice, and if he is damned, at least Rome is saved.

II

In terms of a rational psychology it is difficult to make sense of Cleopatra,[2] but within the total structure of the play, her role is perfectly consistent. In the tradition which came down to Shakespeare he found a Cleopatra who could symbolize in the first four

---

[1] It may be this fact which has led some critics to find a weakness of tragic effect in these plays. Bradley refused to include them among the great tragedies. He acknowledged their mastery in poetic conception, but he found in them defects which he attributed more to their historical sources than to a decline in Shakespeare's powers. See 'Antony and Cleopatra', *Oxford Lectures on Poetry* (London, 1909), pp. 279-305; 'Coriolanus', *Proc. of the British Academy*, v (1911-12), 457-73.

[2] Levin Schücking, *Character Problems in Shakespeare's Plays*, p. 132, for instance, has argued that the harlot of the first four acts can never be reconciled with the noble queen of the final act. W. B. C. Watkins, *Shakespeare and Spenser*, p. 30, is among the very few commentators who have found 'her characterization, with its human inconsistencies, remarkably coherent from beginning to end'.

acts both the magnificence of physical beauty and the debilitating seductions of lust, and in the fifth act a self-sacrificing love. Of all the stories which descended to Shakespeare's age from classical antiquity, that of Antony and Cleopatra was one of the most often retold. To the moral Plutarch it had afforded an example of how a man's self indulgence and lack of public spirit might bring disaster to his country. A great soldier and a brilliant statesman, with the vast Roman empire resting upon his shoulders, Marc Antony had sacrificed the cause of his country in the pursuit of his own pleasures. Cleopatra had not been the cause of Antony's downfall; she had merely stirred up the vice already within him. From the very first Antony had shown an inordinate love of vice and dissipation, of which Plutarch gives ample illustration. Cleopatra, for her part, had been a prize which might well tempt a man:

> Now her beauty (as it is reported) was not so passing, as unmatchable of other women, nor yet such as upon present view did enamour men with her: but so sweet was her company and conversation, that a man could not possibly but be taken. And besides her beauty, the good grace she had to talk and discourse, her courteous nature that tempered her words and deeds, was a spur that pricked to the quick. Furthermore, besides all these, her voice and words were marvellous pleasant: for her tongue was an instrument of music to divers sports and pastimes, the which she easily turned to any language that pleased her. She spake unto few barbarous people by interpreter, but made them answer herself, or at least the most part of them . . . whose languages she had learned.[1]

Plutarch's Cleopatra, 'at the age when a woman's beauty is at the prime, and she also of best judgement' (II.38), is a creature of marvellous vitality and charm. This does not excuse Antony's defection from duty, but Plutarch, in spite of his strong moral purpose, could look upon the Egyptian queen with some degree of reverence.

As the story was told and retold by Christian moralists of the Middle Ages it began to assume a different cast. Coming down to the Renaissance we find the love of Antony and Cleopatra used as a moral *exemplum* to teach the evils of lust, with Cleopatra as the embodiment of animal lechery and Antony the drunken, prodigal fool ensnared by her duplicity, discarding an empire and damning

---

[1] *Shakespeare's Plutarch*, ed. Tucker Brooke, II. 40.

his soul.[1] In this view we no longer have Cleopatra the magnificent, but Cleopatra the devil, and her blackness, the traditional colour of the devil, is accordingly emphasized.

With this lecherous Cleopatra and Plutarch's magnificent Cleopatra there came down to Shakespeare also the tradition of Cleopatra as love's martyr, the faithful sweetheart who had followed her Antony to the other world rather than live without him. This view also was perpetuated in medieval legend. We may find it most notably in Chaucer's *Legend of Good Women*, where Cleopatra's name leads all the rest, the first of love's martyrs. The inconsistency so often seen in Cleopatra stems from the fact that Shakespeare for his larger thematic purposes drew upon three different attitudes towards Cleopatra, all of which were a part of literary tradition: (1) the symbol of lust and treachery, (2) the majestic queen, awe-inspiring in her beauty and magnificence, and (3) the faithful martyr to love who had followed Antony to the other world. A character reflecting these divergent views could not easily be rendered psychologically consistent, but all three are reconciled with one another within the larger artistic unity which is the play.

For the first four acts Shakespeare's focus is upon Antony, and here the dramatist combines a medieval with a classical view of Cleopatra. On the one hand she is a symbol of lechery, 'with Phoebus' amorous pinches black' (I.v.28), the traditional colour of lechery, as we have seen in *Titus Andronicus* and *Othello*.[2] As such she emphasizes the sinfulness and folly of Antony's infatuation. On the other hand, 'Age cannot wither her, nor custom stale / Her infinite variety' (II.ii.240-1); she is a magnificent figure, and in our admiration for her we sympathize with Antony's tragic weakness, and our sense of his own magnanimity and grandeur is heightened. For these four acts we have Antony's steady downfall, with the two motifs playing against one another, Antony's folly and Antony's magnanimity. Cleopatra is used first to emphasize the one and then the other.

At the end of the fourth act Antony has died fully embracing the cause of his downfall. The delusion that Cleopatra is dead and

[1] Franklin M. Dickey, *Not Wisely But Too Well*, pp. 159-60.

[2] In this very statement of her blackness, however, there is an indication also of her magnificence. She is the immortal lover of the sun god, Apollo, the paragon of manly beauty, as she must be of womanly beauty to merit his love. See S. L. Bethell, *Shakespeare and Popular Dramatic Tradition*, p. 127

the inefficient manner of the suicide itself accent his folly, but his forgiveness of Cleopatra and his dying concern for her welfare again assert his magnanimity. Although he dies on this heroic note, there is no regeneration in Antony's death, no victory over the force which has destroyed him. Such regeneration Shakespeare tried to portray in Cleopatra, and in order to do this he had to cast her in a new role. In the final act she is no longer the symbol of Antony's vice; she is now herself the centre of attention. Her regeneration comes in a movement from sinful lust to self-sacrificing love. This is the substance of the fifth act, and for it Shakespeare availed himself of the third tradition in which the story of the lovers had come down to him, that of Chaucer's 'love's martyr' who had followed Antony to the grave rather than live without him.

In this sense *Antony and Cleopatra* is two plays in one. For four acts it is a portrait of a great man's self-destruction through devotion to a sin which is itself heroic and magnificent. In the fifth act[1] it is a portrait of a great queen's awareness of sinful lust, her casting it off, and her dedication of herself instead to a love to which her death is a sacrifice in expiation for former sin. The final feeling of the audience is not one of sordidness; rather it is one of the grandeur and nobility of triumphant love. But whatever triumph Antony and Cleopatra may achieve is in defiance of the Christian moral order, and that we should emotionally share in this sense of triumph while we perceive that it is rooted in sin is a reflection of the paradox which this play in its totality embodies.

III

With the opening lines of the play we know that Antony is already a fallen hero, shameful to his lieutenants, Demetrius and Philo, by his own abdication from his former greatness:

> Nay, but this dotage of our general's
> O'erflows the measure: those his goodly eyes,
> That o'er the files and musters of the war
> Have glow'd like plated Mars, now bend, now turn,
> The office and devotion of their view

[1] This final act covers the ground to which Samuel Daniel had devoted all of his *Cleopatra* of 1594, a play with which it is virtually certain that Shakespeare was familiar. See Kenneth Muir, *Shakespeare's Sources*, I, 209-215; Willard Farnham, *Shakespeare's Tragic Frontier*, p. 157; A. M. Z. Norman, 'Daniel's *The Tragedie of Cleopatra* and *Antony and Cleopatra*', *SQ*, IX (1958), 11-18.

> Upon a tawny front: his captain's heart,
> Which in the scuffles of great fights hath burst
> The buckles on his breast, reneges all temper,
> And is become the bellows and the fan
> To cool a gipsy's lust.
>
> (I.i.1-10)

He now 'reneges all temper', abandons his normal heroic qualities.
The cause of his defection is a 'tawny front', a woman not beautiful, who in her darkness of complexion symbolizes lechery. Gipsy
is used in the double sense of Egyptian and harlot. Philo presents
the typical medieval view of the evil seductress Cleopatra and the
Antony who is now 'The triple pillar of the world transformed /
Into a strumpet's fool' (I.i.11-12).

When Antony enters leaning upon the arm of Cleopatra, the
audience is shocked and dismayed by his effeminate servility, but
no sooner does he speak than the note of grandeur and magnanimity enters: 'There's beggary in the love that can be reckon'd'
(I.i.15). It is an enfeebling love which makes the strong man subject to the shrill mocking taunts of Cleopatra and which leads him
to neglect his duty to the great Roman empire, but we admire
nevertheless the magnanimity which scorns to measure passion's
cost. This magnanimity is again reflected in the powerful lines
with which Antony expresses his unconcern for the messengers
from Rome:

> Let Rome in Tiber melt, and the wide arch
> Of the ranged empire fall! Here is my space.
> Kingdoms are clay: our dungy earth alike
> Feeds beast as man: the nobleness of life
> Is to do thus; when such a mutual pair
> And such a twain can do't, in which I bind,
> On pain of punishment, the world to weet
> We stand up peerless.
>
> (I.i.33-40)

Here the two motifs are neatly juxtaposed. The worldly magnificence of the 'ranged empire' which Antony scorns is evoked for
us, and at the same time we see the sinful folly which negates the
difference between man and beast. Rationally we perceive that in
rejecting 'the ranged empire' Antony is setting himself on the level
of the beast with whom he shares the dungy earth. But the magnanimity of such rejection overwhelms this feeling, and although

we may gasp at Antony's folly, we admire him only the more: 'His taints and honours / Waged equal with him' (V.i.30-31).

Since Antony is fallen when the action opens, we can have no struggle between good and evil for his soul, as we have in *Othello*. His particular sin can evoke for Antony no such horror as the prospect of Macbeth's crime evokes. Antony, unlike Othello but like Macbeth, is always aware of his own sin, and he can from the first perceive its consequences: 'These strong Egyptian fetters I must break, / Or lose myself in dotage' (I.ii.120-1). Shakespeare endows him with a moral sense. Antony knows that he should break his Egyptian fetters, but he knows also that he can never break them, and it is part of his grandeur that he accepts his sin with full awareness of what its final cost must be. When the shirt of Nessus is upon him, he rails upon himself and upon Cleopatra, but this is merely a part of the suffering which he must undergo, and his wildest outcries of shame and despair lead him always to a willing reunion with Cleopatra, the source of his sin, but also his only solace.

Antony is enthralled by the magnificent Cleopatra who holds him in bondage, but he sees also the scheming seducer, 'cunning past man's thought' (I.ii.150). His full awareness of this side of her breaks forth when, in the face of his imminent defeat, he sees her treacherous dalliance with Caesar's lieutenant:

> You have been a boggler ever:
> But when we in our viciousness grow hard –
> O misery on't! – the wise gods seel our eyes;
> In our own filth drop our clear judgements; make us
> Adore our errors; laugh at's, while we strut
> To our confusion.
> .   .   .   .
> I found you as a morsel cold upon
> Dead Caesar's trencher; nay, you were a fragment
> Of Cneius Pompey's; besides what hotter hours,
> Unregister'd in vulgar fame, you have
> Luxuriously pick'd out: for, I am sure,
> Though you can guess what temperance should be,
> You know not what it is.
>
>   (III.xiii.110-22)

But even this outburst is followed by the inevitable reconciliation both to love and to dissipation:

Do so, we'll speak to them; and to-night I'll force
The wine peep through their scars. Come on, my queen;
There's sap in't yet. The next time I do fight,
I'll make death love me; for I will contend
Even with his pestilent scythe.   (III.xiii.190-4)

We see the evil seductive side of Cleopatra in her taunting of
Antony (I.iii), in her lascivious dallying with her maids and eunuch
(I.v, etc.), in her beating of the messenger from Rome (II.v), and
in her flirtation with Caesar's lieutenant (III.xiii), but her beauty
and magnificence are held also before us, largely through Enobarbus. His description of her passage down the river Cydnus
(II.ii.295-323) is too familiar to need repetition. The sentiments of
the audience are reflected in Agrippa's 'O, rare for Antony' (II.ii.
210) and his 'Rare Egyptian' (II.ii.224), and we agree with Enobarbus when he tells us why Antony can never leave her:

                              Never; he will not:
Age cannot wither her, nor custom stale
Her infinite variety: other women cloy
The appetites they feed; but she makes hungry
Where most she satisfies: for vilest things
Become themselves in her; that the holy priests
Bless her when she is riggish.

                                        (II.ii.239-45)

But in this very eulogy Shakespeare reminds us also of her powers
of intrigue; she can use her sensual appeal for insidious purposes:

                                        Royal wench!
She made great Caesar lay his sword to bed:
He plough'd her, and she cropp'd.

                                        (II.ii.231-3)

The magnificent Cleopatra is never entirely separate from the
scheming harlot until her final renunciation in the fifth act of her
baser nature in a selfless sacrifice to love.

The alliance with Octavius Caesar and the marriage to Octavia
are Antony's attempts to break his Egyptian fetters. That these
efforts must be futile has been implicit from the play's beginning.
Antony must 'to his Egyptian dish again' (II.vi.134). With his
return to Egypt his decline is accelerated, but always the twin
motifs of folly and magnanimity are kept before the audience.
Antony's end is mirrored in his decision to fight Octavius by sea.

Here he is cast as a kind of morality hero. On the one side Enobarbus and the old soldier urge him to fight on land, as common
sense demands; on the other side Cleopatra, with the voice of
folly, seconds his decision to fight by sea. That this is an abdication of reason is made clear by Enobarbus:

> Most worthy sir, you therein throw away
> The absolute soldiership you have by land;
> Distract your army, which doth most consist
> Of war-mark'd footmen; leave unexecuted
> Your own renowned knowledge; quite forego
> The way which promises assurance; and
> Give up yourself merely to chance and hazard,
> From firm security.   (III.vii.42-49)

It is Antony's abandonment of all which has made him great as a
soldier. He does not deny the folly of the move, but in the very
foolish reason which he asserts, 'For that he dares us to't' (III.
vii.30), there is a quality which wins for Antony a large measure of
sympathy as a man, while we know that he is dooming his own
army to defeat. Cleopatra shares both in Antony's grandeur and
his folly by her endorsement, 'By sea! what else?' (III.vii.29), as
though no other course were thinkable.

IV

We have already noted Enobarbus in his role as dramatic chorus.
He has further functions as well, for his own tragedy serves to
heighten that of his master, and at the same time to point up the
grandeur and folly which Antony reflects. His desertion of Antony
stems from a clear-headed, rational appraisal of the hero's conduct.
His had been the voice of reason from the very beginning. He had
at once seen the results of the marriage to Octavia (II.vi.133-9).
When Cleopatra asks him after the defeat at sea, 'Is Antony or we
in fault for this?' his reply is a just appraisal of Antony's folly:
'Antony only, that would make his will / Lord of his reason' (III.
xiii.3-4). His decision to desert is prompted by reason:

> Mine honesty and I begin to square.
> The loyalty well held to fools does make
> Our faith mere folly: yet he that can endure
> To follow with allegiance a fall'n lord
> Does conquer him that did his master conquer,
> And earns a place i' the story.   (III.xiii.41-46)

Here he is wavering, sustained in his loyalty only by the greatness of heart which is also part of his make-up, and which reflects the similar greatness of Antony. But reason finally prevails:

> when valour preys on reason,
> It eats the sword it fights with. I will seek
> Some way to leave him.
>
> (III.xiii.199-201)

But this desertion arouses in Antony only a magnificent display of magnanimity; he sends Enobarbus' treasure after him. This touches not the rational Enobarbus, but the man of feeling:

> I am alone the villain of the earth,
> And feel I am so most. O Antony,
> Thou mine of bounty, how wouldst thou have paid
> My better service, when my turpitude
> Thou dost so crown with gold! This blows my heart:
> If swift thought break it not, a swifter mean
> Shall outstrike thought: but thought will do't, I feel.
> I fight against thee! No: I will go seek
> Some ditch wherein to die; the foul'st best fits
> My latter part of life.
>
> (IV.vi.30-39)

We grieve that so noble a soul as Enobarbus should die thinking himself a traitor unworthy to live. His death not only affirms the greatness of Antony in spite of all, but also it heightens our sense of the tragic consequences of Antony's folly. For Rome in the abstract we can have little real feeling, but Enobarbus we have come to know and love.

Octavius and Octavia together stand for a cold, rational morality which the audience may intellectually approve, but which emotionally it must reject as lacking the warmth and vitality of the immoral and foolish Antony and Cleopatra. Octavius represents the necessity of empire. To the forward march of an expanding Rome he will sacrifice everything, including his own humanity. Such a man is impervious to the attractions of Cleopatra. Octavia represents a private morality whose signs are chastity and loyalty. She is good, beautiful, and truly loving to Antony. With her he might have gotten 'a lawful race, / And by a gem of women' (III. xiii.107-8). Octavius in his victory attains what Antony casts away, and Octavia represents an ideal of womanhood against which the abandonment of Cleopatra to unlawful passion may be measured. They are victorious, but the emotional impact of the play emphasizes the hollowness of their victory. Who would be Octavius in spite of all, if he could be Antony? If Octavia has the knowledge of her virtue to sustain her, she is also abandoned, unloved, and alone. Her modesty and 'chaste conversation' are admirable in the abstract, but beside the vitality of Cleopatra she is an unappealing figure, and emotionally no audience can fail to second Antony in his desire to leave her, much as we may recognize the sin of such desertion, and much as we sorrow for Octavia's unfortunate plight.

Octavius Caesar reminds us that *Antony and Cleopatra* is a political tragedy as well as a personal one; the lovers are destroyed not only by their own sins, but by the force of political necessity to which these sins are opposed.[1] As Octavius stands for an expanding Rome and the monarchic ideal, we have as a theme of the play the conflict between world empire and human love. The sensual and wasteful opulence of the East is opposed to the cold, bare efficiency of the West. Egypt stands for passion and human weakness, Rome for duty and self-denial: the world of sense against the world of reason. The love of Antony and Cleopatra cannot prevail against the power of Octavius. We recognize the justice of Rome's victory, but emotionally we regret such victory. Octavius at the end of the play has indeed attained the mastery of the world, but Shakespeare leaves us also with the feeling that this world, in spite of its far reaching magnificence, is small and insignificant. To further this impression Shakespeare uses the meeting on Pompey's barge and the campaign of Ventidius in Parthia.

The feeling of the world's magnitude is sustained by the poetic imagery, with navies sailing the seas, armies marching over vast expanses, and a rapidly changing locale in the brief shifting scenes to further the sense of vastness and movement. But while Shakespeare shows us the magnitude of what Antony abandons and Octavius wins, he also shows us its smallness and insignificance. On Pompey's barge we see the pillars of this world merely as drunken revellers, and the world for which they struggle subject to a single stroke of a pirate's knife. We are drawn to Antony in his sacrifice of this world. His good-natured magnanimity lends attraction to what otherwise might be a very sordid episode, and

---

[1] See Lord David Cecil, *Poets and Storytellers* (London, 1949), pp. 3-24; J. E Phillips, *The State in Shakespeare's Greek and Roman Plays*, pp. 188-205.

our renewed affection for him is heightened by our sense of the smallness of those to whom he stands opposed.

The Menas-Pompey relationship parallels the relation of Enobarbus to Antony.[1] Pompey, like Antony, has a certain magnanimity. He will not knowingly betray his honour for the entire world, and Menas deserts him for his folly (II.vii.87-90). Antony and Pompey each throw away a chance to rule the world, but Antony attains heroic stature in his failure, while Pompey comes to naught. The difference is that Antony has magnanimously devoted himself to an immoral end which is itself heroic, whereas Pompey succumbs to a small sense of morality which, like the 'reputation' of Iago, is implicit only in outward appearance:

> Ah, this thou shouldst have done,
> And not have spoke on't! In me 'tis villainy;
> In thee't had been good service. Thou must know,
> 'Tis not my profit that does lead mine honour;
> Mine honour, it. Repent that e'er thy tongue
> Hath so betray'd thine act: being done unknown,
> I should have found it afterwards well done;
> But must condemn it now.
>
> (II.vii.79-86)

Such a morality has no grandeur or magnificence. We know that Menas in his coming desertion will never suffer the remorse which comes to Enobarbus. Pompey's cause, unlike Antony's, is lost without a compensating gain of any sort.

Plutarch (II.49-53) had described the defeat of the Parthians with the note that 'Ventidius durst not undertake to follow them any further, fearing lest he should have gotten Antonius's displeasure by it'. The reason for such possible displeasure is Shakespeare's own:

> Caesar and Antony have ever won
> More in their officer than person: Sossius,
> One of my place in Syria, his lieutenant,
> For quick accumulation of renown,
> Which he achieved by the minute, lost his favour.
> Who does i' the wars more than his captain can
> Becomes his captain's captain: and ambition,
> The soldier's virtue, rather makes choice of loss,
> Than gain which darkens him.

---

[1] See Brents Stirling, *Unity in Shakespearian Tragedy*, p. 170.

I could do more to do Antonius good,
But 'twould offend him; and in his offence
Should my performance perish.

(III.i.16-27)

The speech is Shakespeare's satiric commentary on the hollowness
and insignificance of the world; the soldier will damage his country's cause to please the vanity of his general. Coming immediately
after the barge scene, this portrait of the soldier in action serves
also to emphasize the contrasting pettiness of those who rule the
world.

The episode further underscores the wide-reaching effects of
Antony's dereliction of duty. His lieutenant fears to accomplish
more than his general, and thus he neglects the chance of a magnificent victory for his country. Caesar's lieutenant, Shakespeare
tells us, would have acted in accord with the same principle.
Antony's own shortcomings are made responsible for the loss
of further triumph in Parthia, and thus these shortcomings are
thrown into larger retrospect, while at the same time, in the futility of the Parthian campaign is shown the insignificance of the
world of politics and conquest which Antony rejects. Shakespeare
simultaneously reveals the far-reaching consequences of Antony's
folly and gives us a sense of the world's insignificance which wins
a measure of sympathy for that folly.

V

As Antony moves towards his destruction, we feel his own pain
with a steadily mounting intensity. He cannot bear to think that
he has 'offended reputation, / A most unnoble swerving' (III.xi.
48-49). We share his anguish as he dwells on his own former greatness and on the contrasting smallness of Octavius who has defeated him:

he at Philippi kept
His sword e'en like a dancer; while I struck
The lean and wrinkled Cassius; and 'twas I
That the mad Brutus ended: he alone
Dealt on lieutenantry, and no practice had
In the brave squares of war: yet now – No matter.

(III.xi.35-40)

He sees Cleopatra as the cause of his downfall, and with his final
military defeat he turns upon her utterly:

Vanish, or I shall give thee thy deserving,
And blemish Caesar's triumph. Let him take thee,
And hoist thee up to the shouting plebeians:
Follow his chariot, like the greatest spot
Of all thy sex; most monster-like, be shown
For poor'st diminutives, for doits; and let
Patient Octavia plough thy visage up
With her prepared nails.
                                    'Tis well thou'rt gone,
If it be well to live: but better 'twere
Thou fell'st into my fury, for one death
Might have prevented many. Eros, ho!
The shirt of Nessus is upon me: teach me,
Alcides, thou mine ancestor, thy rage:
Let me lodge Lichas on the horns o' the moon;
And with those hands, that grasp'd the heaviest club,
Subdue my worthiest self. The witch shall die:
To the young Roman boy she hath sold me, and I fall
Under this plot; she dies for't. Eros, ho!

                                    (IV.xii.32-49)

The sense of loss is now so great that it overwhelms even his
passion for Cleopatra, which had reconciled him always to his
own sinful defection. At this point the audience may expect that
he will renounce the passion which has destroyed him. When,
however, he hears the lying report that Cleopatra has slain herself,
he prepares to die embracing fully the source of his ruin:

I will o'ertake thee, Cleopatra, and
Weep for my pardon. So it must be, for now
All length is torture: since the torch is out,
Lie down, and stray no farther: now all labour
Mars what it does; yea, very force entangles
Itself with strength: seal then, and all is done.
Eros! – I come, my queen: – Eros! – Stay for me:
Where souls do couch on flowers, we'll hand in hand,
And with our sprightly port make the ghosts gaze:
Dido and her Aeneas shall want troops,
And all the haunt be ours.

                                    (IV.xiv.44-54)

It is to the treacherous Cleopatra, practising a desperate and deceitful stratagem, that Antony dedicates his life. That he will walk
'where souls do couch on flowers' is part of his delusion. The

N

bungling inefficient manner of his suicide emphasizes only further the ironic folly of it all. Antony dies still the 'strumpet's fool' he had been at the play's beginning.

This folly, however, is tempered by his magnanimity in the monument scene where Antony dies in Cleopatra's arms. His greatness of heart permits him to forgive Cleopatra, and his dying concern is only for her safety. Even here Cleopatra is still the selfish cause of his destruction, for when Antony dying asks that he may, 'Of many thousand kisses the poor last / I lay upon thy lips' (IV.xv. 20-21), this last symbol of union she refuses out of concern for her own safety:

> I dare not, dear, –
> Dear my lord, pardon, – I dare not,
> Lest I be taken.
>
> (IV.xv.21-23)

Only after Antony's death does Cleopatra begin to rise to the spiritual height which will reshape her character in the final act.

There is in Antony's death no rejection of the sin which has destroyed him. He is from first to last a composite of sinful folly and heroic magnanimity. The sorrow we feel for him is a kind of emotional rejection of the moral order which we know demands his death. 'The gods rebuke me,' says Octavius as he weeps at the news, 'but it is tidings / To wash the eye of kings' (V.i.27-28). The paradox of the play is implicit in the rejoinder of Agrippa: 'And strange it is, / That nature must compel us to lament / Our most persisted deeds' (V.i.28-30).

The final act is concerned with Cleopatra's regeneration, her rejection of lust and her acceptance of a love which is all giving and self-sacrifice. In this act she becomes for the first time a tragic figure. In the manner of Othello or Macbeth, but not of Antony, she is torn between opposing forces. On the one hand is the urge for self-preservation. She has used her female charms on Pompey, Caesar and Antony; she can now reassert her customary role and conquer Octavius, or at least make the effort. This would be an affirmation of the lust and deceit which she has for four acts represented. On the other hand she may now abandon what she has been, and in a gesture of self-sacrificing love attain a new heroic stature and a victory over the force which has destroyed both her and Antony.

Between these two poles Cleopatra moves back and forth until love finally triumphs. Cleopatra instinctively shrinks from the necessity of following Antony to the grave; she struggles for her life even while she longs to die. This adds to the illusion of reality in her characterization; and it is part of the conflict which makes of her a tragic figure. In Cleopatra's raging at Seleucis we are reminded of her earlier beating of the messenger from Rome, and thus we see that the earlier Cleopatra is still much a part of her, and that against this she must struggle before her regeneration is possible.

Cleopatra's initial impulse to die had come at the close of the fourth act, immediately upon the death of Antony:

> Noblest of men, woo't die?
> Hast thou no care of me? Shall I abide
> In this dull world, which in thy absence is
> No better than a sty?
>
> (IV.xv.59-62)

She now has 'no friend / But resolution and the briefest end' (IV. xv.90-91). She will 'do that thing that ends all other deeds; / Which shackles accidents and bolts up change' (V.ii.5-6). But the impulse to self-preservation is also strong within her, and Shakespeare shows the conflict of these opposing forces.

As the fifth act progresses Cleopatra's determination to die grows stronger and receives the fuller poetic emphasis. She has already so decided before she is disarmed by Porculeius and faced with the threat of a Roman triumph. This merely enforces a resolution already made. Cleopatra's opposing impulse to self-preservation, so necessary for the tragic conflict, appears in the Seleucis episode, in her use of Dolabella, and in the momentary flirtation with Octavius implicit in her 'Master, and my lord!' to be rebuffed only by Caesar's blunt 'Not so, Adieu' (V.ii.190). These are necessary interruptions in the movement of the act which leads steadily to a willing self-destruction, not to avoid the Roman triumph – although the illusion of Cleopatra's humanity is heightened by her need for this final impulse of fear to drive her towards the end she wishes but still dreads – but to unite her soul to Antony's.

Wearing her crown for the last time, and with her regal robes around her, she rises at the last to a new spiritual height:

Give me my robe, put on my crown; I have
Immortal longings in me: now no more
The juice of Egypt's grape shall moist this lip:
Yare, yare, good Iras; quick. Methinks I hear
Antony call; I see him rouse himself
To praise my noble act; I hear him mock
The luck of Caesar, which the gods give men
To excuse their after wrath: husband I come:
Now to that name my courage prove my title!
I am fire and air; my other elements
I give to baser life.

                                                    (V.ii.282-93)

It is to her husband that she comes, and this is the first time in the
play that she so calls him. The speech is one of self-sacrifice in
spite of fear, a casting off of all which she has been. Her end, as
Charmian tells the audience, 'is well done, and fitting for a prin-
cess / Descended of so many royal kings' (V.ii.329-30). We are
reminded at the end of her regality. Upon this note of royal triumph she dies, and in her death she attains a new nobility and a
victory over Caesar's world. Hers is the redeeming *peripeteia*, and
it is possible that Shakespeare intended this to suggest a kind of
redemption for Antony as well. To such a feeling our emotions
urge us, although we know that Antony has in no way rejected
his sin like Cleopatra.

The play is a powerful and moving experience, but in its intellectual statement it confirms only a paradox: that in a sinful path
to destruction there may be a heroic grandeur which assures the
sinner a kind of triumph in spite of all, that the public spirit of an
Octavius and the private morality of an Octavia may seem small
and insignificant in the light of such heroic destruction, and that
the great world and its moral order may at times seem scarcely
worth the preservation.

VI

In *Coriolanus* Shakespeare returned to the paradox already faintly
sketched in Octavius of the earlier play: a man so devoted to a
public ideal as to exclude all of the human feelings which had led
to Antony's fall, and thus ultimately to deny his own nature as a
man.[1] Coriolanus is far nobler than his forerunner, for there is

---

[1] If *Antony and Cleopatra* was completed in 1607, as seems fairly certain, *Coriolanus*
must have followed sometime between 1608 and 1610. See Chambers, *William
Shakespeare*, I, 475-6, 479-80; MacCallum, *Shakespeare's Roman Plays*, p. 462.

about him none of the self-seeking craft and guile of Octavius. He is straightforward and honest; the ideal to which he devotes himself, and of which he is dramatic symbol, is a glorious and heroic one, as consuming patriotism often may be, and as particularly in the Renaissance it might be regarded. But the virtuous path of Coriolanus is as surely the way of his destruction as the sinful path of Antony is the cause of his, and we are left at the end with a similar paradox: that the way of public dedication may be the way of public ruin and personal damnation. Antony and Coriolanus are equally damned for contrary reasons; Antony in his destruction attains heroic stature, and Coriolanus is partly redeemed by a spontaneous welling up within him of a human affection which is, in turn, the immediate cause of his death.

There is no moral choice for the hero, for the play opens with Coriolanus, like Antony, already committed to the way of life which will be his destruction. He is an embodiment of the aristocratic ideal, noble, generous to his friends, a fearless warrior, devoted utterly to the good of Rome. As an aristocrat he is always aware both of the gulf which separates him from the common man and of the paramount importance of his personal honour. This aristocratic ideal the Elizabethans could appreciate in a manner of which we, with our opposing democratic and egalitarian traditions, are often incapable, and this is why it is so important to see this play within the historical context of the age in which it was written.

But the aristocratic ideal, virtuous as it may be, involves a separation of man from man and thus a denial of those human affections which link all of humanity in spite of social rank. It leads at last to the sin of pride. Coriolanus, like the earlier Titus Andronicus, acts from motives which are themselves great and noble, but in whose very nobility evil is implicit. Out of his goodness springs his vice, and this vice, in turn, breeds his virtue.

In theological terms pride involved a rejection of the supremacy of God, and as its corollary a denial of one's own nature as a man – of those very human feelings which Antony and Cleopatra had exalted beyond reason to their own destruction. One of the best descriptions of pride, as the Renaissance conceived of it, is found in *The French Academy* of Pierre de la Primaudaye. Here is described that alienation from humanity which is its cardinal symptom:

And indeede God hath made man of a mild and communicable
nature, apt to societie, and to liue with companie not solitarily, as
sauage beastes vse to doe. Therefore there is nothing more contrarie
to his nature, and to that ende for which he was created, then this
vicious pride, whereby he is so puffed up and swelleth in such sort,
as if he were of some other nature and condition than humane, and
as though he meant to liue in some other estate and degree then of
man.[1]

This is not to say that Shakespeare had read *The French Academy*.
It is simply that La Primaudaye describes certain common human
qualities which in the Renaissance were encompassed by the theological concept of pride, and to which Coriolanus in a large measure conforms.

He is a great hero who embodies the aristocratic ideal, but he
would deny his common humanity and 'live in some other estate
and degree then of man'. These two sides of Coriolanus are held in
constant juxtaposition, like the folly and magnanimity of Antony.
The other characters serve primarily to illustrate first the one facet
of Coriolanus and then the other. The hero never wavers from the
ideal to which he is initially committed, although his decision to
seek the consulship involves a momentary flirtation with a way of
life to which he stands opposed. It recalls Antony's decision to
marry Octavia, and it can lead only to similar disaster.

Coriolanus pursues a steady downward course which culminates in his expulsion from Rome and his consequent delusion that
Rome must be destroyed in retribution for the supposed wrongs
it has done to him. His sinful side destroys in him those very
elements of greatness, centred in his devotion to Rome, out of
which his pride itself had sprung. Rome for her sins, as he sees it,
has merited destruction. Like Othello as he murders Desdemona,
Coriolanus sees his crime as an act of justice. To spare Rome
would be weakness, a desertion of the duty with which he regards
himself as charged. Pride has coloured the worst of sins so that
it appears to him as virtuous. When his mother, wife and child
appear – those natural symbols of man's bond with humanity – he
steels himself with the thought that duty and honour (the aristocratic virtues) exceed the claims of all human ties:

> My wife comes foremost; then the honour'd mould
> Wherein this trunk was framed, and in her hand

[1] *The Second Part of the French Academy*, trans. by T. B. (London, 1594), p. 330.

The grandchild to her blood. But, out, affection!
All bond and privilege of nature, break!
Let it be virtuous to be obstinate.
What is that curt'sy worth? or those doves' eyes,
Which can make gods forsworn? I melt, and am not
Of stronger earth than others. My mother bows;
As if Olympus to a molehill should
In supplication nod: and my young boy
Hath an aspect of intercession, which
Great nature cries 'Deny not'. Let the Volsces
Plough Rome, and harrow Italy: I'll never
Be such a gosling to obey instinct, but stand,
As if a man were author of himself
And knew no other kin.

                                        (V.iii.22-37)

The opposing forces in the play are in this speech neatly displayed; on the one hand the ties of nature (the bond which Cordelia had asserted) and on the other a sense of duty (already perverted by its negation of that bond) which asserts itself by a denial of man's subjection to God and his tie to humanity: Coriolanus would 'stand, / As if a man were author of himself / And knew no other kin'. But at this point, with his alienation from humanity destroying the very virtue inherent in the aristocratic ideal, the human feelings within him, which in spite of himself he cannot utterly deny, 'affection' and 'instinct', emerge in spite of all, and this emergence must breed his own death. Volumnia prevails by her evocation of the natural affections, and Coriolanus, in spite of himself, sacrifices his life to the bonds of human affection, and through them to the preservation of Rome, for the two ends are seen at last as closely interwoven. Coriolanus knows that his decision to spare Rome must also mean his own death:

                    O mother, mother!
What have you done? Behold, the heavens do ope,
The gods look down, and this unnatural scene
They laugh at. O my mother, mother! O!
You have won a happy victory to Rome;
But, for your son, – believe it, O, believe it,
Most dangerously you have with him prevail'd,
If not most mortal to him.

                                        (V.iii.182-9)

This is not a renunciation of sin by Coriolanus. In his delusion he sees his yielding to his mother as the sinful act, as a denial of the duty and justice by which he has lived.

When he returns to the camp of the Volscians he is still blinded by pride, hoping for praise from his allies for his betrayal of their cause, as full of his own righteousness as ever:

> Hail, lords! I am return'd your soldier,
> No more infected with my country's love
> Than when I parted hence, but still subsisting
> Under your great command.
>
> (V.vi.71-74)

And he recounts the supposed triumphs he has won for the Volscians. That he is still the soldier of his enemies is Shakespeare's reminder that Coriolanus is still the victim of his pride. His behaviour in the enemy camp parallels closely that in Rome which had led to his banishment. The taunting of Coriolanus by Aufidius corresponds to his earlier baiting by the tribunes in the market place of Rome, and he reacts to it in the same manner, breaking forth in the violence which must assure his death. He will not acknowledge the treachery which has been his mark since first he left Rome, treachery first to his own country and now to the Volscians. He dies as firm as ever in his own blind sense of righteousness, glorying to the last in his personal renown:

> Cut me to pieces, Volsces; men and lads,
> Stain all your edges on me. Boy! false hound!
> If you have writ your annals true, 'tis there,
> That, like an eagle in a dove-cote, I
> Flutter'd your Volscians in Corioli:
> Alone I did it. Boy!
>
> (V.vi.112-17)

The 'alone' is emphasized in his death, and there is pathetic irony, for the audience knows that the future will not read of him primarily as the conqueror of Corioli, but rather as the man who turned against his country and brought it almost to destruction.

The decision to spare Rome is a momentary triumph of a deep-seated tie with humanity inherent in the very nature of man; this even Coriolanus cannot entirely destroy. In the realization of the power of this inescapable humanity the audience may experience some of the reconciliation essential to the tragic experience. There is some attempt by Shakespeare to assert a moral order to which the very nature of man contributes. But this is not the kind of affirmation we have in *King Lear* or *Macbeth*, for the paradox remains: that in the noblest attributes of man may be an inherent evil which can overcome the nobility from which it springs, that justice, valour, and public dedication may lead the commonwealth to the brink of destruction, and that it may be saved instead by an unthinking emotional response to the basic impulses of humanity.[1]

VII

Both the aristocratic virtue of Coriolanus and the evil of his alienation from humanity are revealed in the battle scenes before Corioli. Three generals are shown in action: the hero, Cominius, and Titus Lartius, the other two being used to reflect the twin aspects of Coriolanus which Shakespeare wishes to make clear. Two divisions attack the city, the one under Cominius and the other under the joint command of Coriolanus and Titus Lartius. Both divisions fight bravely, but both are driven back. Cominius reveals the attitude of a great general, aware like an earlier Henry V of the human bonds which link him to his men:

> Breathe you, my friends: well fought, we are come off
> Like Romans, neither foolish in our stands,
> Nor cowardly in retire: believe me, Sirs,
> We shall be charged again.
>
> (I.vi.1-4)

This speech throws into fuller light the opposing attitude of Coriolanus, hungry only for victory and personal renown, and cut off from any fellowship with those he leads; they are not his 'friends'. His negation of his human bonds is implicit in the curses which he hurls at his men who have suffered similar defeat:

> All the contagion of the south light on you,
> You shames of Rome! you herd of – Boils and plagues
> Plaster you o'er, that you may be abhorr'd
> Further than seen and one infect another
> Against the wind a mile!
>
> (I.iv.30-34)

---

[1] Hermann Heuer, 'From Plutarch to Shakespeare: A Study of *Coriolanus*', *Shakespeare Survey 10* (Cambridge, 1957), pp. 50-59, traces the evolution of the story from Plutarch through Shakespeare and notes that North's version poses also an 'inexplicable paradox'.

Coriolanus achieves his victory, but it is a solitary one. The closing of the gates of Corioli behind him is a symbolic reminder of his separation from his soldiers and from humanity. His feat alone within the city walls is stupendous in its heroism and magnificence, and this Titus Lartius is used to underscore:

> O noble fellow!
> Who sensibly outdares his senseless sword,
> And, when it bows, stands up. Thou art left, Marcius:
> A carbuncle entire, as big as thou art,
> Were not so rich a jewel.
>
> (I.iv.52-56)

Thus simultaneously are portrayed the magnificence of the hero's victory and also the alienation from humanity implicit in those very things which make his victory so great. Coriolanus must always be the solitary fighter. He can never be a great general.[1] In the very greatness of his military prowess are the roots of military inadequacy, and this is true as well of every other aspect of his life.

His rejection of the well-meant praises of Titus and Cominius emphasizes again both the greatness of Coriolanus and his alienation from his fellow men. There is contempt for man in the self-sufficiency which makes him reject as base flattery the praises which come from Titus and Cominius in the openness of their hearts and in an awesome appreciation of his achievements:

> May these same instruments, which you profane,
> Never sound more! when drums and trumpets shall
> I' the field prove flatterers, let courts and cities be
> Made all of false-faced soothing!
> When steel grows soft as the parasite's silk,
> Let him be made an overture for the wars!
> No more, I say! For that I have not wash'd
> My nose that bled, or foil'd some debile wretch, –
> Which, without note, here's many else have done, –
> You shout me forth
> In acclamations hyperbolical;
> As if I loved my little should be dieted
> In praises sauced with lies.
>
> (I.ix.41-53)

---

[1] See P. A Jorgensen, 'Shakespeare's Coriolanus: Elizabethan Soldier', *PMLA*, XLIV (1949), 221-35. Granville-Barker, *Prefaces to Shakespeare*, II, 151, contrasts Coriolanus with Antony in this respect.

This is not mere modesty; there is something far stronger in the connotations of 'profane', 'false-faced soothing', 'lies'. The rejection of human comradeship in the lines is fully perceived by Cominius:

> Too modest are you;
> More cruel to your good report than grateful
> To us that give you truly: by your patience,
> If 'gainst yourself you be incensed, we'll put you
> Like one that means his proper harm, in manacles,
> Then reason safely with you.
>
> (I.ix.53-58)

There is a perfect epitome both of the hero's grandeur and his vice in the little episode – altered from Plutarch – following the victory, when after refusing the lavish gifts of Cominius, Coriolanus pleads for the life of a Volscian who has been taken prisoner.

> I sometime lay here in Corioli
> At a poor man's house; he used me kindly:
> He cried to me; I saw him prisoner;
> But then Aufidius was within my view,
> And wrath o'erwhelm'd my pity: I request you
> To give my poor host freedom.
>
> (I.ix.82-87)

He is not a poor man in Plutarch; Shakespeare makes this change to further reveal the redeeming grandeur of his hero. But when Coriolanus is asked the name of the man who has so befriended him, he has already forgotten it:

> By Jupiter! forgot.
> I am weary; yea, my memory is tired.
> Have we no wine here?
>
> (I.ix.90-92)

His magnanimous impulse is destroyed and vitiated by his alienation from humanity. Just as his wrath had o'erwhelmed his pity, it is now o'erwhelmed by an essential unconcern. He has forgotten his friend's name, and he turns to other things without an effort to remember.

VIII

Like the earlier Roman plays, *Coriolanus* is rich in political implications. As the hero destroys himself he brings the state also to
the verge of destruction.[1] The political issues in the play emphasize the ethical paradox which is its theme. They give to *Coriolanus*
a wider range, as they do to *Antony and Cleopatra*, but in both these
plays the essential questions involve not political forces, but the
forces of good and evil within the soul of man. The political tragedy of *Coriolanus* is that the hero's negation of the bonds of
humanity makes him incapable of accepting the normal relation of
ruler to ruled which was the political creed of Shakespeare's age,
and which all of his history plays affirm. This was a position of
power tempered by responsibility. Coriolanus attempts to assume
the role of absolute power without the attendant responsibility,
and such a political act must lead inevitably to tragedy.

To make this clear Shakespeare uses Menenius Agrippa. The
fable of the belly and the members is an ancient political parable
which Shakespeare found in Plutarch, but of which he might have
read versions in many other places.[2] It illustrates the system of
obligations and duties which binds a people to its rulers, and as
Menenius tells it, it reflects the Elizabethan ideal which Englishmen still asserted in the face of the emerging Stuart tyranny. The
belly, or king, must have the service of the members, or people,
because it in turn keeps them alive; the services which the king
receives return in greater measure to the people:

[1] It is wrong, however, to regard *Coriolanus*, like J. E. Phililps (pp. 172-88), as a
kind of political morality play, with Rome as the true hero, in which Shakespeare
argues the superiority of monarchic to aristocratic government. Nor can we regard
the play in that manner which so alienated nineteenth-century audiences: as a
diatribe against the lower classes by a newly wealthy playwright eager to identify
himself with the aristocracy. E. C. Pettet, '*Coriolanus* and the Midlands Insurrection
of 1607', *Shakespeare Survey 3* (Cambridge, 1950), pp. 34-42, has suggested that
Shakespeare may have been particularly concerned with the problem of rebellion
because of the Midlands insurrection of 1607 which affected his own Warwickshire.
But the attitude towards rebellion does not differ essentially from that in the earlier
plays. Nor is the attitude towards the common people any other than he has expressed before: as individuals they are still lovable, but as a mob seeking to rule the
commonwealth they are monstrous in their potential for evil. Brents Stirling, *The
Populace in Shakespeare* (New York, 1949), has shown that Shakespeare's attitude in
Coriolanus and earlier plays is a conventional one in his age. Granville-Barker,
Prefaces to Shakespeare, II, 153, has indicated Shakespeare's sympathy for the plebeians
in the play.
[2] See Kenneth Muir, *Shakespeare's Sources*, I, 223-4.

and fit it is,
Because I am the store-house and the shop
Of the whole body: but, if you do remember,
I send it through the rivers of your blood,
Even to the court, the heart, to the seat o' the brain;
And, through the cranks and offices of man,
The strongest nerves and small inferior veins
From me receive that natural competency
Whereby they live.

(I.i.136-44)

Weak and strong alike, the belly says, are nurtured by the central source of all bounty, to which the weak and strong contribute as they may. And then the point of the parable is made clear:

The senators of Rome are this good belly,
And you the mutinous members; for examine
Their counsels and their cares, digest things rightly
Touching the weal o' the common, you shall find
No public benefit which you receive
But it proceeds or comes from them to you
And no way from yourselves.

(I.i.152-8)

Tudor and Stuart political theory enjoined unquestioning obedience upon a people, but as the representative upon earth of a just and beneficent God, the king must rule for the benefit of his people. When he did not he became a tyrant, and Elizabethan moralists held that a tyrant must be destroyed by God. A ruler corrupted by pride cannot acknowledge the supremacy of God, and thus he can have no sense of his awful responsibility. Coriolanus must inevitably be a tyrant.

To oppose a tyrant by rebellion, however, was the worst of all sins. Menenius argues the folly of such rebellion, the omnipotence of the Roman state, the care for the commons by the patricians who wield this omnipotence, and the ancient Tudor argument that it is God who sends misery to a people, and that only by prayer, and never by rebellion, can their conditions be improved (I.i.65-80). Coriolanus represents an opposite position. He would have the unquestioned authority of the lawful ruler, but he will not assume the responsibility which must go with this role. He is named in the first scene of the play, with its important function of dramatic exposition, as 'chief enemy to the people' (I.i.5), just as

Menenius is called some lines later, 'one that hath always loved the people' (I.i.52). We cannot doubt the deliberate contrast which Shakespeare here intended. Coriolanus is again epitomized in the words of the tribune:

> You speak o' the people,
> As if you were a god to punish, not
> A man of their infirmity.
>
> (III.i.80-82)

He has negated his tie to humanity, and of this fact his political stande is a positive reflection.

That attitude of Coriolanus is made clear by his greeting to the crowd, contrasting so markedly as it does with the kindly solicitude of Menenius:

> What's the matter, you dissentious rogues,
> That, rubbing the poor itch of your opinion,
> Make yourselves scabs?
>
> (I.i.167-9)

The very imagery reinforces the speaker's attitude of loathing and contempt. There can never be for Coriolanus a sense of responsibility to those from whose humanity he has so alienated himself. They are:

> Beneath abhorring. What would you have, you curs,
> That like nor peace nor war? the one affrights you,
> The other makes you proud. He that trusts to you,
> Where he should find you lions, finds you hares;
> Where foxes, geese: you are no surer, no,
> Than is the coal of fire upon the ice,
> Or hailstone in the sun. Your virtue is
> To make him worthy whose offence subdues him
> And curse that justice did it. Who deserves greatness
> Deserves your hate; and your affections are
> A sick man's appetite, who desires most that
> Which would increase his evil. He that depends
> Upon your favours swims with fins of lead
> And hews down oaks with rushes. Hang ye! Trust ye?
> With every minute you do change a mind,
> And call him noble that was now your hate,
> Him vile that was your garland.
>
> (I.i.172-88)

The vehemence of the language emphasizes the hero's lack of that human sympathy so necessary to the ruler, but it must be noted also that what Coriolanus actually says of the populace – their fickleness, untrustworthiness etc. – reflects commonplace Renaissance attitudes, and probably would have been regarded by Shakespeare's audience as accurate. The people left to govern themselves would indeed turn Rome into a chaotic wilderness, with men preying upon one another like beasts. The paradox is that Coriolanus stands for political truth, but it is truth without human feeling.

The satisfaction with which Coriolanus greets the news of war as a 'means to vent / Our musty superfluity' (I.i.229-30) would have sounded as inhumanly cruel to Shakespeare's audience as it does to a modern one. The solitary man of pride, living in a world of his own, negating the bonds which tie man to man, can never accept the responsibility for his fellow men which was so vital an aspect of the Tudor ideal of government. Such a man should never aspire to a position of rule, and this Coriolanus himself affirms for the audience: 'I had rather be their servant in my way / Than sway with them in theirs' (II.i.219-20).

The price of the consulship which Coriolanus seeks is to 'ask it kindly' (II.iii.78). He need only obey the ancient Roman tradition, show his wounds to the people, and ask them for their consent. This Volumnia and Menenius urge him to do. He is tragic in his attempt to follow their counsel, but his alienation from humanity will not permit him to show his inner self to other men any more than it had permitted him to accept the praises of Cominius and Titus Lartius. To 'ask it kindly', as a member of human kind, is for him to forfeit for the moment his aristocratic isolation. This he cannot do:

> Better it is to die, better to starve,
> Than crave the hire which first we do deserve.
> Why in this woolvish toge should I stand here,
> To beg of Hob and Dick, that do appear,
> Their needless vouches? Custom calls me to't:
> What custom wills, in all things should we do't,
> The dust on antique time would lie unswept,
> And mountainous error be too highly heapt
> For truth to o'er-peer. Rather than fool it so,
> Let the high office and the honour go,
> To one that would do thus.   (II.iii.120-30)

We feel pity for Coriolanus, but we feel also the magnificence of his unwillingness to compromise, his inflexible honesty and devotion to principle. The horror of flattery and his refusal to stoop to it lead Coriolanus to the outburst in the market-place and to his consequent banishment. This refusal to be sullied by what was in Renaissance terms among the basest of political vices gives to Coriolanus a heroic grandeur with which we sympathize while we lament the stupidity of his political behaviour. We share in the judgement of Menenius when Coriolanus has provoked the crowd to fury:

> His nature is too noble for the world:
> He would not flatter Neptune for his trident,
> Or Jove for's power to thunder. His heart's his mouth:
> What his breast forges, that his tongue must vent;
> And, being angry, does forget that ever
> He heard the name of death.

(III.i.255-60)

In the market-place of Rome as in the battle scenes before Corioli, the two aspects of Coriolanus are again held before us, the sinfulness of his alienation from humanity, and the magnificence of his unbending aristocratic ideal. To emphasize this latter aspect, Shakespeare dwells upon the petty viciousness and scurrility of the tribunes, Brutus and Sicinius. They represent a total absence of the aristocratic ideal; they control and manipulate the populace as Coriolanus can never aspire to do. What they represent Shakespeare brands unmistakably as evil, and this serves to set the grandeur of Coriolanus in fuller retrospect. The entire episode of his outburst against the tribunes in the market-place when they deny him the consulship is Shakespeare's invention. This is what the tribunes need to drive from Rome her greatest hero, cause him to renounce his greatness by embracing the cause of his enemy, and bring Rome to that final edge of destruction, from which only a spark of unthinking human emotion within that very hero can save it.

IX

Menenius serves as a chorus; he comments upon the action and directs the sentiments of the audience, making clear the positions both of Coriolanus and his adversaries. He helps us to see that the tribunes are in their own way as fully corrupted by pride as Coriolanus: 'You talk of pride', Menenius says, 'O that you could turn your eyes towards the napes of your necks, and make an interior survey of your good selves! O that you could!... Why, then you should discover a brace of unmeriting, proud, violent, testy, magistrates, alias fools, as any in Rome' (II.i.39-49). The tribunes are destructive forces in the commonwealth. It is ironic that such men should condemn Coriolanus for his pride, 'who, in a cheap estimation', as Menenius tells them, 'is worth all your predecessors since Deucalion, though peradvanture some of the best of 'em were hereditary hangmen' (II.i.99-101).

In spite of this, the tribunes' fears of Coriolanus are justified[1]; he would make precisely such a ruler as they fear, and they are, in a sense, guardians of the public welfare. But the tribunes have no real concern for the people. They represent self-seeking pride, without honour or principle, and they are offered as a contrast to the honourable, aristocratic pride of Coriolanus. The tribunes are used to make clear the political realities of the hero's position from the plebeian point of view. For this purpose none of the patrician characters, not even Menenius, will serve, and thus Sicinius and Brutus, in spite of their own debasement, must speak political truth. These separate dramatic uses of the tribunes need not be rendered consistent with one another in terms of character, and Shakespeare makes no attempt to do so, for such concern was not a part of the dramatic tradition in which he worked.

Tullus Aufidius also was designed as an instrument by which certain functions in the total dramatic design might be executed. Aufidius is used first as a contrasting foil to Coriolanus: the fearless warrior seeking personal glory who is, however, untouched by the sense of honour and the aristocratic ideal which enobles Coriolanus. He will use whatever means he can, fair or foul, to destroy his foe:

> By the elements,
> If e'er again I meet him beard to beard,
> He's mine, or I am his: mine emulation
> Hath not that honour in't it had; for where
> I thought to crush him in an equal force,
> True sword to sword, I'll potch at him some way
> Or wrath or craft may get him.   (I.x.10-16)

---

[1] See MacCallum, *Shakespeare's Roman Plays*, pp. 532-3; Kenneth Muir, 'In Defense of the Tribunes', *Essays in Criticism*, IV (1954), 331-3.

o

Aufidius stands for the enemy. He will destroy Coriolanus by any means, and he represents those very forces within the hero himself which overcome his nobility and breed his destruction. Just as Coriolanus is unaware of his own pride, he sees Aufidius as noble, and he gives him his admiration:

> I sin in envying his nobility,
> And were I any thing but what I am,
> I would wish me only he.   (I.i.234-6)

These are ironic lines, for one side of the hero is in fact Aufidius, and this part will destroy him. Here Coriolanus embraces the idea of his own destruction, as he later is to embrace it in actuality. In joining with Aufidius Coriolanus gives himself to the evil side of his own personality, negating the noble elements which had counterbalanced it. Their alliance is much like that of Othello with Iago, a symbolic union of the hero with the source of his destruction. Finally, after Coriolanus spares Rome, it is Aufidius who strikes the death blow. He is a dramatic symbol of the hero's sin.

To Aufidius also Shakespeare assigns the role of commentator to make clear for the audience the meaning of the hero's life-journey:

> First he was
> A noble servant to them; but he could not
> Carry his honours even: whether 'twas pride,
> Which out of daily fortune ever taints
> The happy man; whether defect of judgement,
> To fail in the disposing of those chances
> Which he was lord of; or whether nature,
> Not to be other than one thing, not moving
> From the casque to the cushion, but commanding peace
> Even with the same austerity and garb
> As he controll'd the war; but one of these –
> As he hath spices of them all, not all,
> For I dare so far free him – made him fear'd,
> So hated, and so banish'd: but he has a merit,
> To choke it in the utterance. So our virtues
> Lie in the interpretation of the time:
> And power, unto itself most commendable,
> Hath not a tomb so evident as a chair
> To extol what it hath done.
> One fire drives out one fire; one nail, one nail;
> Rights by rights falter, strengths by strengths do fail.
>   (IV.vii.35-56)

Aufidius states the paradox of the play.

Volumnia is as inconsistent psychologically as Aufidius. She performs primarily a thematic function, in which she is seconded by Virgilia and Valeria, and the alliteration of the three names accents the ritualistic nature of their characterization. Shakespeare gives to Volumnia most of the role which in Plutarch had been performed by Valeria, preserving that lady largely for the sound of her name.

Volumnia is used for three specific dramatic functions: to serve as the author both of the grandeur and the sinful pride of Coriolanus and thus to illustrate them; to point out the insufficiency of her son which leads to his banishment; and finally to evoke in him that last spark of human feeling which saves Rome. Of these functions, for only the last is there much warrant in Plutarch, where she receives little attention before her final plea for Rome, and where even the embassy of the women is undertaken at the suggestion of Valeria.

Volumnia is seen as the source both of her son's valour and his pride when with Virgilia she awaits his return from the wars: 'Hear me profess sincerely: had I a dozen sons, each in my love alike and none less dear than thine and my good Marcius, I had rather had eleven die nobly for their country than one voluptuously surfeit out of action' (I.iii.23-27). This is a heroic sentiment, but it is also a negation of the human ties of maternal love, and Virgilia serves to emphasize the normal horror of a wife at the prospect of her husband's blood: 'His bloody brow! O Jupiter, no blood!' (I.iii.41). The image which Volumnia evokes in reply is a rejection of the human bond which Virgilia asserts:

> Away, you fool! it more becomes a man
> Than gilt his trophy: the breasts of Hecuba,
> When she did suckle Hector, look'd not lovelier
> Than Hector's forehead when it spit forth blood
> At Grecian sword, contemning.   (I.iii.42-46)

Valour and inhumanity in Volumnia are fused. Valeria is used in this scene to emphasize the unnaturalness of such an attitude by her description of how the son of Marcius destroyed a butterfly:

> I saw him run after a gilded butterfly; and when he caught it, he let
> it go again; and after it again; and over and over he comes, and up
> again; catched it again; or whether his fall enraged him, or how 'twas,
> he did so set his teeth and tear it; O, I warrant, how he mammocked
> it!   (I.iii.65-71)

This, as Volumnia says, is 'One on's father's moods' (I.iii.72).
Volumnia stands for glory and heroism, but its pursuit to such a
degree that it destroys the simple human values of tenderness and
beauty – symbolized in the butterfly – which make life livable.

When in a later scene Volumnia says to her son, 'Thy valiant-
ness was mine, thou suck'dst it from me, / But owe thy pride
thyself' (III.ii.129-30), Shakespeare is not denying what earlier he
had made explicit. He is using Volumnia for a different dramatic
purpose. She must now point out to Coriolanus and the audience
the results of his own pride, and to do so she must divorce herself
from that pride she is censuring, and of which the audience has
already seen her as source and symbol. 'You might have been
enough the man you are,' she tells her son, 'With striving less to
be so' (III.ii.19-20). This is an important measure of her son's
failure. While we second the wisdom of Volumnia's advice, we
feel the grandeur of the manner in which Coriolanus rejects it:

> I'll know no further:
> Let them pronounce the steep Tarpeian death,
> Vagabond exile, flaying, pent to linger
> But with a grain a day, I would not buy
> Their mercy at the price of one fair word;
> Nor check my courage for what they can give,
> To have't with saying 'Good morrow'.
>
> (III.iii.87-93)

Volumnia in this role urges him to deny those very elements of
his own nature which in her earlier role she had implanted in him.

At the end of the play, with Virgilia and young Marcius beside
her, Volumnia, the unnatural mother, comes finally to stand for
the common bonds of human life. She now makes clear the gross
perversion of nature to which the delusion of Coriolanus has led
him:

> Making the mother, wife and child to see
> The son, the husband and the father tearing
> His country's bowels out.
>
> (V.iii.101-3)

Volumnia saves Rome, but she cannot save her son, for the
impasse to which he has been led by his aristocratic virtue, in
conflict with an alienation from humanity sprung directly from it,
can resolve itself only in his own destruction. Volumnia's plea

itself is a statement of the impossible: 'no; our suit / Is, that you reconcile them' (V.iii.135-6), and it is not to her rational argument that he yields, but to the blind supplications of his child:

> Nay behold's:
> This boy, that cannot tell what he would have,
> But kneels and holds up hands for fellowship,
> Does reason our petition with more strength
> Than thou hast to deny't.
>
> (V.iii.173-7)

The aside which Aufidius addresses to the audience makes clear the impossible separation of human feeling from aristocratic honour which is implicit in the hero's yielding, and that in this his doom already is implicit:

> I am glad thou hast set thy mercy and thy honour
> At difference in thee: out of that I'll work
> Myself a former fortune.
>
> (V.iii.200-2)

The demands of the honour he has pledged to Aufidius call for Rome's destruction; his forfeiture of honour in response to normal human feeling must be his own destruction. He cannot maintain at the same time both his aristocratic ideal and his common humanity. In this great climactic scene is dramatically affirmed the paradox which is the theme of the total play, and to which all of its diverse elements contribute. For Coriolanus there can be no meaningful renunciation of evil nor any regeneration, for the sin which destroys him is the inevitable concomitant of all which makes him great. To this intellectual impasse Shakespeare came at last, after his long years of relentless probing into man's relation to the forces of evil, from his hesitant beginnings in *Titus Andronicus*, through his great positive affirmations in *King Lear* and *Macbeth*, and now to the final unanswerable questions. After *Coriolanus* there is no further ground. Shakespeare's tragic vision is complete.

Index

DATE DUE

OCT 0 2 1990			
3-18- 2:40			
MAR 2 1 1991			
4/16-1991			
4/17-1991			
4/30 11:00			
5/1 1:15			